CU00906750

Let

us

Follow the Clyde

*Discovering the communities
along the course
of the river
from its source at Watermeetings
to the estuary at Ardmore Point*

James Denham

Let us Follow the Clyde

ISBN 978-1-291-69199-3

Glenmore Books
Galashiels, Scotland, UK.

http://www.glenmorebooks.yolasite.com

format by E.W. Paterson

Acknowledgements

Paul Dobie
Paul Fishlock
Carol Walker
David Dixon
Gavin Laird
William Starkey
Patrick Mackie
Bill Millar
Ian Sykes
Graeme Yuill
David Hamilton
Graham Murdy
Tommy Thomson
Andy Fleming
Jonathan Oldenbuck
Andy Paterson
Bill Sim
Chris Wimbush
Mark Donnelly
Elizabeth Paterson
M.J. Richardson
Stephen Craven
Clyde Football club

A great big thanks too, to my wife Elizabeth who was with me every step of the way, and, because of my disability, she did so much 'walking' research for me and virtually all the typesetting.

Thanks too, to every other person who took the time to speak to me on my way but who did not wish to be mentioned. Without you all, without your kind words and photographs, this book would not have been possible. Thank you all, every single piece of help is so much appreciated - James

Photograph Front Cover : The river and the Clyde Arc – courtesy of David Dixon © 2010
Photograph Back Cover : The old Garrion Bridge – James Denham © 2013

Introduction

Let me say from the outset, this book is NOT a definitive history of the communities of the Clyde I have visited but simply an overview of each. To do all the towns and villages full justice, each would require at least one volume of their own and Glasgow? that would require a small library. I have always believed, to truly tell the story of a town, you need to have lived there most of your life. I do not live in any of the communities I have visited but I do have strong family connections with Glasgow, through my father and both grandfathers. I grew up in a mining village in East Lothian but from the beginning, I was immersed in the waters of the Clyde and began to feel as though I belonged there. I never tired of my dad's stories of his trips 'doon the watter' and his charabanc days down the Clyde Valley. For me, this is my way of seeing so much of what I had been told of during my childhood days. For my dad and his dad, Glasgow and the Clyde, were their passions and a great part of that has passed on to me.

The story reaches back in time, looking at the ongoing invasions of the area from the Britons, Saxons, Romans, Danes and the English. We take a look at how it all developed from those times through to the present day. I know, in some sections, you will think that you have 'already read this part or another', and that is the case but it is important to speak of each town or village as if it was on page one, they deserve nothing less. So, if you feel at points, it is a little repetitive, which I guess it is in places, I apologise.

I have cited some history of a national nature in various areas in an attempt to put the story of our journey, and the area in to context.

Where I have expressed an opinion, it is entirely my own opinion and where I have addressed individual persons, there has been no intention to cause hurt. If you feel I have been critical or offensive to anyone, alive or dead, then I am truly sorry, no attempt has been made to hurt nor demean anyone. I must also apologise in advance for the inevitable typing error here and there.

I do hope you enjoy this rendering and you find it of some interest. I have had so much enjoyment travelling the course of the river and thinking of all I had learned from so long ago though I have had the privilege of sailing doon the watter to Rothesay twice in my younger days. Visiting Glasgow has always been a pleasure for me, to see relatives, and follow my beloved football club, Clyde, when they played at Shawfield and I always drove through the city to get there.

It has been so reassuring meeting so many nice people along the way who have given me so much help. I have been touched by the friendliness of the folk I have met and some of the sights I have seen.

The estuary was a bitter sweet experience, sad I had reached my destination and my trip was over but exhilarating watching the dashing waters of the river crash in to the oncoming tides of the Firth of Clyde but now I have said enough, *Let us follow the Clyde* together.

Many thanks for reading, and my warmest regards, James.

Contents

Dedication

After reading my introduction you may have guessed what I am about to say. I would like to dedicate this offering to my dad John and to his dad, also John who have instilled in me everything I am today. Their passions are mine, Glasgow and the full flow, from source to estuary, of the great River Clyde and, of course Clyde Football Club.

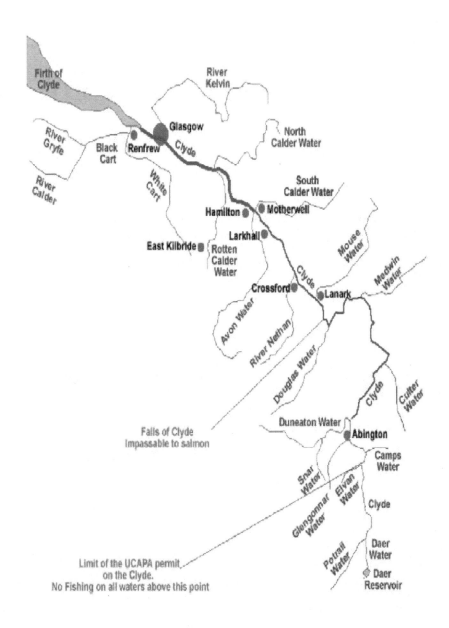

Firth of Clyde

River Kelvin

River Gryfe

River Calder

Black Cart

Renfrew

Glasgow

Clyde

White Cart

North Calder Water

South Calder Water

Hamilton

Motherwell

Larkhall

East Kilbride

Rotten Calder Water

Mouse Water

Crossford

Clyde

Lanark

Medwin Water

Avon Water

River Nethan

Douglas Water

Falls of Clyde
Impassable to salmon

Duneaton Water

Clyde

Culter Water

Abington

Camps Water

Snar Water

Glengonnar Water

Elvan Water

Clyde

Potrail Water

Daer Water

Limit of the UCAPA permit
on the Clyde.
No Fishing on all waters above this point

Daer Reservoir

Courtesy of fishingnet.com

8

Section One

The Southern Hills – Source to New Lanark

Let's pull up our socks, fasten our boots, rucksack on? then let's go, we have places to go and people to see, as we meander north in the company of the imperious River Clyde. First we must find the source and that may be more difficult than meets the eye since many have their own views on the subject. Is it the source of the Potrail Water which rises to the south in the Lowther Hills? Or is it the Daer Water which first meets the light of day at Daer Head on the slopes of Earncraig Hill, a few kilometres west of Beattock before creating the great Daer Reservoir. While others may say otherwise, we make our start at Watermeetings in South Lanarkshire where the Daer and the Potrail meet in the company of Glenochar Burn in the shadow of Brown Hill. The meeting of the waters is a haven of peace, sitting blissfully among the Lanarkshire hills, a peace giving no indication of the nature of one of Scotland's great rivers, renowned the world over.

To the west of the confluence at this point is the ruins of the once mighty bastle and fermtoun of Glenochar, which may have been in the own of one of the Douglas family in days long gone. From early times, many families built 'strong houses' as a defence against faceless foes and not just of the English variety. Reiver families, from both sides of an ever changing border, murdered and looted in their efforts to widen their own possessions and gain supremacy. In 1603, when James VI became king of England, he took huge steps to wipe out the carnage of never ending wars of attrition along the length of the Scoto/Anglo border and to a large degree he succeeded. As peace took hold, many of the bastles or strong houses were no longer required and subsequently abandoned, as was the case at Glenochar.

Watermeetings - Courtesy of Chris Wimbush ©2010

From this point, the infant Clyde flows in a generally north easterly direction being joined by the Annanshaw and Blakeshaw Burns before reaching Crooked Stane Farm near an ancient standing stone and where another small flow, the Crookedstane Burn joins the river from the east. Others like the Clydes and Newton Burns rush in from the east, eager to join us near the start of journey north.

River Clyde

*S*oon the first settled community on our journey north on the river's flow, Elvanfoot, is reached and where the Elvan Burn meets with her mother water. A foot bridge, not in use at the moment, crosses Clyde in the village where a fine 19th century church exists along with an old toll house, once visited by the immortal bard, Robert Burns. Sadly the church is no longer in use and has been registered as a 'building at risk'. Elvanfoot was a junction of old, for both road and rail and where a branch line once left for the lead mines of Wanlockhead and, while its old importance has gone, the beauty and serenity remain. At this stage, the river flows virtually parallel to an old Roman road, indicating the importance of its course, and source of fresh water. From ancient times, men have travelled the route in search of food, a place to live or to wreak havoc on anyone who dared stop them. Clyde leaves the Elvan in the shadow of the heavily afforested Wellshot Hill as she heads on her way over a ford then past the old curling ponds of Stoneyburn on her way to another old staging post off the A74 motorway, Crawford. Before reaching Crawford, another two waters, the Harry and Collins Burns, join a deepening river as she makes her way onward.

*C*rawford has been one of the most important stopping points on the route from Carlisle to Glasgow for centuries though is now a much quieter locale, and no longer on the principal route. The Romans built a marching fort just to the north of the ancient settlement near the site of the ruins of Crawford Castle which had strong association with William Wallace, patriot and Guardian of Scotland. It is a lovely little village hemmed in a peaceful valley between Ellershie and Corbury Hills and is where the Stoney and Camp Burns introduce themselves to Lady Clyde along with the Midlock Water. The village contains a post office, village shop, two hotels and a fine church of 1871 which is the descendant of an ancient kirk. The first church was built in the 10th century and dedicated to St. Constantine the Martyr who was a disciple of both St. Columba and St. Mungo (Kentigern) In medieval times, the lands and church were granted, part to Newbattle Abbey, a daughter house of Melrose, part to Holyrood Abbey but sadly, like so many churches in the modern age, it is no longer in ecclesiastical use.

*W*hile no longer of the importance of bygone years, Crawford is by no means a lost and forlorn backwater and contains many clubs and organisations which help create a great spirit within the community. There is a bowling and carpet bowls club, toddlers group, a branch of the Scottish Womens' Rural Institute, a fine primary school, medical centre and a much used village hall.

*I*n the earlier part of the 12th century, Crawford was said to be in the hands of Thor Longus, a benevolent and pious laird who founded several churches in Lothian and the Scottish Borders; he was also the first man to be granted the lairdship of a new form of local government known as a parish by David I, making Ednam in Roxburghshire, the first such ecclesiastical foundation in Scotland and the forerunner of things to come. The castle of Crawford, and barony, were granted to the Lindsay family by King Robert II in the 14th century before it passed to the mighty Douglases. At various times, the Carmichael family were keepers of the castle as were the Dukes of Hamilton. While that was the

The Southern Hills

case, the barony itself was still in hands of the Lindsays evidenced by Crawford being elevated to a burgh of regality and an earldom awarded to the Lindsay family by Robert III in 1398 and, remarkably, is still in that illustrious family; the present holder of Scotland's premier earldom, is the 29th of the line, Robert Alexander Lindsay.

*Wi*thin the village bounds, the river swings left under the road bridge below Crawford Castle and heads under an old rail viaduct before taking in the Ellershie Water and reaching the ancient hamlet of Kirkton on the left bank, where the remains of an old church can be seen near the farm of the same name. Veering right, the river is squeezed between Castle Hill and White Hill near where the Gair Gill Water joins, as she heads north toward Abington. On Castle Hill, there is much evidence of ancient forts, enclosures and homesteads dating from early in the first millennium through to the early Middle Ages. From Laggerengill Rig, where more ancient activity has been identified. Next, the baby Glengonner Burn sees her first light of day before heading north-east to meet the Clyde south of Abington. Southwood and Raggengill Burns are soon to 'join up' as they rush from the hills east of the village.

River Clyde looking downstream from Crawford

*A*bington, formerly in the parish of Crawford, is yet another favourite watering hole on the main route through south-west Scotland and home to Glengonnar School where many Scots' children have had the times of their lives, and former home of the Colebrooke family, baronets of Crawford and hereditary constables of Crawford Castle. Another lovely village, with shop, hotel, village hall and the most wonderful church, Glencaple Parish Church, founded in 1898, and hidden from view in the most peaceful setting on the west side of the main thoroughfare. Until the early 1960s, Abington was home to a station on the west coast line but Dr. Beeching, during his 'cut the railway network' era, closed Abington as he did so many stations, not just in Lanarkshire of course, but all over the United Kingdom.

A little to the north, the river pays a courtesy visit to Abington services on the

11

River Clyde

A74 and to Cold Chapel Farm where another hill water joins the river near the tiny community of Nether Abington. Apart from the award winning services, there are signs of ancient settlements including the mound remains of a motte & bailey castle adjacent to the motorway facilities and situated between the A703 road and the Clyde. The motte, thought to be built by John of Crawford in the 12th century, sits some 30 feet above the river with the former bailey some six feet higher. There too, is a monument to Matthew McKendrick, a local man and weel kent fisherman on that stretch of the river.

Clyde continues to head north below the mighty White Hill, still following the route of the Roman road and soon, on the left bank, she welcomes the Duneaton Water. Only yards to the north at that point are the sites of a Roman camp and fortlet. Clyde then flows under Clyde's Bridge (below) which carries the A702, and is the first major road bridge on her flow. That bridge has replaced an older brother of the 19th century, which still carries traffic on a local minor road.

After a sharp bend to the right, the river passes Moat and a river island, home to abundant wildfowl, below Harten Hill. Moat Farm near Roberton is home to an ancient motte (hence the name) where many interesting artefacts have been found over the years.

Another large river island splits the river in time to welcome the Beer Burn before the Wandel Burn becomes the next to join the growing family of Clyde Waters. A little further downstream, other waters have rushed from the hills to join the party, the Ladygill and Woodend Burns, are now fully fledged members of the bludgeoning 'river clan'

The next port of call is Roberton, an ancient settlement below Devonshaw Hill, which sits astride the Roberton Burn, another local guest about to join the river. Roberton is an ancient barony granted to an imported Flemish family during the reign of David I, but who lost their lands and title at the command of Robert I (the Bruce) after Stevene de Roberton swore fealty to Edward I of England in 1296 at Berwick. Seems to be a strange assertion to some, since Robert was still nowhere near being king in 1296 and he, himself, swore allegiance to the dreaded 'Longshanks'. Roberton Parish, it's said, became the largest Flemish enclave in the south of Scotland before the lands were passed to Sir James Douglas, the king's trusted right hand man and were later in the hands of the Douglas, Earls of Dalkeith. A chapel was founded in Roberton in the early 12th century and was, until 1153, in the dependency of Wiston before being granted, by Wice de Winston, to Kelso Abbey. It became a parish church in its own right in the 13th century but was abandoned by 1885. The impressive church (see below) of today was built in 1905 and still dominates the village amidst its own kirkyard on the site of the ancient chapel of which no vestige remains. The Knights of St. John of Jerusalem also owned local lands during medieval times and would almost certainly build a 'spittal' (hospital) nearby. A fine hall exists, where much of the local activities take place in a village, where, in more recent times, a congregation of the Relief Church assembled. Roberton too, was the site of early habitation leaving some evidence of what may have been a fort on the lands between the A73 and the kirk. In later times, the village boasted a shop and a primary school

*A*cross the river from Roberton is the remains of a tower at the Bower of Wandel dating from the 15th century. There are also many signs of ancient workings including what is believed to be an Iron-Age fort. Wandel was once the home of a medieval kirk which was situated just to the north of the Bower at Hartside but that church was left to nature when the parish united with Lamington in 1608.

*G*entle, soothing waters of Lamington Burn on its way to the Clyde, flow through an area of rich, fertile farming lands, while majestic hills, the highest of which is Lamington Hill (493m) occupy the right bank. Before reaching the village, an old two arched bridge of 1836, crosses the river carrying the B7055 road. The ancient parish of Lamington or, formerly, Lammingtoune, contains the conservation village of the same name and is where the wife of William Wallace, Marion Braidfute (Broadfoot) heiress of Lamington, was said to be born. To the north of the village stand the fragile remnants of Lamington Castle, a fortified home of the notable Baillie family of Lamington who believe they are descendants of the Braidfute family, the original owners of the old tower house. Certainly the Baillies, who also owned tracts of land in East Lothian, at Penston and Hoprig, were said to be descendants of the de Baliol family, important contenders for the Scottish throne during the Wars of Independence and, indeed, one of them. King John I reigned from 1292 until 1296. The so called *Toom Tabard,* was the son of John, founder of Baliol College at Oxford University. The son of King John, Edward, reigned briefly in the 14th century but was never truly recognised as king.

River Clyde

Lamington was, of old, a market town, having been granted the right to hold markets every week and two annual fairs, during the reign of Charles I who ruled from 1625 until his execution in 1649. His execution was the result of his ongoing feud with the English Parliament and the stubborn Stuart belief of their *Divine Rights of Kings.*

There are two churches in the parish, St. Ninian's Church and Trinity Church though neither is in regular use and are now owned by Biggar Museum but ancient St. Ninians Well still exists nearby. St. Ninian's, the former parish church, was built in 1721 to replace its decaying 12th century predecessor while Trinity was built in 19th century as an Episcopal Chapel.

Lamington parish is also rich in ancient artefacts and many signs of Roman activity including sites of a marching fort, camp and fortlet are still extant. The village boasts a fine primary school and a community hall which hosts many local events and special occasions. On the left bank of the river there once existed a railway station but like so many others, has long since, blown its 'final whistle'.

Apart from Marion Braidfute, many of the philanthropic family of Baillie were born in the parish as was the Olympic curler, Willie Jackson, in 1871.

It would seem, the proud district of Clydesmuir was now lying derelict having lost its industry, the mills and quarries, and the railway stations but not a bit of it. Throughout the area, there have been many fine homes built in recent times and there is an air of optimism among the local folk. There is a large percentage of retired people that's true but of the others, most are quite happy to commute to the larger centres each day for work, in the knowledge they return each evening to one the most peaceful of settings. On the river's flow, and in the village itself, there is a peace which is quite tangible and comforting, a setting to behold and, when the sun is shining, the river sparkles in approval of its heaven sent environs. It is such sweet repose before the challenges ahead but treasures like the scene at Lamington parish will linger in the heart for many a day. It is time now to push on to Symington, passing the confluence with Garf Water, Langholm Farm and the old, deep pond of the now disused Lamington Quarry on the way.

To the north, above Symington Mains Farm, is another Castle Hill covered in earth workings of ancient men. It is not difficult to understand why ancient people were attracted to the southern reaches of the Valley of Clyde, food pickings would be forever near at hand, in forest and river. Abundant wood for home, fortification and warmth with the added benefit of fresh running water for bathing and refreshment. On past Coulterhaugh and Coulter Mains on the right bank and Symington House on the left flowing over Sandy's Ford in the process. Culter village is a pretty little place with a school, church, many fine houses and a restaurant in the old mill where a warm welcome always awaits. The most notable houses are Culter Allers, which boasts one of the finest gardens in the south of the country and Culter House. The present church of 1810 is a lovely old building and is the descendant of an ancient foundation of the 12th century during the reign of King William I (the Lion); the church was a rectory in the Deanery of Lanark, part of the Diocese of Glasgow. Its most famous preacher was Master Pieres Tylliol,

The Southern Hills

Parson of Cultre, who swore fealty to Edward I of England at Berwick in August, 1296. Many more ancient homesteads can be seen on the hills above the village, which is traversed by the Culter Water on its way to Lady Clyde.

*T*ime now to cross the river of dreams, to admire another place which has withstood the tests of time, Symington. The village was the home of one of the earliest branches of the railway network in Scotland, when the local line linked with Biggar and Peebles in 1858 but first we must cross the old bridge at the quaintly named Wolfclyde, home of the ancient Culter Motte Castle and nearby Cornhill House, an award winning hotel and restaurant.

*W*olfclyde Bridge is an unusual structure of the early 19th century in the sense that it contains two large arches and no less than six flood prevention arches. There is also, to the north, the columns of the old railway bridge (photograph below) which stand as sentinels awaiting the return of the aforementioned railway which crossed the Clyde at this point and was one of Scotland's earliest rail bridges. Nearby is Cormiston, home to all occasions from weddings to gymkhana events and, just a few yards to the west, is Cormiston Towers where the most 'important' days were during the life of the now long gone tower. That tower was in much demand over the years and passed at various times through the hands of the Cormistones, Chancellors, Somervilles and Douglases though the last known resident was Sir Widham Carmichael-Anstruther in 1882.

*T*he peace of the day is broken only by fishermen chattering to themselves as they become increasingly agitated in their constant vigil awaiting a catch and the excited calls of gulls and ducks hoping for a quick 'steal' from the fishers. I am sure many of those waterproofed men  will 'boast' of the one that got away and blaming those damned gulls for their bad luck.

*I*n the modern day, there are no howlings of the preying wolves as they wander the countryside as they once did, indeed, it is claimed, on the site of the nearby Wolfclyde Farm, the last ever wolf in Scotland was killed in the mid 18th century though I have got to say, other areas too, lay claim to that 'illustrious' event.

*S*ymington, though not a large village, covers a lot of ground and contains many fine houses, with large, well kept gardens. The facilities of the village include a post office and village store which provides for everyday needs, a fine community hall where many of the village activity takes place and the old kirk and its hall, another venue for local meetings. There is also a well respected primary school, the Tinto school, which caters for the local children and others from the surrounding countryside. Tinto School of course, is so called in the name of the highest hill in the area. The villagers are proud too, of their local football team, Symington Tinto AFC who boast an excellent clubhouse, yet another place to pass the time of day. The club enters two teams in the Caledonian Amateur League while their youth teams, three of them, play in the local age group, youth leagues, a really good set up which many senior teams would be proud of.

The old kirk at Symington was founded in the 12th century by Symon de Locard, a lord, one of many imported by King David I in his quest to modernise Scotland, to bring governance and a new 'pecking' order to the land. Over the years, the de Locards patronised the church but, following a legal battle with the Bishop of Glasgow and the monks of Kelso Abbey, the local lord, initially confident of success, was forced to consign his thoughts to defeat. The church remained in the hands of Kelso though still part of the Deanery of Lanark, within the Glasgow Bishopric. The present church, with much renewal over the years, still retains great sections of the original giving us a greater insight in to the past; it is set within its kirkyard which contains many fine stones including symbolic and table. The body of the founder, the pious Sir Symon, was buried within the chancel of the kirk but re-interred, still within the church, during renovations of the 19th century. There is also a very interesting mort house which was built during the days of the resurrectionists as protection against body snatching during the 18th and 19th centuries.

The de Locards (Lockhart) who were thought to have two houses in the area, the place (palace) near the kirk and a tower atop the nearby Castle Hill, were an interesting family and a descendant of the said Symon. Another Symon, wrote himself into the annals of Scottish history following the death of Robert I (the Bruce) in 1329. Bruce had requested his heart be cut from his body and taken to the Holy Land, Symon Loccard was one of the chosen few charged with carrying out the king's last wish. Leader of the pack, Sir James Douglas (the good Sir James) was entrusted to carry the casket containing the precious cargo while Symon was entrusted with the key. During their journey through Spain, they encountered a Moorish army at Teba and, during the affray, James Douglas was killed. Locard was one of two men given the task of returning the body of Douglas home to Scotland with the casket containing Bruce's heart firmly placed in the grip of the dead knight. Sir James was buried at St. Bride's Church at Douglas while the heart of the Bruce was buried in Melrose Abbey.

Today's Symington, where once stood a prosperous rail station, the renowned Hartree Arms Inn and busy mills with the associated hustle and bustle, there is but peace in the shadow of the surrounding hills, the tallest, Tinto standing at some 2,400 feet and the most famous of local land marks. I must add however, a sand

and gravel pit still exists in a parish where the surrounding castles and forts are laid bare. Little remains of the past with the exception of what is said to be the ruins of a Druid Temple at the summit of Tinto and the scant remains of Fatlips Castle near the foot of the hill.

The village is still though, the destination of those wishing to have the wedding of a lifetime at nearby Tinto House Hotel which joins other buildings of note including Symington House, a palatial mansion with surroundings to match and Symington Lodge.

Nearby is St. John's Kirk and cemetery of which the centrepiece is a burial aisle of the prominent local family of Waugh situated within the roofless ruins of the old church. The graveyard also contains many men of the Polish army who were based nearby during the Second World War. Back at Wolfclyde the river twists to the left below Cormiston

The old Mort House in Symington Kirkyard
Marytn Gorman ©2012 Geograph/1779110

near Netherton, before bending once again at Eastfield in time to welcome on board the Clachan Burn. Opposite the lands of Cormiston Towers are the ruins of Annieston Tower looking rather dilapidated and probably another lodge of the Locards. What is more interesting is Annieston Farm where, in recent times, an ancient homestead and other earthworks were found giving up ancient treasures, including a bronze arrow head, which had been hidden from sight for up to two thousand years.

Another twist is in sight with the Cleave Burn sweeping its way from Crawhill to the river in time to go hand in hand with another burn pouring in from Muirhouse Farm on the left bank. There are so many farms populating this section of the county undertaking all forms of farming, particularly pastoral with cattle the most important. Arable fields too, are commonplace as is fruit farming, including apples, pears and berries, while tomatoes are another important crop. Indeed the entire Clyde Valley, stretching ever north, is famed for its fruit farms.

Now we flow in the shadow of daunting Quothquan Law, a pyramid shaped hill to the north standing more than 600 feet above the river. That hill, said to mean *Beautiful Hill* is topped by an ancient hillfort and an interesting lump of stone known as *Wallace's Chair* which, legend tells us, was used by William Wallace when he held his war council before the Battle of Biggar in May, 1297.

River Clyde

On the right bank below, in the shadow the great hill, is a much more gentle scene at Quothquan Law Farm. Now it is sharp right to Thankerton and the old 'Boat Bridge' as the bridge is known since it carries the boat road from the village on the left bank across the river to the right. Why the boat road? It seems, in the days before the stone bridge was built in 1798, people were ferried, or they carried their own boats to the narrowest point of the river. That road to the river became known, in times long ago, as *The Boat Road,* a name which has survived to the present day.

*T*hankerton, or Thankeston as it was once known, boasted its very own parish church but when the parishes of Thankeston and Covington were cojoined, the old kirk at the village on the Clyde, was allowed to die and now there is no vestige to show it ever existed. There is no school in the village and while, in days of old, the children attended Covington Village School, they now make the short journey to Symington.

*T*he village is thought to have been so named in honour of an early proprietor of the parish, Tankred or Thankard from the 12th century, who was granted the lands by King Malcolm IV, grandson of the saintly David I. In those days of renewal in Scotland, many Norman knights were invited to rule over many areas in the south of the country but it seems to me, Tankard is not exactly a Norman name nor is it Flemish so I can only speculate, he was from an earlier time, a descendant perhaps from one of the many Viking invasions. As we shall see, Thankerton's sister village, Covington, was so named around the same period from another of Malcolm's charters, to a man known as Colbran or Colban and that, in my mind is definitely Viking since another of that race founded Colbrandspeth or Cockburnspath in Berwickshire. It is not beyond the realms of wishful thinking that Tankred and Colban were of Scandinavian descent, considering the Danes controlled much of the Scottish coast, particularly the western islands, for nigh on 200 years. Another spelling for the parish crops up in the so called *Ragmans Rolls* of 1296 when Symon de la More knelt before Edward of England, paying homage on behalf of the *vill de Thaugarston.*

*T*oday's Thankerton, is, like so many other villages along the Clyde's flow, pretty and peaceful. Many lovely cottages line the road and more populate the village centre where there is a good village store and an inn. A village hall provides a focal point for all the local groups including a volunteer group, ready and willing to help anyone in need. Thankerton bowling club on Sherifflats Road is another popular venue where many social functions take place and encourages, mainly the elders of the village, to enjoy some sport in their twilight years in the company of many younger enthusiasts.

A little to the north, Covington is much smaller than before and there is not really too much left in the village; the school, now a private residence, has closed, as has the fine church which was first founded and dedicated to St. Michael in the 12th century but still can be seen and admired. A new town of Covington was built and is now the larger of the two settlements but the two communities co-joined, would barely make a reasonably sized village. While the glories of old

The Southern Hills

Colbandstoun are consigned to the past, there is still much to see including the ruins of the tower and doocot to the north.

*I*n the late 13th century when Edward Longshanks became obsessed with overpowering his northern neighbours, he held court twice at Berwick, in 1291 and 1296 for the purpose of landowners and churchmen to come, kneel before him, kiss his feet and swear homage to him, their 'rightful sovereign'. Covington was represented by three local dignitaries, Edmund, Isabelle and Margarete all designated as 'de Colbanston'. Another of note to swear allegiance at the same time was the local cleric, Huwe de Chastel Bernard, Parsone de Colbanston.

*T*he fairly extensive ruins of the 15th century tower, is part of a formidable site which was most definitely built for defence and, judging by the extensive trenches all around, in at least two circles, the proprietors took their safety very seriously. There too, are signs the castle was built atop an earlier motte mound suggesting

this area has been fortified since the days of Colban in the 12th century. Nearby, the beehive style doocot would provide food during the winter for the occupants of the castle since, in those far off times, there was no way food could be kept fresh all winter. In fact many of the animals were slaughtered at the onset of the bad weather since not enough food could be stored

above : Clyde at Thankerton
right : Covington Tower

to feed them while grazing was interrupted by snow and ice. Keeping pigeons was a way of feeding the family during those months when winter was a much harsher season than it is in the modern day.

*R*everend Donald Cargill, the redoubtable Covenanting minister, spent a few nights at Covington Mill in 1681, when one morning, 12th July, he, with two colleagues, was arrested by James Irvine of Bonshaw and charged with traitorous behaviour towards his king. The minister, generally a shy and retiring gentleman, was taken to Glasgow before a fearful trip to

River Clyde

Edinburgh where he was charged, 'tried' and sentenced to death. Such a man, quiet and sober by nature, was a lion in defence of the established Church of Scotland and was totally committed to opposing the foolish Stuarts' attempts to impose the Episcopacy on the people of Scotland. As he stepped on to the gallows on that fateful morning, 27th July, 1681, he was heard to say "*I go up this ladder with less fear, confusion or perturbation of mind, than I did entering a pulpit to preach*" Within minutes he was executed, his head cut off and pinned to a stake and placed on show at the Netherbow near the head of his friend and colleague, Richard Cameron, the founder of the Cameronian Church. James Irvine was rewarded with 5,000 merks for bringing Cargill 'to justice'. There is a monument to the great man on the roadside at Covington Mill and a cairn monument at Rattray in Perthshire, where he was born.

Just north of Covington is another tiny village, Pettinain, which we shall discover later but time now to head back to the right bank of the river. The summer of 2013 has seen little rain and the Clyde is at its lowest level for some years. Wading across looks so inviting but I think the more sensible route is to head back to the Boat Bridge at Thankerton and make the crossing there.

Over the Boat Bridge and, taking the next left, we head along the Shieldhill Road, below the Quothquan Law, for the village of the same name. The river appears more fragmented at that point with many overgrown river islands obstructing a smooth flow. It is a lovely route below the green grass and thick vegetation of the hill, occupied by great herds of cattle on one side, and the scenic river below. Soon after passing Parkshouse on the left and Loanhead on the right, look out for the ruins of the Quothquan Church situated on the left behind the lovely little village hall where many groups meet, including the local branch of the Womens' Rural Institute.

The church of 'Cuthquen' is thought to have been founded in the 12th century but the first solid mention of it came in 1345 when Master Henry, the rector of the church, bore witness to a charter of Alan, bishop of Argyll at Paisley Abbey on the feast day of Saints Cosmus and Damian, the martyrs. The church was described as a parsonage with Pencaitland in East Lothian in the deanery of Lothian and the diocese of St. Andrews. Quothquan Kirk, which was united with nearby Libberton in 1669, fell out of ecclesiastical use in 1724 then, for many years thereafter, acted as the schoolhouse for the local children. When the school closed, the church fell in to ruin and was used as a burial vault. The walls stand to full height though it is more than likely a great deal of work has been done to make this possible and of course to enclose the burial vault of the prominent Chancellor family of Shieldhill Castle. On the west gable is the most delightful belfry still, remarkably, with a bell dated 1641. When the church closed after unification with Libberton, the church's website tells us, it was planned to move the bell to the church to the north but the villagers dissented, pulled the bell from its fittings and hurled it in to the River Clyde crying out, *"Lang may ye weel"* Later it was recovered and returned to its rightful location and, interestingly, that area of the river is forever known as the *Langly Weel.* There are many fine stones in the graveyard but, sadly it is not so quiet and peaceful as it could be. Immediately to the rear of the church, there is a major animal feed producer on Roadhead Farm but, on a happier note, that provides work for local people and contractors from far and wide. A little further on is a major dairy produce centre providing even more work and, for such a small village, is a major filip for the local economy.

Quothquan is a dainty little place with a many fine houses in the centre and more, including affordable housing, built on the east side near Eastertown Farm. The houses, cottages and other buildings, are lovely and so befitting such a bonnie rural locale but one notable building in the hamlet though, is a real eyecatcher. Known locally as the *Tin Tabernacle,* it was, formerly, the school then village hall, but the building has the appearance of a little chapel where local services may have been held after the unification with Libberton though now it appears to have been converted to a private residence.

Time now to head for the other half of the parish, Libberton, but before we do, let's journey further along the Shieldhill Road and visit the castle, once home to the mighty Chancellor family. Shieldhill Castle was originally built in 1199 during the reign of William I but, in later times, the family moved in to a new mansion house nearby. Sadly, following the fateful Battle of Langside in 1568, when the Chancellors sided with the queen, Mary of Scots, their new home was sacked and burnt to the ground causing them to move back to their tower house which meant much refurbishment. The family, of course have long since left their beloved hall which is now an award winning hotel, conference centre and a much sought after wedding venue. Sections of the old tower remain as does the old chapel, allowing the beautiful building to retain some of its grace and dignity, in the most heart warming surroundings, above the gracious River Clyde.

| The Tin Tabernacle in 2008 | Libberton Kirk |

Head back now to Quothquan and take the road to the right just at the entrance to the village. Libberton lies beyond the farms at Burnfoot and Quothquan Mill...and the village school. Past the school, there are a few houses but the Carnwath junction must be reached before arriving at the pretty little village deep in the Vale of Clyde. To the east of the school is Quothquan Lodge

River Clyde

built in 1939 by Sir Alexander Erskine Hill. We soon cross the Craigie Burn which, on its way to the Clyde, flows in to a loch on the Libberton Moor offering good fishing for the local fisherfolk. Ancient workings have been found near the loch giving us more indication of early man settling here, always with food and warmth on his mind. The parish of Libberton stretches back in to the mists of time and early tribal families are known to have lived in the nearby forests and the fertile lands watered by the Medwin Water and the Clyde, as we have seen all along the course of our journey. The church arrived early and there is mention of the parish, including Carnwath, in the earlier part of the 12th century making Libberton among the oldest parishes in the county. Indeed so well founded was the church, it was decided to allow Carnwath to leave its oversee and form a parish of its own in 1186. The first note of a parson was William who appeared as a witness to a charter of Kelso Abbey in 1210. Huwe of Dunoum was another parson of note and it was he who swore allegiance to Edward of England at Berwick in 1296, not his most pleasing act. Edward I, the so called *Hammer of the Scots,* was among the most hated men in the eyes of ordinary Scots but he was well looked after by the aristocrats of the country who were ever eager to gain reward or award from the English king. Yet another parson of note, who not only preached the Gospels but also busied himself in the politics of the area, was Sir Thomas Gray who, according to Blind Harry, author of the life of Wallace, was a joint author of the original story of the Patriot's life. The Knights Hospitaller of Jerusalem owned lands in Libberton and, and like many other places, may have built a place of refuge for the poor and weak and that could be the case here since a farm community just to the north of the Medwin Water is known as Spittal.

From very early times, the lands around Libberton belonged to the mighty Somervilles who owned great tracts of land all over southern Scotland from the Firth of Clyde to the German Ocean (North Sea) However, the most enduring landlords in the parish were the aforementioned Lockharts who bought huge areas from the 4th Earl of Carnwath, John Dalzell in 1676. Sir George Lockhart, the purchaser of that land was later elevated to Lord President of the Court of Session in Edinburgh but was brutally assassinated in March, 1689.

The residents of the wee place on the right bank, are happy with there seclusion, their peace and well being. Unlike their ancient forebears, they do not have to hunt for food, larger centres with good shops are nearby but some do still fish the river, but more in the name of sport than a hunt for dinner, but still, of course, with a fishy tale to tell. They have so many wonderful walks all around and good clear air to breathe. I wonder, as I look towards Quothquan Law, what William Wallace would say if he could look down now and see the many fine communities which exist where once, when he viewed the valley in 1297, there was very little and what did exist was full of poor people scurrying around looking for food or defending themselves from unwanted visitors.

Today, Libberton, apart from the church and school, boasts a village hall which is now situated within the manse of the church. The folk of the small village are fortunate to still retain their old kirk, since, as we shall see in the coming paragraphs, many of the churches in this area are now united, meaning some of the old kirks closing their doors to regular services.

On we flow of the river as she prepares for extreme windings where, in the matter of a few miles, she sweeps in every direction of the compass. From north-east approaching Libberton she now curls to north-west between the lands of Muirhouse and Northholm Farms before looping south, then north en route to the Meetings where the substantial Medwin Water floods in to the old lady before yet another series of twists and turns. To the north, slightly off our principal route, is Carnwath a place of ancient standing with one of the oldest mercat crosses in Scotland which dates from the days of James V in 1514, who had granted the 5th Lord Somerville, by charter, the lands of Carnwath with the stipulation he erected a cross, which he did two years later. It was merely a natural progression since the toun had been erected to the status of Burgh of Barony in 1451 during the reign of James II of Scots.

The Somervilles were ardent followers of the Scottish monarchs since the days of King David and William, 1st Baron Somerville, was a close associate of Robert I (the Bruce). The Somervilles were responsible for the building of the first church dedicated to St. Mary, a church which was extensively reworked in 1346 before being raised by the lordly family, in the latter part of the 15th century, to collegiate status. In those days, wealthy families were increasingly applying to the bishops of the day, or the pope, to employ a provost, a group of priests and choristers to pray and sing for the lord's family, his ancestors and descendants. This worrying trend was being carried on throughout Scotland without too much

regard for the ordinary parishioners. The remains of that church, St. Mary's Aisle, (left) the burial place of the Somervilles, the earls of Carnwath and the Lockharts, still stand proud in the town. The beautiful Gothic building is situated immediately adjacent to the parish church of the 19th century which is covered by an interesting roof, modelled on Parliament Hall in Edinburgh but, sadly the old church closed 'for business' in 2012.

The ultra powerful Somervilles built a motte castle in the 12th century which was added to and strengthened over the years. It was abandoned sometime in the 17th century as peace descended across the land but the last remnant, the motte mound, still remains on Carnwath Golf Course. The meaning of the name, Carnwath is said to derive from an old cairn which stood to the west of the village and a ford (or *wath* in the Saxon language) over the local burn, therefore Cairn or Carn Wath; that burn, the Carnwath, runs through the golf course then between the motte and the parish church. Another Somerville possession, formerly a Douglas bastion, was Couthally Castle, the remains of which lie to the north of the small town.

The main industry from very early times, has been arable farming and it was indeed an area which participated to a great degree in the agricultural reforms of the 18th century. Some weaving was undertaken but mostly for local use while a few flocking weavers worked in the employ of larger companies in Glasgow. At nearby Wilsontown, within Carnwath parish, there was an extensive iron foundry which employed many of the local population then, in much more recent times, the town was home to a railway station but that went by the wayside during the Beeching cuts of the 1960s.

Today, Carnwath is still reliant on agriculture but to a much lesser degree than before and most must travel for employment. The town itself is self sufficient in everyday needs with various shops, bank and post office, while halls, including the town hall, hotels and inns provide for all occasions. One such inn, the Wee Bush Inn, was the last thatched roof inn in Scotland until fire swept through the premises in the mid 1980s. On visiting the inn, Robert Burns inadvertently gave name to the pub when he, the world's most famous graffiti artist, scratched on the window, *Better a wee bush than nae beild at a'* – beild meaning shelter. Sports and recreation are catered for at King George's Park, the bowling club and the golf course.

Carnwath is home to one of the oldest traditions in the country, *The Red Hose Race,* the oldest foot race in Scotland having been founded in 1508 and still going strong. When James IV, the ill fated king who died at Flodden, granted the manor to the third lord of Carnwath, John Somerville, he added a clause stating 'The

Crown's vassal (Somerville) should award one pair of long, red hose (stockings) to the man running *the most quickly* from the east of the town of Carnwath to the cross known as the *'Cawlo Cross'* That race is still held every July during the town's agricultural show at the Show Ground.

Let's now reach out for Carstairs to the west but first we must pass West End Carnwath, very much a village in its own right, near where the Carstairs State Hospital is situated. To the north of West End

A scene at Carstairs Village

24

is the White and Red lochs, a 'Mecca' for fishermen from a' pairts, but it is to Carstairs we now head. Carstairs Village is in a fine situation and contains all needed for comfortable everyday living, shops, inn, hotel, community centre and lovely old church. At the centre of the village is a beautiful and well used village green, adding to all the other ingredients of the traditional village settlement, mixed well, to form the tranquil nature of the wee place.

Carstairs from Old Welsh *Caer* (fort) and *stair* (possession within a fortified settlement) which could mean there has possibly been a settlement since before the Romans arrived in early AD. We do know the Romans built forts at Castle Dykes and Corbie Hill while much of the route of their ancient roads have been uncovered nearby. Other artefacts have been found over the centuries including pieces of weapons and coins. Experts believe the site of the tribal Damnonii town of *Coria,* was situated near Corbie Hill and the Carlisle road which ran through the settlement en route to the Antonine Wall.

From the 12th century, the advowson of the parish was with the Bishops of Glasgow, a situation of great importance to the diocese but in terms of Carstairs, their day was still to come. Towards the end of the 12th century, the Bishop, Robert Wishart was called to help mediate in the ongoing quarrel between the de Baliol and de Brus families as they vied for the crown of Scots in the wake of the deaths of Alexander III then his grand daughter, Margaret, *Maid of Norway.* Wishart's reward for his help was the right to build a castle near the church of Carstairs.

The present day church, of the latter part of the 19th century, is the descendant of that ancient church of Casteltarres (another old name) which was founded before 1170 and was in the deanery of Lanark until the Reformation. In 1508, another bishop of Glasgow, Robert Blackadder, founded another chapel in the parish, St. Mary's of Welbent of which no vestige remains.

Many groups, of all ages, exist in the wee village and the community centre is a well used venue. Sport too, comes in the shape of a bowling club and the magnificent Kames Golf and Country Club which offers two courses to the enthusiasts. Pity to leave the lovely wee place but I must take a quick look at Ravenstruther to the west before we make our way to Clyde's left bank and the old parishes of Pettinain and Carmichael.

Ravenstruther, south of the Mouse Water, is home to a large coal terminal, a caravan and camping park and a fine, busy village hall. It is an ancient settlement and was granted to, who else? the Somerville family in 1517. In days gone by, a flourishing quarry was busy on the banks of the Mouse as were several mills grinding out the fruits of the soil. Now that area, comprising large ponds and a fast running stream, is home to a very popular Deer and Trout park. The sights and sounds around the old eastern ward of Carstairs are soothing but soon our thoughts turn to Carstairs Junction on the north bank of Clyde.

The village grew following the opening of Carstairs railway station at the junction where Edinburgh trains heading down the west, joined the main west line of the old Caledonian Railways in 1848; the line was electrified in 1991. The village has grown ever since and now contains an inn, primary school and a parish church which is now united with the church at Carstairs Village. It may not have the same lovely layout as its big sister up the road but still, it is neat and very functional. Being on the banks of the River Clyde does add a scenic backdrop and, of course, attracts a multitude of fishermen. Through the village we go until a magical scene meets the eye, another north to south loop in a river searching for the low grounds as she meanders through the hills. The loop is the perfect place to tarry, reflect on where we have been and anticipate the next port of call, Pettinain, yet another ancient parish in the lands of Clydesdale but I could not leave without mentioning magnificent Monteith House. The great house, also known as Carstairs House, was built in 1823 by William Burn, one of the pre-eminent architects of his day, for Henry Monteith MP but in 1899, the house was purchased by a former Lord Provost of Glasgow, Sir James King 1st Bart. However, the house was later sold to the Roman Catholic Archdiocese of Glasgow who renamed the mansion, St. Charles Institution and was used to house and care for children with mental illness. Carstairs House was again sold in 1983 and returned to the name 'Monteith' and is now used as a nursing home. The house and grounds are probably more famous as being the site of Scotland's first electric railway when Joseph Monteith, grandson of Henry, built a small electrified railway from the house to Carstairs Station, to 'ferry' himself and his guests back and forth.

Now to Pettinain, (Old British – *Peithynan* – meaning a stretch of flat cleared land) which originated in the reign of David I (1124-1153) when the king granted lands to his clerk, Nicolas, with the rights of pasture, however a problem arose...the lands were entirely covered in woodland. Nicolas took the king to his word, and cleared the forest to create pasture on the wide open spaces, thus the name.

The church at *Pedynane,* was, from its foundation in the 12th century, a free parsonage with the king himself the patron. David granted the tithes of the church to Dryburgh Abbey though it remained firmly part of the Diocese of Glasgow. The ancient church stood on the same hillock as the present with its village built around which is still the case, an old village huddling around the pretty divine, in the company of Bank Farm. Around the year 1200AD, a grant of land at Pettinain, was made to William de Asseby which was granted in perpetuity for his heirs. However, William's son, Peter, felt he had no rights to the land and gifted it to Dryburgh in the witness of Lady Christian de Morville, daughter-in-law of the founder of that abbey. In much later times, the possessions of Pettinain were granted to the Johnstone family of nearby Westraw as reward for their capture of the Lord of Douglas at the Battle of Arkinholme (Langholm) in 1455. The lands, in time, passed to the Earl of Hyndford then, on his death, to the Anstruthers. In the wake of the Reformation some of the lands passed on to the earl of Mar. Laurence de Petyn was a local man who was sent to Berwick in 1296 to do 'the deed' at Edward's feet. All around Pettinain are reminders of times long gone with various sites of ancient workings, of forts and homesteads which were built before and after the period of Roman aggression. The hillock on which the church stands

The Southern Hills

is widely believed to have been the site of a Roman fort.

The gracious old church has the most wonderful and unique belfry which was retained from the previous church of the late 17th century. Another piece of antiquity is a grave slab inserted with an engraved image of sword and shears, is fitted to one of the lintels on a window on the south façade. Sadly the church is no longer in use as more 'centralisation' of churches takes place.

Tiny Pettinain sited round the church has no facilities at all, no school nor shop where once there was in times gone by, no community hall and, of course, now no church. A few hundred yards to the south of the old village, many new houses have been built in more recent times but still there is no new arrivals by way of facilities. If ever there was a community, where the great days are long in the past and with no prospect of ever returning, it is lovely Pettinain.

Clyde continues to weave a pretty fabric through the gentle hills and rich farmlands before sweeping south between Cobblehaugh and Easter Hills as she

approaches the parish of Carmichael. On past the dam opposite Millhill and the confluence with the burn of the same name, she reaches Carmichael Mill on the left bank. Wonderful gardens and the mill itself attract thousands of visitors throughout the year and is certainly worth a look. Next on the route is quaintly named Carmichael Boat, an old ferry point, at the crux of a sharp left hand bend as the old Hyndford Bridge (above) comes in to view. The great bridge of four arches and several flood, segmental arches, was built in 1773 in the Carmichael Estates and has served road traffic crossing the Clyde between Carmichael and Lanark ever since. It is one of the most photographed...and famous of Scotland's rural, river crossings. Now we are in the domain of the notable Carmichael family, literally, everything south of the river at this point is truly Carmichael in name and deed. That family have served king and country, both Scotland and the United

River Clyde

Kingdom with distinction, for nearly 1,000 years. The title, Lord Carmichael was bestowed on the family in 1579 and the Earldom of Hyndford was the honour bestowed on the 2nd Lord, John Carmichael in 1701. Later the title passed by marriage to the Anstruther family whose origins lay in Fife though they assumed the name Carmichael-Anstruther but the earldom became extinct in 1817 on the death of the unmarried 6th earl, Andrew, which appears strange, since there would be no shortage of claimants. The present chief of the name and arms of the Clan Carmichael, is Richard Carmichael of Carmichael having dropped the Anstruther, thus returning the name to its original form. Incidentally, there is an impressive monument of 1774, on Carmichael Hill, dedicated to Sir John Carmichael, 3rd Earl of Hyndford and a distinguished commanding officer in the British army.

The name is said to derive from a church built on a hill and founded by the saintly Queen Margaret in 1068 soon after her marriage to Malcolm III. The Princess of Wessex was a highly pious lady and the church she founded on Kirkhill, was only one of many of her foundations across Scotland. In earlier times, that hill was home to a hillfort, or *Caer* from the old Welsh and, since the queen dedicated the church to St. Michael, the name Caermychel or Carmichael was born. The hill stands less than one kilometre to the east of Carmichael House but no vestige of the old divine remains though an 18th century burial vault stands on the site. Slightly north-east of Kirkhill is Chesters Hill another home of Roman fortifications.

The Carmichael family held many castles and lands at various times during their history including, Maudlsie, Eastend, Fenton Tower, Castle Craig, Crawford and of course, Carmichael. Carmichael House, described as the Caput of the Barony, was built in 1734 but sadly is now a ruin. The magnificent house was last occupied by the 25th Baron Carmichael, Sir Windham Carmichael-Anstruther but, during the 2nd World War, the house, like many other mansion houses across the country, was used to house troops of the Polish army. Sadly, like so many other houses I have come across in Scotland, the house was badly neglected during those soldiers' stay. Rather than repair the house to its original glory, Sir Windham sold the building which was converted to a nursing home. The home folded in 1950 and, after the good baron repurchased it, he removed the roof to save on heavy taxation. If nothing else the house was saved from total ruin but in recent times, much restoration has helped save the building for future generations to see and admire what, there is no doubt, was nothing short of supreme. On a much happier note, the Carmichaels still reside on the estate and Clan Carmichael Gatherings are now held annually, when the clan gathers at the old house before going on various tours where Carmichaels have resided and made their name.

The parish of Carmichael, one of the largest of the old parishes of the region, was a busy and industrious place of old, part of which, the mill, we have already seen. It was a prodigious producer of fine leather, contained an iron foundry with cast iron works for all needs, including all the local threshing mills while many weavers were kept busy all year round. Local inns flourished because of the industry as did travelling retailers. Of course, farming was so important among the hills of Carmichael but, as we can see, there was more to the parish than simply agriculture.

Following the demise of the church on the hill, founded by St. Margaret, a new church was built in the most populated area of the parish, Carmichael Village. Of the old church, we know one of the earliest of the parsons, Robert de Jeddeworthe (Jedburgh) in 1286 and it was he who paid homage to Edward I in 1296 at Berwick being named as *Parfone de Eglife de Kermighel del comte Lanark*. Soon after, the church of *Chermeildch* was given in to the patronage of Sir James Douglas by Robert I and for centuries the patronage stayed within that family until it eventually passed to the Carmichaels.

Today's kirk is known as the Cairngryffe Parish Church (left) named after a local hill and is now one of only three churches in the region still serving the local congregations of Carmichael, Libberton, Covington, Quothquan, Symington and Pettinain. It is sad, in the modern day, that so many churches must close their doors for the last time due to a general lack of interest in Sunday worship, a malaise sweeping the entire country. While there are isolated cottages and farms dotted all around Carmichael, the village itself is but small with barely 30 houses though there are more within the great Carmichael Estate.

While there is no shop, the community is still home to a very fine primary school and village hall where many local functions are held and local groups meet including the SWRI.

Another popular destination is the Carmichael Visitor Centre. Opened in 1994, the centre contains Scotland's only wax model museum, as well as farm, shop, coffee shop, adventure playground and wonderful estate walks. It really is an experience and where the finest venison is offered for sale. Walking and cycling are very important pastimes in the vicinity and are well catered for, especially those tackling Tinto Hill, the highest in a very hilly parish. Hill runners are drawn from many parts to participate in Tinto races and are, as are spectators, suitably catered for with extensive car parking facilities and cafés at the site and on the

River Clyde

Carmichael Estates and it would be a delight to stay a little longer and admire the beautiful countryside, staring at the rolling hills standing as pinnacles, silhouetted against the afternoon sun; again though, it is time to head on and back to the river just to the north of Hyndford Bridge where the lovely village of Hyndford Bridge awaits. To the west of the village stands the sites of ancient crannogs which were found and excavated in the late 19th century. While now on dry land, the island dwellings gave up many interesting artefacts from an extremely long period of time stretching from the Bronze Age, through Roman times right up to the early medieval period. The site of the crannogs is thought to be what was an artificial lake near the small Lang Loch near Hyndford quarry. Just to the north of Hyndford, at the meeting point of the A73 and A70 trunk roads, is the old Winston Barracks, for some time, the home of the famous Cameronians. The barracks have been heavily renovated to provide more housing for the local people.

Now swinging sharply to the left, Clyde takes on Carmichael Burn, before passing the ruins of Boathaugh, an old coaching inn on the right bank near Prett's Cornmill and the oddly named Crookboat near the site of a dismantled railway. Crookboat is thought to have been the site of an old ferry but rather than, as some would say, the ferryman being tarnished with charging too much for the crossing, it was so named as the place of the crook in the river where she changes directions sharply from south to north welcoming the substantial Douglas Water in the process. That crook in the river really is a bonnie spot, where we can spend some time, have a seat, tea and biscuit in the comforting arms of nature's beauty. From this point, the sparkling waters are headed for the most exciting section of their entire journey, the world famous Falls of Clyde at New Lanark. No longer will the peaceful river 'dilly dally', she is in a great hurry to reach 'home' whether the fishermen on her banks like it or not. The cattle, busy on the north bank don't seem to realise the importance of Clyde's hurry as they stoop for some refreshment.

The first port of call on this section is Harperfield Farm on the left bank before reaching the remains of Old Tillieford Village where once was a ferry across the river and the site of Tillieford Mill which was depicted on Pont's map of 1596. Now sweeping on a north-westerly flow below Drummond's Hill, Clyde prepares for the next 'left hander' where she meets Bonnington Linn. The countryside ahead is beginning to drop to a much lower level and, here at Bonnington, it shows, quite dramatically. In the space of a few yards, the river falls more than 36 feet over quickly dropping rock formations, all providing the most wildly exciting scene at the beginning of the legendary *Falls of Clyde*. The crashing waters, created by the linn, power a local hydro electric power station and provides the first powerful sign of what's to come. The ruin of an old iron footbridge can barely be seen through the thick vegetation as the river hurries on regardless. Though still fast flowing, it seems a much more leisurely water flow beyond the farms at Parkhead, Damhill and Corehouse on the left bank and Robiesland on the right. Now it is time to meet the daunting Corra Linn which, in the most awesome fashion, causes the water to fall an incredible 90 feet over eroding rock strata hewn over millions of years, it is one of the most dramatic scenes in the entire country. No matter how often you see them, they never fail to amaze as they crash down towards the power station which they drive, and the old mills where the wheels turned and business flourished. Corra is said to be named as the place where Princess Cora, daughter of William III and Queen Margaret, rode to her death after being shunned by a prospective lover.

On the left bank, high above the basin, lies the mournful ruins of Corra Castle which is widely believed to have been a fortified farm house, the type we witnessed near the source of the river. This one however, was protected on three sides by cliffs overlooking the daunting gorge of the Clyde below. On the landward side there is evidence of a ditch and an enclosed courtyard. Whoever built this powerful defence of the 15th century was obviously a man of some substance and, perhaps, with a power making ransom on his head. Almost directly opposite is the substantial ruin of Bonnington Pavilion, or the *House of Mirrors* as it is sometimes known. Built in 1708, by a proud James Carmichael of Bonnington, who would take his guests to the pavilion, his summer house, to view the rip roaring waters crash, level by level, towards its basin in the depths of the canyon below. Mirrors were hung around the walls so as to allow friends to see the falls no matter which way they turned.

New Lanark Mills, are the recipients of the great flowing of waters crashing off the linns, formerly of great industrial excellence, a stepping stone for mankind and the pride of 18th century Scotland. Here is where a new concept was born, where people were cared for in every way, from cradle to grave; they had work, a home, church, education, solace, warmth and food, there was even a burial ground which, in 18th century Scotland, was still a rarity for the common people. This is where David Dale and his son-in-law, Robert Owen, created something which had never been tried before, respect for all men regardless of their station. This was Owen's dream, *Utopian Socialism* had arrived and the two men proved, great profits could be made from industry by treating their employees with the utmost respect, a staggering new stepping stone in the history of human relationships. From the moment a new babe was born in to the community, they were taken under the 'company's wing', baptised in the community church, attended kindergarten and school then worked, were housed, and paid too!

At New Lanark, there were and are, all the ingredients of a down to earth, caring culture. If only other industries had followed New Lanark's lead, like the coal industry where men, women and children were consigned to a hellish life in the *Devil's Dark Chamber* and the ship builders who worked all the hours God sent, with paltry reward for their lifetime efforts. Of course that applies to all industries but what Dale and Owen proved, happy workers are good workers and more productive to boot. They built their mills, harnessed the power of the Clyde through tunnels and lades in order to drive the waterwheels which in turn provided the power for the weaving looms in order to create the finished material. One of Robert Owen's meaningful, 'before-their-time statements' was "*To train and educate the rising generation at all times should be the first objective of every society"* A statement which would come as shock and horror in some quarters. Owen's politics and outlook would, one day, turn the world on its head.

The amazing concept drew a collective 'gasp' from the rest of the known world or at least, the upper classes of the world. The system used had so many benefits both for employee and employer who could now rely on a greater sense of loyalty from the workforce. However, in more modern times, the great economic upsurge in Japan copied, in so many ways, the philosophy of New Lanark by harnessing the loyalty of the workforce.

The great revolution at New Lanark began in 1786 and survived until 1968 when it closed its doors for the last time, as the downturn in the Scottish textile industry began to bite. Every other similar area in Scotland, producing wools, cottons and other textiles, soon followed in New Lanark's footsteps.

As time passed, the old village and its mills began to deteriorate and that was the case until the New Lanark Conservation Trust was founded in the mid 1970s. Now known as the New Lanark Trust, they set about restoration, on a grand scale and, by 2006, their efforts began to reap rich rewards. The newly refurbished village and 'industrial estate' was now attracting visitors from all over the world. Of course visitors had been arriving before but, in the present day, numbers are still increasing year on year to this, one of the UNESCO World Heritage Sites, the highest possible accolade and a fitting tribute to all New Lanark stands for.

Present day New Lanark is not simply a tourist attraction, it is still a real, living village with a vibrant community of more than 200 souls. There are shops including the Village Shop, eateries, visitor centre and a fine hotel, all ingredients of a thriving community, which is the envy of many other villages in the region. It is situated in one of the most inspiring locations anywhere; a beautiful valley, enclosed in tree curtained hills overlooking the sparkling, dashing waters which still provide the power for heating and lighting in the visitor areas. The Bonnington and Corra Linns have provided power for more than two centuries but they are not the only sections of cascading waters, there is another one in the deep gorge, the Dundaff Linn. On the opposite bank from the mills, the left, there exists a wildlife nature reserve and many more fine walkways. One feature of the Clyde, for a great part of its course, is the wonderful walkways providing leisure amidst some of the most beautiful settings. One of the great periods of life at the village, is the annual Victorian Festive Fair on the lead up to Christmas; a time for joy, happiness and bargains at New Lanark where so much has been achieved for the betterment of mankind.

**Lower falls of the Corra Linn
at New Lanark**

**Mill Lade
at New Lanark**

River Clyde

**St. Nicholas Church at Lanark
with statue of the Patriot, William Wallace
Scotland's greatest hero**

**The Main Street
Crossford**

Section Two

The Orchards – Lanark to Cambusnethan

*A*s you can see, a more than interesting day can be spent in this beautiful environ at New Lanark but time now to carry on with the flow and visit one of the most historic towns, not only on the river, but in the entire country, Lanark, the former county seat and where the *'Free Scotland'* revolution began.

*T*hough home to a Roman encampment, a little to the south of the town centre on Castle Hill, Lanark is thought to be much older with roots in the Mesolithic period, but the first mention comes from Ptolemy, the Roman cartographer and geographer, who identifies Lanark as Colænia though the present name is thought to have been *Lanerc* from the old Cumbric language, meaning *'a clear space in a forest glade'*

*F*rom those early times, though tiny, Lanark has been of great importance and was for many years, a country seat of kings, indeed the town grew slightly to the north of a royal castle which was built below the confluence of Clyde and Mouse Water, on the aforesaid Castle Hill. The first mention came in 978AD when the king, Kenneth II, held the first known parliament at Lanark Castle. (though some say, the castle was not built until 1140) From the time of Kenneth, Lanark grew in size and importance. While many believe, David I granted the town Royal Burgh status, it is more likely his brother, Alexander I granted that honour some time earlier. In those times, there was something of a power struggle within the royal family, nothing ever seemed to run smoothly with Scottish royals. When King Edgar died in 1107, younger brother David, Earl of Huntingdon, was desperate to succeed him though he was by no means the next in line. Edgar knew this and made a request of Alexander, his other brother and heir. Edgar wanted David to have some power in the south of Scotland and he created him Prince of the Cumbrians or, as some may say, the titular King of Strathclyde. Though David was a very pious man, he was determined to gain power at any cost and would have happily taken the crown off his brother's head. As it happened, when Alexander died, he needed the help of Henry I of England to provide forces allowing him to 'steal' the throne from his nephew. Still, David did renew Lanark's royal status as did nearly every monarch up to Charles II, such was the royals' love of the little town on the Clyde which had become one of the most royal of all Royal Burghs. There is a school of thought, David renewed the castle around the time he ordered the planning of a market place where feu holders could ply their wares. The town also boasts one of the oldest schools in Scotland and almost certainly the most enduring, a source of pride for everyone who has attended Lanark Grammar School which was founded in 1183 or before...a school still renowned for its excellence. There is simply no doubting Lanark's early standing and importance.

*O*f course, Lanark's single greatest claim to 'immortality', rising higher than the parliament or the deeds of kings, was the day William Wallace, Scotland's greatest hero, rose from the shadows to avenge the savage murder of his wife

River Clyde

Marion Braidfute of Lamington. Wallace seemed to have a desire to kill any Englishman he stumbled across 'just for fun' but at Lanark, his role in life took a dramatic turn. He assassinated the sheriff of the town, commonly thought to be Sir William Heselrig but others believe it was more likely to have been Sir Andrew Livingstone, a Scot in the service of Edward I, as most Scottish nobles were at that time, including Robert de Brus, the future king. Wallace's followers then proceeded to push the English garrison out of the town. His quest now, was not simply revenge for Marion, though that was the spark which ignited the fire, it was to rid his beloved homeland of the unwanted aliens from the south. Here was a man, more common than noble, to whom the ordinary man could associate with, a man they could follow. They did not follow him in search of riches and power, they followed him out of blind belief and trust. His quest was theirs, the English must go and so should all the Scottish lords who followed Edward Longshanks for favour and power. Wallace's fight, was not for fame nor wealth but freedom and, after his barbaric execution at Smithfield in London in 1305, freedom did arrive, but it would be a long and painful process. He had earlier been captured and betrayed at Robroyston by one of Edward's Scottish 'lachies', Sir John Menteith, Sheriff of Dumbarton, as we shall see in a later chapter. The man had gone in body but his spirit and legend lives on, he was simply the *Flower of Scotland* who became, sadly, yet another, *flo'er o' the forest.*

Wallace's death was really one of the greatest turning points in Scotland's history. The Central Belt, the Lowlands, the Borders and Southern Uplands began to unite more than ever before though the Highlands would take a little longer. It was a slow and sometimes bitter process since large parts of southern Scotland were still in English hands, off and on, well in to the 15th and early 16th centuries and for ten torrid years during Cromwell's Commonwealth in the mid 17th century. There is even mention of Lanark itself when Edward II of England is still seen as granting favours and patronage of churches in the town in 1319, long after Bruce ascended the Scottish throne. If truth be told however, the Highlanders, Lowlanders and Borderers could not, in general terms, agree on the colour of grass but now things were beginning to change, even if just a little, all thanks to that fateful day at Lanark in 1297.

Old Lanark was always busy and industrious particularly through the 19th century when industry and orchards flourished. Weaving, lace manufacture and shoemaking were all very important as were the three breweries which existed in the town. Around the town, many mills, more especially flour mills were providing for larger centres and were joined by nearby coal mines, quarries and iron works. Other works included the production of artificial manure, a wood craft factory, a tannery, spinning factory, several orchards, and a mineral oil works. Add all that to the impressive set up at New Lanark and we find ourselves in one of Scotland's more affluent societies.

As we have seen, education came early and so did the church. St. Kentigern's was founded, some believe, by the great man himself and, considering he died in 614AD, would make it one of the earliest church foundations in the country. It is

The Orchards

not beyond the realms of possibility, that is the case since the same saint is widely believed to have established the church at Glasgow with others at Stobo in Peeblesshire and St. Aspath in Wales. The beautiful ruins of the great church, which was granted to Dryburgh Abbey in the 12th century, stand amidst its own burial ground just off the Hyndford Road to the south-east of the town centre. Strangely, that church is one of only two churches I know of, the other was in old Haddington, which was dedicated to the saint in his birth name rather than his pet name 'Mungo' but we shall hear more of that holy man in later pages. There is also a beautiful cemetery chapel in St. Kentigern's Kirkyard. The old church was abandoned in the 17th century but there is another kirk of 1884 which was dedicated to Kentigern on Hope Street though, in 1993, united with Cairns Church and is now known collectively as Greyfriars Parish Church.

Another early church was St. Nicholas' Chapel which stood on the site of the present St. Nicholas Parish Church which is situated near the Cross at the foot of the High Street. That chapel was founded by the early 13th century and contained an altar dedicated to St. Catherine. In slightly later times, the canons of Dryburgh founded another altar in the chapel and dedicated that to the Blessed Virgin. Approaching the Reformation in 1560, Sir Thomas Godsel, chaplain at St. Nicholas, mentioned in a financial report of the day, of another two altars in the church, dedicated to the Holy Blude and St. Michael; a huge statue of Wallace dominates the front façade of today's church. A Franciscan Friary was also established during the reign of Robert Bruce with its church sited on, what became the New Inn then Clydesdale Hotel. The Franciscans, or Grey Friars, were renowned as teachers and founded many schools around the country including Haddington Grammar School and, possibly, Lanark Academy.

Yet another holy establishment was endowed in the parish, St. Leonard's Hospital, which was said to have been founded by the king, Robert I but there is mention of an hospital during the reign of William I and it could be, that Bruce granted funds to renew the old hospital rather than found it. Over the centuries, Lanark was famed for its hospitals and care homes for the infirm, under privileged and mentally ill, indeed the Roman Catholic church was very heavily involved and, at one stage, oversaw at least two establishments in their care. To this day, all the denominations are served by some fine churches and, apart from the ones already mentioned, there are St. Mary's Roman Catholic Church and Christ Church serving the Scottish Episcopalian congregation. There is also a Congregational Church in the town and a Jehovah's Witnesses' Kingdom Hall at Kirkfieldbank. Happily, the caring still goes and the town still boasts a small hospital, the Lockhart, on Whitelees Road.

As the former county town, administration of the county was carried out, as was local justice meted out at the Sheriff Court. Gallow Hill in the town was often a gory place and where the more serious offenders met their maker at the end of a rope. As a Royal Burgh, the town held weekly markets and annual fairs including the *Lanark Lanimers* which is held in the town every June. Like many burghs, the burgesses were required to ride the bounds of their lands to ensure no encroachment had occurred. Stones marked the spot of the boundaries and each stone had to be ridden to and inspected. In bygone days, that ritual would have

Young riders at the Lanimer
Courtesy of David Hamilton ©2007

taken place several times a year but in the modern era it is an annual ritual with processions, bands, fancy dress and anything else of interest. In the past, the burgesses and the men of the crafts, and there were six incorporated trades in the town all with their own Dean of Guild, competed to be the 'head' man or *Lord Cornet* at the Lanimer but nowadays, a committee selects the lucky lad. There are several ride outs including the important perambulation of the Burgh Marches (bounds) There is the Lanimers Ball and finally the crowning of the Queen and the great procession through the town before the fun begins in Castlebank Park ending with the Queen's reception in the Memorial Hall. Hundreds of visitors join the local people to enjoy one of the great days in South Lanarkshire. As colourful pageants go, the people of Lanark can hold their heads high, theirs is one of the finest of all. Another annual celebration is held every year on March 1st and involves children running round St. Nicholas' Church. At the stroke of 6pm on the church clock, the children take off, racing round the building swirling paper balls on a string around their head. Members of the Community council then throw coins in to the throng causing a great scramble amongst the kids. The festival is known as the *Whuppity Scoorie* which dates back some two centuries but no one really knows the origins, but knowledge of the ceremony or not, the celebrations carry on for a week thereafter bringing joy and laughter to the people.

Lanark contains many facilities for sport and leisure and covers nearly every sport imaginable. From fishing and walking at Lanark Loch and the River Clyde to horse riding, from bowls to tennis, from football to fitness and swimming to sauna...and a golf club, the list is nigh endless. Many halls and sports grounds are available and widely used. Lanark United, the town's football team, were founded in 1920 and have competed with distinction ever since. They play at Moor Park where the record attendance is an amazing 10,000. Another famous club, Lanark Thistle Bowling Club, ply their craft on Castle Hill where it all began all those centuries ago. Many groups provide for the young and not so young and

The Orchards

there is simply always something going on somewhere around the town. From the mother and toddler group to the rotary club and chess club to curling club, it is all in place in a wonderfully caring community.

Many varied shows are held at the local showground which is one of the top venues in the county. The famous Lanark racecourse closed in 1977 after centuries of horse racing, in fact it is said to have been founded during the reign of William I (1165-1214) The greatest of all races held at Lanark was the *Lanark Silver Bell* which was, reputedly, gifted by that same king but had to be replaced in the 17th century. Traditionally, the last race of the Scottish flat racing calendar every year was held at Lanark, *The William the Lion Handicap.*

A wide selection of independent shops offers a varied shopping experience meaning townsfolk are catered for their every need. Good pubs, restaurants, cafés and hotels cater for both locals and visitors alike and provide venues for some chitter chatter when old friends meet, and don't be surprised on visiting, if a local stops and bids

Lanark Loch courtesy of Graham Murdy ©2008

you a good day, such is the friendliness of the residents of the Royal and Ancient Burgh. Looking around the town and surrounds, it is a little difficult to imagine so many groups of warring men who have assembled there. From the early Cymric tribes, the Roman legions, the English invaders, the followers of Mary of Scots and her foes, both sides during the Bishops Wars and the more friendly Cameronian Rifles, Lanarkshire's Own.

People with association to the town, and we shall get rid of the 'baddy' first, are, the dastardly Irvine of Bonshaw, who profited from sending the Rev. Donald Cargill to his death, now lies in St. Kentigern's graveyard, Robert McQueen who, as Lord Braxfield, served as an 18th century High Court judge, was born near Lanark, William Smellie, a ground breaking obstetrician, was born in the town in 1697, John Glaister, forensic scientist was born in 19th century Lanark, the motoring family of McCrae lived nearby, and many footballing figures too had association. Those include the legendary Rangers' manager Walter Smith born in the town, Dougie Imrie who played for Lanark before moving to Clyde and Lee Miller who plays for Carlisle United. Finally, a local landlord who may have lived at Bothwell Castle was Fynlaw de Twydyn of Lanark who swore allegiance to Edward of England in 1296.

River Clyde

*O*ne other note of interest is, Lanark was the headquarters in Scotland for weights measures using the town's *'Troy Stone'* system before standardisation to the national Imperial system.

*I*t is with some regret, we have to leave the historic town, full of fine buildings and, more importantly, nice people, so, now we head back to the river and set sail for pastures new. We are soon to enter the most prolific section of an area renowned for its vegetables and fruit, especially apples and pears. The Clyde Valley fruit industry is renowned in every corner of the planet and is the principal reason so many lovely villages have grown along the next stretch of the river.

*C*lyde flows north out of the town before swinging left below the bridge carrying the A72 trunk road. As you cross this bridge, the old three-arched, Clydesholm Bridge comes in to view; it was opened in 1699 and, though still open, was superceded in 1859 by a new single-span bridge. Once across the heavily tree-lined river, we are in the old village of Kirkfieldbank, so called since it occupies the old kirk's land (the glebe) on the left bank.

*I*f I was describing Kirkfieldbank or Kirkland as it was sometimes known, in the latter part of the 19th century, I would be describing a village consisting of two rows of houses lining the main road with a shop, post office, library, school and church. That village contained a weaving factory, a horticultural society, curling club, horticultural society and an angling club. Today, the village appears a little longer, there are more houses and still there is a church (of 1871) a shop, school, a well used hall and an inn; a plastics factory is situated between the village and Linnville on the A72. The houses on the north side of the street have the most lovely backdrop with gardens (above) reaching out to the river below as it is joined by the unusually named Mouse Water which has busied itself with mills, quarries and exasperated fisher folk on its journey through the hills to the north and east. As she reaches her confluence with the historic Mother Clyde, Mouse has carved out the deepest of gorges and is sometimes difficult to pick out, hidden

The Orchards

as she is, in deep, rich vegetation. On the right bank is an excellent caravan park which I know from experience, huddled between the two rivers with Chapel Knowe and My Lady's Well to the north.

My Lady's Well, or The Mary Well is situated near East Nemphlar junction with the Cartland Bridge road. The straggling little village of Nemphlar is stunningly beautiful and each year the friendly folk open up their village to visitors wishing to view the delights of their gardens, every cottage garden is a treasure in its own right. Proceeds raised from the visitors always go to a deserving charity, the residue of a simply cherished community in the gentle hills above the River Clyde. The village is also home to a village hall and an ancient Bastle house. In times gone by there was a school and a library but more centralisation over the years has caused them to close. Even deeper in to the past, Nemphlar was home to a chapel of the Knights Templar and another which survived up to the Reformation. The village was blessed with the birth of William Gardner on 3rd March, 1821 in humble surroundings, growing up on a farm, he had strong desires to travel. In order to achieve his dreams, he joined the army where he saw armed combat at the Crimean War and the Indian Mutiny. William was a colour sergeant in the 42nd of Foot (Black Watch) when, during active service in India, he saved the life of his commanding officer amid fierce attack from the enemy. He was wounded in the affray but later was awarded the highest accord possible, the Victoria Cross. William died at Bothwell in 1897 and that hero of Scotland, was buried in Bothwell Park Cemetery.

A little north-west, sits the magnificent Lee Castle, a former stronghold of the Lockhart family which was recently sold in to American hands. That castle is also particularly renowned for its handsomely landscaped gardens in which an ancient chapel, dedicated to St. Oswald, is said to have stood. The scene over the river from the hills in this part of the county, is quite breathtaking but time to make a quick descent as Clyde visits another lovely little place, Linnville on the left bank overlooked by Hakespie Hill on the right. Beyond Linnville is the Black Hill viewpoint where some spectacular views are to be had and well worth the detour.

Down at the river, things are beginning to hot up again. First we find an iron grid bridge though not for transport, it is used to carry a pipeline over the river but a little downstream, there is some damaged rock strata over where the river starts making waves but rougher waters lie ahead. Within seconds, the river has reached the final section of the Falls of Clyde, Stonebyres Linn, so dramatic, so exciting and yet, only trepidation takes over. From the top shelf, where a watermill once stood, the white rapids crash over rock after rock which has suffered so much erosion ensuring the waterfall becomes even more exciting. The waters, crash over 80 feet in total, before clattering on with gay abandon as they drive on the turbines of Stonebyres Power Station on the right bank. Clyde suddenly becomes a little more placid after passing the station below Nemphlar, but this is as far as any fish would dare reach, ensuring no salmon can reach nor witness the Lanimers Fair at Lanark.

Onward and northward flows the old river, below the ruins of Stonebyres

River Clyde

Castle built by the de Vere family in the 13th century and though remodelled in the 18th century, is now just another wreck. Castles and great houses come but ultimately go, saying goodbye to a world they once knew, but the eternal Clyde

**The exciting
falls
at
Stonebyres**

**Courtesy
of Graham
Murdy ©2008**

moves on regardless. Below the ruins, the Linn Burn is the latest addition, flowing down from the western hills in time to meet Hazelbank but there are more rapids to negotiate before flowing under Arthur's Craigs and past the beautiful village. Hazelbank is surrounded by farms and rolling hills flanked, on the east, by the gracious waters sailing past in all their majesty.

Particularly, on this stretch from Lanark, the banks of the Clyde are dotted with glass houses, fruit farms, nurseries and garden centres as all year round efforts are made to uphold a special pride in the Clyde, one of the great 'bread baskets' of Scotland and there are more to come. Sadly, just beyond Hazelbank, there is the sorry scene of dereliction as a huge area of glasshouses lie empty and broken on the banks of the river at Underbank. Even though, there is still a garden centre there, some lovely houses and a primary school, that sight is quite sorrowful on the road to Crossford but yet there is still a sense of beauty rising above the dereliction. On our way north, we pass a beautiful old school, now private homes, on the opposite bank of the river from the Valley International Park, a wonderful fun park for all the family and includes an atmospheric, narrow gauge railway, all set in the most beautiful surrounds, formerly known as Carfin, the park, for fun and relaxation, is unsurpassed.

The Clyde, the wonderful Clyde, has reached Crossford, which, as the name suggests, is the site of an old ford over the river where now stands a bridge. Crossford is a lovely wee place, situated as it is, below Craignethan Castle, Hallbar Tower and enclosed by the waters of the Clyde, Braidwood Burn and the River Nethan. The village itself is good place to live, with so many lovely walks and the alluring Crossford Park. There is a gracious church, shop, two inns with the local school not too far away.

Craignethan Castle is a ruin of some magnitude and, while built as a show piece artillery fortress, the last of its kind, it was never tested. The lands were in the hands of the Douglas family (the Black) until 1455 when they were made forfeit and the lands granted to the Hamilton Earl of Arran. He in turn gifted them to is illegitimate son, James of Finnart and it was he, being a master of fortified buildings, who built the castle. James Hamilton was executed in 1540 for conspiracy and the castle later came in to the own of his uncle, 2nd Earl of Arran. This was the man who negotiated Princess Mary's marriage to the Dauphin of France, at the Treaty of Haddington in 1548 before being created, in the French aristocracy, Le Duc de Châttelherault. We shall hear more of him in later pages.

A few years later, the Hamiltons were forced to surrender their castles at Craignethan and Cadzow. The castle later changed hands more often than the Queen's guards change at Buckingham Palace, from Hamilton to Hay to Douglas and so on. The magnificent ruin is now in the hands of Historic Scotland and is a must see attraction in the midst of the Clydesdale hills. Restored Hallbar Tower, or Braidwood Castle, is now available as a holiday home with mesmerising views over the Clyde Valley, in the most heavenly setting. The lands at Braidwood were granted by Robert the Bruce to John de Monfod but changed hands continually until 1681 when it passed to the Lockharts of Lee. Amazingly the old tower, beautifully restored, is still owned by the Lockharts.

*B*raidwood is another fine village situated on the old Roman, Watling Road and former home to stone quarries including fine marble. It contains a good mix of private and social housing, a school on hand for the local children who later attend Carluke High School, a good, well used hall and an inn on Station Road. While in the vicinity, we simply must look, though not quite on our route, at Carluke the parish town which contains Braidwood. Several other sections of this parish have been mentioned in other sections including Lee and Maudslie.

*W*ithin Carluke, there is a district known as Roadmeetings and that is such an apt description for this place, so many roads, some major, meet in the town and that may have been the case for centuries at this great meetings point in the southern hills.

*C*arluke is sometimes thought to mean an eminence and a church dedication to St. Luke as in *Caer Luag* though there are several other versions of the town's name. The first church was granted by Robert I to Kelso Abbey and there is some evidence, monks of that abbey worked and lived at Carluke. That church was said to have been situated much nearer the Clyde, about two miles west of the present church which eventually replaced that original. The old church, was replaced in the late 14th century, though known as St. Luke's, was dedicated to St. Andrew and belonged to Lesmahagow Priory. That church was ruinous by 1650 but was repaired to the point it was able to hold a new belfry and the Maudslie loft which were added in 1715. The old church was finally abandoned when the present parish church, the third of Carluke, was built in 1799. Today, there are three Church of Scotland kirks in the town. Apart from St. Andrew's, there are Kirkton and St. John's, while there is a Roman Catholic church, St. Athanasius; a congregation of the United Reformed church and a Gospel Hall also flourish in

River Clyde

Carluke.

The town was created a Burgh of Barony in 1652 during the reign of Charles II and it seemed, the settlement which existed before the coming of the Romans, through the years known as Kirkstyle, had finally 'arrived' and was duly recognised but there is so much history associated with the parish. That history includes the mysterious *'Kirk o' the Forest'* where William Wallace was declared *Guardian of Scotland* after his famous victory over the English at the Battle of Stirling Bridge in 1297. There were three claimants to that notable title, St. Mary's of the Lowes and Selkirk Old Kirk, both in Selkirkshire and the original church in the parish of Carluke. The answer may never be known, each church has a legitimate claim to hosting that great event but the jury, as they say, is out.

Carluke is well endowed with schools with no less than six primary schools and a high school ensuring the children receive good education with not so far to travel. Sport and leisure too are other areas in which the town excels with a fine leisure centre, including pool, baths and many halls and pitches covering many sporting activities. Add to that, dance classes, toddlers groups and function suites, no one need go out of town for sport, leisure or fun in general. Many outdoor facilities are catered for too including rugby, stand up Carluke Tigers Rugby League club, football in the shape of Carluke Rovers, the local junior team who play at the John Cumming Stadium while two bowling clubs, Carluke and Castlehill vie for the town's 'bragging' rights. Golf is not forgotten either with a fine golf course just on the edge of the town and always willing to welcome new members and visitors. But there are so many other societies, groups and sporting clubs making for a thriving and happy community. That is not all though, there are so many other centres and halls ready and willing to accept all kinds of meetings whether it be for leisure or business including Lifestyles, a venue for all and where a section is used to house St. Athanasius School. The library too is a busy and popular venue where many spend hours reading, learning and computing

Carluke is an old town with so many fine buildings but is well prepared for modern life. No one need ever travel for their needs with so many fine shops and supermarkets catering for all, and on their own doorstep. It is also the centre for many surrounding villages, making for a very busy locale. The markets of old may have gone but the hustle and bustle which has replaced the old 'buzz' gives the impression of a market day, every day of the week. The parks and gardens of the town simply add to the atmosphere and of course, provide quiet, welcome walks away from the busy atmosphere of the town.

The industries of old, like weaving, iron foundry, mining, corn mills, brick and tile works, engineering and timber operations may have largely left but there is still work to be found in and around the town including a jam factory, chocolate refinery, bacon curing and other excellent food producers. All the trades of the modern age are situated in what has become a very fine and well equipped town, well able to look the future in the face, with confidence.

So many good and notable people have association with Carluke but pride of place must go to three men, all war heroes, all made of steel, all men of Carluke

The Orchards

who went on to receive the highest accolade in the British army, the Victoria Cross, they are :

William Angus VC a former professional footballer who lived in Carluke
Thomas Caldwell VC, born in Carluke but later emigrated to Australia
Donald Cameron VC born in Carluke and who died of his wounds

Carluke War Memorial

Our humble gratitude is offered to those gallant who helped create a better world meaning everything we now take for granted is due, in no small measure, to those brave laddies of Carluke.

Others include, Dr. Daniel Rankin, Carluke's doctor, geologist and student of pre-historic culture, Major Thomas Weir, adherent and soldier of the *Solemn League and Covenant* and, allegedly, a warlock, General William Roy, the great man of maps, John Cumming, Hearts and Scotland footballer; other footballers include, Joe Dodds and Dougie Arnott.

To the west of Carluke is the village of Law, for long part of Carluke parish. Law was a noted mining village but the pit has long departed the scene meaning the local folk must travel for work but not, alas by train, the station closed some years ago as has the well known Law Hospital. The village itself is like most former mining communities, compact and practical, full of solid, down to earth people.

For its size, Law's facilities are excellent, good shops, small supermarkets, a pharmacy, coffee shop, hairdressers, a village inn, hot food takeaway and a post office. More importantly for people with younger families, there is a good primary school and plenty park area. The local community centre provides a great meeting place and caters for functions and meetings for all the local groups. Finally there is a nice little church and its church hall which are totally immersed within the community and provide the space for more groups to meet, like the mums and toddlers, a voluntary action help group and the boys and girls brigades. The village bowling club is another very busy venue all year round.

Local notables include, Roy Henderson, Mark Weir and Ryan Finnie, all professional footballers.

While in the area, Overtown, now an administrative part of Wishaw, is another place we can take a quick look on our way back to the river. Overtown is a trim little place, another former mining village, boasting a lovely 19th century Gothic style church with an atmospheric three-stage tower. There is also a Gospel Hall, primary school, petrol station, a few shops, post office, community centre and ample parkland adding to a health centre, a major bus depot and the Clyde Valley High School which is situated nearby.

Overtown once contained a very unusual walk, the walk to a local disused mine. To reach the destination, the adventurous locals had to scale a steep brae with some steps near the lower reaches. That walk was known as *Jacob's Ladder,* and though now, no more, a street in the village has been so called as a reminder of the great wee meander. Maybe though that will not be the only reminder, local people are campaigning to have one of the greatest local landmarks restored, and why not?

Time now to get back on course, back to Crossford to board my waiting raft then push on, helped on by the gentle downstream flow of the river, feeling, first the confluence

Overtown Parish Church

with the Braidwood Burn pushing us over a little before negotiating the more affluent flow of the River Nethan joining us on our voyage of discovery, we may need our life jackets here as the waters begin to ruffle, testing our 'sea skills' to the limit. On past Poplar Glen and Threepwoodbank before reaching in to the shadows of Waygateshaw House which was originally a property of the Murrays of Touchadam before passing to the prominent Lockharts through marriage. The old castle then became the property of the Weirs before another family, the Steels, took possession. In 1980, the house was gutted by fire but has now been fully restored to its former glories by the Chiswell family. The great house sits in a picture postcard setting high above the gentle waters of the river.

Onward flows the Clyde on her way to the freedom of the open seas in the north. Through the fertile lands and rich green woods of Overton, Sandilandgate, and Miltonhead Farms where she accepts the Townhead Burn as a new friend, and below the monument to General Roy of ordinance and map fame. The monument marking the great man's birthplace, is appropriately, marked by the triangulation point for the OS Grid square NS8249.

Time now for a sharp 'S' bend below Milton Lockhart, greeting more feeder burns on the way through and flowing on, past Rosebank on the left bank. Before going in to the tiny village, let's have a look at one of the most beautiful, yet

The Orchards

unusual bridges in Scotland, the entrance to Milton-Lockhart. The big house was originally built in 1828 on a site and in a style suggested by Sir Walter Scott, who was biographed by John Gibson Lockhart, owner of the house. In recent times, the fairy tale house was purchased, dismantled, shipped to Japan and, remarkably, re-built. The current owners of Milton-Lockhart are in the process of building a new house in the same style. The bridge over the river leading to a turreted and arched entrance gate, is a superb 'disturbance' on the journey and, with the weir on the loop of the river which once serviced Clydes Mill, a wonderful scene is complete; that enchanting vista envelopes the mind, returning us to an age long since departed, sadly never to return. At times like this, imagination runs riot, thinking of the horse drawn barouches or some other elegant carts transporting the owners of Milton-Lockhart and their guests over the river, in all their finery to a dinner or function at the great house before sipping fine wine above the heavenly waters, cascading below.

*R*osebank is another pretty village, simply surrounded by nurseries, garden centres and orchards on the banks of one of the great rivers of Scotland. The gently rolling, wood covered hills around the village exemplifies everything, the peace, goodness and the beauty of the Vale of Clyde. If Utopia arrived tomorrow, it would surely call in

at Rosebank. At the heart of the village is the cutely named Popinjay Hotel which attracts tourists from all over the world. The Tudor style finish to the building blends in well with nearby houses, all adding to another attraction set, perhaps, in times long ago. The scenic Clyde walkway, crossing another tributary, Jock's Burn, on the way,

above: entrance to Milton-Lockhart
left : glasshouses at Rosebank

north, continues along this section where the peace is personified in a glorious little haven. A day on this magical stretch of water is never a day wasted.

Beyond Rosebank we encounter another entrance, similar to that at Milton-Lockhart, this time at Maudslie, let's investigate. Maudslie reaches back in to the depths of Scotland's history and the first mention appears to be in the early 14th century when Robert the Bruce exchanged some lands at the old estate for lands and orchards in Lanark, the bargain was struck with one, Elen Quarently, and, in fact, further exchanges between the Crown and others, decimated the size of the overall manor of Maudslie. By the late 14th century, the lands, or what was left of them, were granted to Sir John of Danielstown and Finlayston. The estate was later owned by Arthur Erskine of Scotscraig before, in the late 18th century, being acquired by Thomas, 5th Earl of Hyndford who built the great house, a house which would match any in the land, in scale and elegance. James Hozier, later Lord Newlands, purchased Maudslie in 1850 but sadly, one of the greatest houses of all was demolished in 1935. All that remains is the stunning entrance and the bridge. Now the river sweeps right, to the meeting with Tod Burn then sharp left with Dalserf on the left bank and Brownlee House and yet more nurseries on the right. You simply must pop in and see Dalserf, one of the most 'olde worlde' villages in southern Scotland, tucked away in blissful seclusion.

Dalserf is the ultimate in one way streets, one way in and the same way out. It is almost akin to entering an estate, down the drive we go and, suddenly, we are met with two lines of cottages one of which is a hall, with a beautiful wee church (right) at the very end. A car park and another couple of cottages make up the scene which would have fitted in well somewhere in a Hans Christian Andersen story. The little church is a much sought after venue for weddings and, on my first visit, I walked in to a wedding ceremony, no one raised a toast to me but they did wave goodbye as I left. I did return and realised, the  couple who were married that day, really did have their dreams come true, in fairytale surroundings. The old church is cruciform in shape, has an unique, square tower and an, almost Grecian style, belfry all painted white, in keeping with the bright nature of the place. Dalserf, thought to mean the *Field of Serf,* relating to St. Serf who, it is believed, founded a chapel near here. The present church was built in 1655 on the site of, what is believed to be the older church. Wherever the old church was situated exactly, is of no real consequence, since today, it is in the perfect setting. History tells us that in 1116, during the time of

The Orchards

the inquisition of David the future king, regarding lands belonging the cathedral church of Glasgow, some were at the haugh lands of Machan otherwise known as Dalserf, which lay between the Clyde and the Avon. It is unclear if a church was in situ at that point, but by the time Malcolm IV became king, there was a chapel dedicated to the Virgin and dependant on the church of Cadihou or Cadzow (Hamilton) Robert the Bruce later granted the chapel and lands at Dalserf to Sir Walter Fitz Gilbert, ancestor of the Dukes of Hamilton, lands which had previously belonged to John Comyn, Bruce's arch enemy in the contest for the crown and whom Bruce murdered in the Greyfriars Kirk In Dumfries. In 1589, beyond the Reformation, James VI granted the patronage of the kirk to James, 4th Earl of Arran. There is said to have been another chapel nearby, at the site of Brownlee House.

A famous son of the kirk, the Reverend John McMillan, the first minister of the Reformed Presbyterian Church and a fervent Covenanter, is buried in Dalserf Kirkyard where a fitting memorial remembers his life and marks his final resting place. To the west of Dalserf is Ashgill and Ashgillhead near Larkhall. They both contain shops, post office, care home and a fine 19th church, the Rorison Memorial Church named in memory of Rev. William Rorison, former minister at Dalserf. Another popular nursery is situated near the church in an area so full of goodness. There is also a good mix of housing and not far from the much larger community at Larkhall but that town can wait just a little longer since I must keep faith with the river and get my feet wet again below the bridges of Garrion. First though, we have to wade across, yet another friend of Clyde, the Dalserf Burn before coming face to face with Stewart Gill where exciting falls can be seen a little upstream of that dashing water. The Garrion Burn too, takes the scenic route and has wasted no time in getting to the party before we flow under the famous old Bridge of Garrion and it's younger companion at the old road junction.

A tiny hamlet has formed around the old Garrion Bridge since the day she was constructed in 1817. For many years, the bridge was a notorious place, well known for traffic bottlenecks but, in 2002, the answer was found to the problem, a new bridge, only yards upstream, was opened thus forming a river roundabout and easing the pressure on local drivers. Apart from the old bridge and some fine houses, there is a popular garden, arts and crafts centre nearby. Beyond the bridge, heading downstream, the surrounding lands are full of yet more orchards and nurseries in this prodigious fruit growing county, sometimes known as the *Garden of Scotland* or, if you like*, Glasgow's Larder.* A little further north on the lands of Skellyton, the Mill Burn meanders down from a beautiful glen of her own to add to an ever growing river as does another three streamlets to the north, on the next crook in the river's flow. More glasshouses can be seen as Clyde swings to the left at Trotterbank and a little further north still, we catch sight of the most beautiful ruin sitting proud and high amidst the trees on the right bank of the Clyde, the ruin is of Cambusnethan House. The great house is described as being *Neo-Gothic of two and three storeys with turrets at each corner, a three storey in the west elevation and a massive square porch.* Turrets all round and pinnacles embellish this elaborate piece of architect James Gillespie Graham's magic. The house was built in the style of so many priories of earlier times and was one of the masterpieces of old Cambusnethan Parish. Cambusnethan House, or Priory as it is sometimes known, of the 19th century, replaced an older house built only a century earlier and stands near the site of an ancient establishment. There may have been houses built from early times including one which featured a tower, four storeys and demolished in 1661 when Sir John Harper built another new house of which, no known vestiges remain. A little to the east of ruined Cambusnethan House, set deep in woodland, is a huge mausoleum of the Belhaven and Stenton family who, though powerful in this particular area, had their principal seat at Biel House near Stenton in East Lothian. Beyond Cambusnethan Woods, Whittrick Burn, Skelly's Gill, Hall Gill and Tammy's Burn, throw their combined weight in to the flow of the graceful river on her never ending flow.

**The ruins
of
Cambusnethan
House**

**Courtesy
of
Graham Murdy
©2008**

A little further downstream and nearer the river, you can find the ruins and kirkyard of the 17th century Cambusnethan Kirk which replaced a medieval church on the same site, and yet another memorial to Lord Belhaven situated near a large pool by the river and yet another wildfowl reserve on the right bank.

*B*efore 1153, William de Finemund granted Kambusnaythen to the monks of Kelso Abbey which was confirmed by Malcolm IV and later by William I but by the end of the 12th century the manor had passed to Ralph de Clerc who granted even more to the abbey on the Tweed. After 1300, the church was transferred to Glasgow by the new proprietor, Sir James Hamilton and was now part of the Deanery of Rutherglen, the principal deanery in the bishopric of Glasgow. During the reign of Robert Bruce, Cambusnethan became the property of Sir Robert Braide (or Baird) but by 1345, that family were forfeited and the lands passed to the powerful Somervilles. 1386 saw the foundation of a chapel dedicated to St. Michael within Cambusnethan Church. As you will soon find out, the direct descendant of the churches of yesteryear, can be found in present day Wishaw.

Section Three

Industrial Heartlands – Larkhall to Rutherglen

*B*efore heading in to Wishaw, let's venture a little to the west and pay a courtesy call to, the 'relatively young' town of Larkhall.

*L*arkhall is believed to have originally been made up of several smaller villages but by the 19th century was becoming very much a town of some standing. It was an industrious place too, busy with weaving, bleaching and coal mining and, in more recent times, iron and steel manufacture. Sadly that has gone and most working people now head for other centres like Hamilton, Motherwell and Glasgow for gainful employment.

*T*he town contains most facilities required of a place its size including a fine leisure centre, many halls, library, sports fields, a total of eight primary schools in the vicinity and the Larkhall Academy offering further education for the local kids. Shopping is a good experience with everything available without the need to travel to the larger centres; cafés, coffee shops, restaurants, hotels and inns are in abundance as are clubs. Those facilities, added to parks and gardens, mean there is always something to do, somewhere to go, in a town which also boasts several sports clubs. There are three junior football teams, bowling clubs, swimming and racquet sports at the leisure centre while the Scottish Association for Country Sports, based in the town since 1994, offers every country sport imaginable for the outdoor enthusiasts. Add all that to a popular golf course and it is easy to see, the people of Larkhall are not short of activities to keep themselves busy. There are more than a few fishermen spotted most days on the

St. Machan's Church, Larkhall
Courtesy of Ian Sykes ©2008

nearby Avon Water, a great playground for all, especially adventurous schoolboys; ample health centres and Stonehouse Hospital all add to the facilities of a very vibrant town. Even if there is a need to get somewhere quickly, Larkhall is not a bad place to be, near a good motorway network and two railway stations, mean you can be in Glasgow within 15 minutes and Edinburgh in less than an hour.

A total of eight churches take care of the spiritual and pastoral needs of the local people, and considering Larkhall's foundation really stems from as late as 1776, the town has come a long way in a relatively short time.

*N*otable people of Larkhall include the footballing McLean brothers, Graeme Dott, World Snooker champion and Mhairi Love who won two silver medals at the 2004 Paralympic Games.

*T*he great river to the east will soon come in to friendly contact with the waters of Avon between Hamilton and Motherwell but I must now head to Wishaw and Motherwell but before I go, let me tell you of an old ghost story of Larkhall, of the Black Lady of Broomhill, wife of Captain McNeil Hamilton. The captain brought her home from one of his trips to a far and exotic location but, when she was at Broomhill, he would not allow her to venture out during daylight hours, no doubt because of the colour of her skin. Soon the captain posted her missing but no one believed him since she still appeared at the window after dark and, some time later, as a ghostly spectre at nearby Morgan Glen. The captain later died at a young age, of unknown causes and soon the unlikely story grew and grew. Later when a huge lintel from the ruinous Broomhill House was being moved to a local hostelry, it took five men to lift it and put in to place at its new home but next day it was found across the road, broken. Stories of spectres abound in the neighbourhood but no really plausible explanations have been forthcoming.

Former Coltness Gatehouse in Wishaw courtesy of Lairich Rig ©2005

Still shivering from the tale, I have reached Wishaw, a town of many districts and a population of just under 30,000 souls, making it the 26th most populated town in Scotland. It was created a burgh as late as 1855 but did not begin to grow until the villages of Cambusnethan and Craigneuk were added in 1874. As the town grew, so did the industry until it reached a peak in the early 20th century when coal mines abounded, as did iron and steel works, sewing factories, construction of railway wagons, a nail works, foundries, a distillery and fireclay works, the list goes on in one of Scotland's most industrious locales. The post office and banks arrived early, eager to capitalise on the growing economy. Inns opened as did hotels, the town hall was built and so too was Victoria Hall along with a library, bowling green and a golf course. Parks and gardens were laid out and soon the local press, Wishaw Press and Wishaw Herald were publishing the local and national news. The number of churches and schools grew with the rising population. Added to the original town were, Netherton, Coltness, Gowkthrapple, Greenhead, Wishawhill, Panther and Waterloo. Soon a weekly market arrived while other fairs were held twice a year, Wishaw was now placed firmly on the map of Scotland and though it was once, with nearby Motherwell, part of a united burgh, Wishaw has always retained its very own identity.

*I*t sounds as if, like Larkhall to the west, Wishaw is a fairly new settlement but it is not, considering reports of communities here stretching back to the 12th century as we have seen, and the old church dedicated to St. Nethan at what became the district of Cambusnethan, one of the original areas of the 'new Wishawtown' which probably means, *town by the water in the woods.* The latest Cambusnethan Church opened in 1840 at the same time as a chapel of ease in Wishawtown. Nowadays, there are many Church of Scotland kirks in the town serving all the various districts, though some of them have united taking in to consideration the fall in church attendance; Wishaw Old and South Wishaw are the churches which serve the centre of the town. Other churches exist in the shape of St. Andrews Episcopal, the Gospel Hall, Baptist, two Methodist, A Christian Outreach congregation and four Roman Catholic Churches dedicated to St. Thomas, St. Ignatius, St. Aiden and St. Patrick joining the church of St. Brigid at nearby Newmains which for administrative purposes only, is joined to Wishaw.

*E*ducation grew to a point today where there are eight schools in the district including five primaries, all ensuring education is retained at a very high standard. The schools both non denominational and Roman Catholic provide primary education before the children move on to Wishaw High School where John Higgins, World Champion Snooker player was educated.

*E*very area of the town contains shops and inns but the town centre, particularly Main Street, is the principal shopping precinct though many national shops are dotted around the outskirts, just like most major towns. Hotels too, are in abundant supply as are restaurants, coffee houses and cafés, amusement arcades and takeaways. Everything from nugget to nails, rolls to rugs and furniture to fun can be bought in Wishaw. Medical facilities are excellent in the town which even has its own hospital, Wishaw General.

*S*port and leisure is important to the people everywhere and Wishaw is no exception, where facilities are more than adequate for the town and its districts. An excellent sports centre including pools, situated in Alexander Street, caters for all areas of fitness, health and multi sports including athletics, ten pin bowling, shinty, badminton,

Scene at Wishaw town centre

gymnastics, tennis and handball, There are other clubs in the town including Wishaw Football Club, several bowls clubs, lawn and indoor, rugby and a fine old golf course. Other sporting clubs exist for pigeon fanciers, walking and fishing and are available to all. Social clubs include the social ex-servicemens' and miners' welfare clubs. Nurseries and play groups are numerous as there are old folks clubs which include their very own weekly tea dances.

Wishaw really is a town with throbbing heart, there is always somewhere to go, something to do including lots of good walks in any of the fine parks where many of the older folk among us are seen walking with old friends and no doubt reminiscing of the old days when everyone had a job nearby. That, of course, is no longer the case since Wishaw like most towns in Scotland's industrial belt, has suffered. Some service industry jobs and local industrial estates have replaced the ones which have gone, but not nearly to the same degree as before.

The Belhaven Park named after Lord Belhaven, one of the old local barons, is a popular place for all the family especially in summer when the kids can take a dip in the paddling pool or swing their way higher and higher. Belhaven Park is also the scene of a new venue recently added to the town's calendar, the '*Be in Belhaven*' Music Festival although in 2012 it was moved to Beltane Park because of traffic disruption in the town centre. This has proved to be a real plus for the economy of the town attracting thousands to a festival where many well known bands have performed. The festival, after six seasons, is destined to become bigger and better, challenging some of the more established festivals of its kind across Scotland.

Wishaw is almost surrounded by water, with the Clyde the most dominant. Temple Gill burn runs through part of the town before joining the larger South Calder Water which runs across Dalzell Park before, in days gone by, joining the Clyde but now flows in to Strathclyde Loch which it helped to form.

Transport in and out of town is good, with excellent and regular bus and rail services. The fact Wishaw is so near to the main motorway hub in the country, the townspeople, like Larkhall before, are within easy reach of the principal centres at Edinburgh and Glasgow.

Nearby Dalzell Park, part of Motherwell, was, once upon a time, a hunting forest which was laid out and landscaped in the 18th century by the prominent Archibald Hamilton. The park features some remarkable trees and plants and, of course, atmospheric walks. There is a an oak tree, reputedly planted by David I of Scotland in the 12th century, an arboretum, a rose garden, a Japanese garden and so much more. The centrepiece though is old Dalzell House or Castle. Let's take a look back to the days long before the landscaped gardens and before moving on in to Motherwell town centre since the story of Dalzell, or Dalziel, really is the route we should follow closely, to track the course of history which led to the modern town just up the road.

In 1846, it was reported Dalziel parish consisted of Dalziel village, Motherwell and Windmill Hill with a total of 1,457 people living in the parish as a whole and, while Dalziel was the main village, Motherwell had the biggest population, a 'staggering' 747 souls in what would one day become the steel capital of Scotland. In those far off days, the principal industry was weaving, though the village of Motherwell was becoming busier year on year with coal mines and iron works.

The origins of Dalzell date from the 11th century when Malcolm III (Canmore) granted the manor to the family of Sandilands but sometime later, came back to the Crown but no details are available why the lands were returned, though some believe they were back in the hands of the Sandilands for some time after 1342. More details are given with the first mention of the church in the 12th century, as we shall see. Some time later, the lands of Dalywele (Dalziel) were granted by the king, William I (the Lion) to a family who adopted the name, and that was the case until 1342, when the family were made forfeit for indiscretions in the eyes of the king, David II of Scots. However, less than a century later, the lands were returned to the family through marriage. One of the family, Sir Thomas of Dalzell fought with valour at the Battle of Bannockburn in 1314 just 18 years after swearing allegiance to Edward I of England in the company of another member of the family, a local churchman, Renaud. Renaud was almost certainly the pastor at the local Dalzell Church which was founded in the 12th century and there is mention of it being granted to Paisley Abbey in a charter witnessed by Bishop Joceline of Glasgow who died in 1199. That grant was confirmed by Pope Innocent III. Before 1232, the church was granted to Glasgow Cathedral witnessed by Walter of Glasgow, and was placed in the Deanery of Rutherglen

Dalzell House near Motherwell
Courtesy and copyright © Jonathan Oldenbuck, Wikimedia Commons

where it remained until the Reformation. In 1798, the old kirk, situated to the south of the tower near the Baron's Haugh, was finally demolished. At the same time a new parish kirk had been built and still serves to the present day but, after unifications within the parish, is now known as Dalziel St. Andrews Parish Church.

As so often happened in medieval times, grant and counter grant became akin to a complicated labyrinth. Dalziel was granted to Malcolm Fleming by David II but we later find, in 1352, the same king granting the same lands along with Modyrwaile (Motherwell) part to the de Vallibus family and some to Robert Stewart, later King Robert II. Not long afterwards, it appears the barony was now owned jointly by Duncan Walys or Wallace and John de Neysbit a local baron. Further grants were made of the lands by Duncan Walys but this time in the name of his wife Elionore de Brus (Bruce) Countess of Carrick who seems likely to have been the widow of Alexander de Brus, Earl of Carrick who died at the Battle of Halidon Hill in July, 1333. It would appear, land could be granted then taken away for any given reason the king saw fit but here the lands were being given to various members of the royal family, and, of course, sometimes taken back.

It is virtually certain a fortified house was in situ from the time, or before, of the church but the building we see today was begun in the late 15th century when a form of tower house was built. A significant change in direction took place in 1645 when the Dalzells gifted the house to James Hamilton a kinsmen of the Hamiltons of Cadzow who wasted no time in adding a large south wing to the tower. In the ensuing period the house was continually added to while older sections were being renovated. The landscaping of the gardens and great avenues of trees followed from 1745 at the hands of Archibald Hamilton, 4th of Dalzell and the gardens we see today owe their existence to Archibald's vision of the mid 18th century. In 1850, the house was entirely reshaped by the architect, Richard Billings, who added a new north wing to his restoration work on the rest of the house. Andrew Cassells, a great landscaper, remodelled the gardens meaning all was in place for the visit of the Duke and Duchess of Rothesay in 1888. In 1952, it all came to an end for the Hamiltons at Dalzell when the 2nd Baron Hamilton died and the house was sold. Soon a section was used as private school but that was short lived before the house was purchased by the local council but lay empty for more than 20 years until they sold it for £1 to Classical House, developers of ancient houses. When they had finished their magical work, the old lady was subdivided in to 18 apartments and sold, however, the classical work of Billings has been retained and, as such, is the great building we see today. The estate of old included the Baron's Haugh but that great wetland area is now owned by the RSPB who have overseen a dramatic turn in fortunes and now, during the season, is swarming with wildfowl and such a wonderful scene it makes, especially on a bright summer's evening as the sun sets over the overwhelming beauty of the waters and surrounding woodlands; it is not clear exactly what are the origins of the name Dalzell but the most popular theory is, *white lands.*

After the splendours of Dalzell Park let's wander around at the south side of the Baron's Haugh, the great haven for migrating birds and, for us mere mortals too, near the confluence of the great river and Dalzell Burn. This really is another form of heaven for us all, such peace, such tranquility yet, without realising, so near to a large town, wonderful. There seems, what appears to have been, a mill lade near the Baron's Haugh but no mention of mill is mentioned anywhere. It is as though all the flat haugh lands at this point, are great sections of flood plain, wetlands awaiting the wild birds who arrive every year.

*T*he Clyde loops around the haugh where there is a peaceful island, yet another home for hungry migrant birds. Another steep bend to negotiate, a great railway viaduct to encounter and suddenly, we are face to face with the Airbles district of Motherwell, home to one of the town's rail stations, time to head in to the old steel town.

*W*e now know Dalzell was the oldest of the villages which made up the original town but Motherwell too is older than some would have you think and, as we have seen, there is mention as early as 1352 when old Modyrwaile was in the hands, at various times, of the Fleming and de Vallibus families. De Vallibus also possessed extensive lands in Haddingtonshire but there, were referred to in the name of de Vaux. Probably one of that family, a knight of old, who swore fealty to Edward at Berwick was designated Adam de Moderual in the county of Lanark and it is more than possible, that was another spelling of Motherwell. The name, Modyrwaile, is derived from an ancient well which was dedicated to the Virgin Mary and known as the Mother's or Our lady's Well; a street in modern Motherwell bears the name, 'Ladywell'. More mention of the district came in the

16th century, in the name of Baillie of Lamington, who were granted the lands of Jerviston during the reign of James V of Scots and from there, a notable branch of that great family grew.

*A*s discussed earlier, the Baillies were descendants of the two de Baliol kings but that branch made

Scene at Airbles in Motherwell

a conscious decision to disassociate themselves from the hated kings by changing, though only slightly, their name. Jerviston later came in to the own of James Canison who built a new house in 1782. In later times the prominent Colville family arrived and it was they who would change the industrial map of Motherwel forever.

*D*avid Colville founded Colville & Sons, an iron and steel producer at Dalzell, in 1871. David and his sons managed the company, a company which paved the way, ultimately, for the great Ravenscraig Steel Works by which time, Motherwell was the steel capital of the United Kingdom. Motherwell became known as the *Steel Town,* the people known along with the local football team, *The Steel Men.* Sadly, the mighty Ravenscraig closed in 1992, the site cleared and is now going through a mammoth regeneration programme where a college has been opened in company with a huge sports complex, the envy of every other locale in Scotland, with further plans afoot to build thousands of houses on the site.

*A*nother great regeneration took place in the early 1920s when the Colville family gifted their house and park, Jerviston, to the workers at the Dalzell plant, for them, their families, indeed for the population of Motherwell, to spend some more quality leisure time. The newly developed Colville Park opened in 1923 complete with golf and tennis facilities and more activities of interest in the new club house, Jerviston House. The club house contained a library, reading room, rest rooms and all needed for dining, meetings and family parties including weddings and anniversaries. At one fell swoop, the family had shown their workers a gesture of supreme benevolence but that was the way they were. We saw earlier of the philanthropic Dale and Owen and their philosophy on how to treat their workers, now here was a 20th century gesture of equal magnitude. There is a now a new club house at Colville Park, and known as, appropriately, New Jerviston House. The golf course was later restructured by the inimitable James Braid and that track remains pretty much unchanged to the present day. Colville Park Golf and Country Club goes from strength to strength and the Colvilles would be so proud of the club's achievements. Their wonderful website tells us, the Colville family were not simply a giver of facilities, great though though they are, they were givers of their hand; they would often pass the time of day with their trusty employees many of whom they knew by first names. It is not often we read of such people, powerful and wealthy though they were, they never lost their sense of humanity, surely near the top of Motherwell's 'great people league'.

*T*here is still a lot of work in Motherwell, including steel works and other associated industries but nothing can ever replace the number of jobs lost at the giant Ravenscraig plant. Facilities in the town as a whole are very, very good and virtually everything imaginable is catered for. We are about to hear of Strathclyde Park squeezed between the town and Hamilton but many other good parks and gardens are situated around the locality. Sport too is important, as we have seen at the 'renewal' taking place at Ravenscraig.

*T*here are many athletic clubs in the town with the long established Motherwell Athletics Club leading the way while the men's hockey club, founded in 1987, vies on the national stage and are currently in division three of the Scottish league. Another well established club, Dalziel Rugby Club are currently in the RBS Championship A league and play their home games at Dalziel Park while cycling too, is very popular, as is tennis but bowls, football and golf are the most popular in terms of numbers playing; swimming, too is high on the list and that sport is very well taken care of in terms of facilities. In fact the people of

Industry

Motherwell can be very proud of their wonderful leisure, sports and community centres, libraries and the concert hall and theatre. However, in terms of sport, leisure and recreation, pride of place must go to the town's premier league football team, Motherwell Football Club.

Motherwell FC was founded in 1886 and beat local rivals, Hamilton, in their first ever game. In 1895, they moved in to their present home at Fir Park on land gifted by Lord Hamilton. In 1932, they were crowned Scottish Champions after a very successful season in which they won 30 of their 38 games and they have also been runners up to the champions on no less than six occasions. They have won the second tier league four times. The Scottish FA cup has been lifted twice out of seven finals and they have qualified to play in European competition nine times. A magnificent total of 39 players have gained international honours while playing for the club adding to many more who have played for their countries before joining, or after leaving the club; they currently wear their famous claret and amber strips in the Scottish Premiership. Some of their most notable players are, Hughie Ferguson, the all time top goal scorer, the late Davie Cooper, who went on to Rangers and Scotland but sadly died so young, Tom Forsyth and Tom Boyd who went to Rangers and Celtic respectively and both played for Scotland, Owen Coyle, now a successful manager who played for Ireland, Phil O'Donnell another internationalist who also died as a young man, Ian St. John and Andy Weir who were members of Bobby Ancell's 'babes' team of the latter part of the 1950s and early 1960s. There are so many more worthy of a place but...

The town is full of fine shops both local, independent and national and shopping is made a little more safe with many centres and a large pedestrian shopping area. Fine hotels, restaurants and inns help make the town more homely and welcoming and of course provides weekend outlets when a week's work is

Motherwell Railway Station – Courtesy of Thomas Nugent ©2013

done. Many fine buildings can be seen around the town, which is the administrative headquarters of North Lanarkshire Council. A few buildings of note and worthy of a second glance include, the public library, Dalzel House of course, Moorings House Hotel and Windmillhill Street Fountain. The town too is well served by so many fine churches including, as previously mentioned, Dalziel St. Andrews. Our Lady of Good Aid Cathedral also known as Motherwell Cathedral which is the seat of the Bishop of Motherwell and head of the Roman Catholic Diocese of the same name. The latest Bishop was the Right Rev'd Bishop Emeritus, Joseph Devine who retired in 2013. St. Mary's Parish Church of Scotland, is another beautiful building in a town full of lovely churches serving all denominations.

*E*ducation of the local children, is given at no less than nine primary schools and six high schools in and around the town with Motherwell College offering a wide range of courses.

*L*ike all the towns in this area, Motherwell enjoys being in the envious position of having some of the best communications anywhere, being near the main motorways, good town, and out of town, buses and three rail stations all of which reflects the population of Scotland's 25th largest town.

*N*otable people include, from the field of entertainment, Alexander Gibson, conductor and fine musician, actor, Paul Higgins, Hamish Imlach, a popular folk singer, actress Katie Leung and opera singer, Anne Sharp. Sport is represented by, Gordon Dalziel, Tommy Gemmell and Scott Veitch, all footballers who join others already mentioned, while Nan Rae competed in the pool at the Olympic Games. Others are, Alan Fisher, broadcaster, Lord Bonomy, a Senator of the College of Justice and last but by no means least, the philanthropic family of Colville of Jerviston

*W*e cannot leave Motherwell without mentioning the beautiful Strathclyde Country Park and its origins but first let's see how the river is coping with her arrival on the edges of the most densely populated area in Scotland. We still have so many places to see and Clyde is becoming impatient, so, once again, it is all hands on deck as we set 'sail' northward. The river bids farewell to the Baron's Haugh as she flows north round several bends before passing under the railway bridge and sweeping to the left at what can best be described as a great peninsula where the magnificent pile of Ross House is situated. The great house possesses a long history stretching back, at least to the 12th century when David I arrived for play in his hunting forests of Cadzow, part of which was later granted to the monks of Kelso Abbey. The lands were then gifted to John Fitz Gilbert, brother of Walter, in one of the earliest charters to the 'to be' Hamilton family. The lands of Ross passed to the Aikmans in the early 18th century, then in 1889, Colonel Robertson-Aikman had the house completely remodelled to plans of the architect, Alexander Cullen.

*R*ound the left hand sweep and suddenly the river crashes head long in to the River Avon which has cut a deep furrow from the hills on the Ayrshire border in her quest to meet Clyde and now, arm in arm, sweep forward together, between the great towns of Hamilton and Motherwell. Only one more bend, sailing under the Clyde road bridge carrying the A723, and is now flowing along the western edge of Strathclyde Loch hemmed between the loch and the M74 motorway.

The loch is the centrepiece of Strathclyde Country Park which has grown to be one the top destinations in the west of Scotland. A look over the loch (right) a walk around the park and beautiful woodlands, inevitably attracts a first impression of something along the lines, "What a  beautiful place, nature harnessed for our pleasure" and yes! It is a beautiful place but the loch itself is entirely artificial having been created during the early 1970s and involved the flooding of the old village of Bothwellhaugh which stood on the Hamilton Palace Low Parks by the South Calder Water, formerly a tributary of the River Clyde.

In the mid 19th century great seams of coal were discovered around the lands of Hamilton Palace, home to the Duke of Hamilton. Many pits were dug until the late 1870s when it was decided to open two new pits, known as Hamilton Palace Collieries. Of course miners were needed but they also required a place to live and so, Bothwellhaugh Farm was bought and the farm house retained for the pit manager. Then more than 400 cottages were built and laid out as other miners' villages were, in lines of terraces. In time a school was built and it would appear that village would exist forever, but, when the pits closed, the end was nigh for the small community and so it came to be, presumably it was abandoned for various reasons other than simply to create the loch, part of a huge leisure facility. Beautiful though Strathclyde Loch is, I am sure many who were born and grew up in Bothwellhaugh would describe a scene, in their eyes, of far greater beauty than a stretch of water. Nothing can be changed now so we really must appreciate what we have and the loch is a wonderful asset on what was once a great industry and home to another branch of the Hamilton family, the Hamiltons of Bothwellhaugh.

The park plays host to so many activities including walking, cycling, sailing, rowing and other water sports, principally, fishing, all being added to by a fine camping and caravan facility, a hotel and M&D's fun park dubbed Scotland's Theme Park. The Commonwealth rowing events were held there in 1984 and will be again in 2014, when Glasgow plays host to the games.

A watch tower is provided as a look-out to ensure safety is adhered to at all times on the loch. There have also been music festivals held at the park and the world famous 'T' in the Park' festival was held there until 1996. So

River Clyde

whatever your reason for visiting, be it a walk, a picnic or simply sight seeing, do visit. Apart from the obvious, why not take a look at some of the plant and woodland life, including the old Bothwellhaugh woodlands and admire the many species of migrating birds on the mainland and the atmospheric island.

As we have seen from earlier in our journey, the Romans were in the area for such a long time and that was the case too at Bothwellhaugh where they built a fort, and bath house at what is now the eastern section of the loch. Not then was it a place of fun but rather a stopping point for invading 'conquistadors'. The fort, of large proportions, was built on both sides of what is now the loch but the most noticeable is to the east where there are expansive remains of their bath house. Nearby, crossing the South Calder Water, is the remains of what is thought be a medieval copy of a Roman bridge. In my opinion it is more of a 16th or 17th century packhorse bridge, the type which can also be seen at Stow in the Scottish Borders but still acts as another attraction from a bygone age.

Contrary to many beliefs, and as we have seen, the loch was filled by the South Calder Water and not the Clyde, the course of which was diverted in order to create the facility, though sections of the original course can still be seen.

Flowing downstream adjacent to Strathclyde Loch

Soon, we shall be making our way through the town of Hamilton but, before crossing the river, let's meander up the Bothwellhaugh Road, heading for Bellshill but first we pass through the small area of Orbiston, where existed a chapel at, what was, the confluence of the South Calder Water and the River Clyde, long before the building of Strathclyde Loch and where now exists a golf course. That church at *Osbernystun* was dedicated to St. Catherine the Virgin and, in 1242, endowed by Walter Olifard (Oliver) Justiciar of Lothian to the sum of ten pounds annually. If that was not paid, the monies came out of the coffers of Bothieuill (Bothwell) Mill. In 1253, that endowment was challenged by Walter de Moravia and, following a court case, the chapel passed to him with the provision he paid to the High Church of Glasgow, 100 shillings for a chaplain at the great church and nine merks to the chaplain of *Obernistun Chapel* which was in the dependency of Bothwell Church. Another chapel, also part of Bothwell Parish, was mentioned around the same time, and dedicated to the same St. Catherine at *Bertram Shotts* (Shotts) but no mention whatsoever of Belshill in old writings. There was however a village of *Belhil,* appearing on Timothy Pont's map of 1654.

Sometime thereafter, a quarry, allegedly owned by the Bell family, was a busy place of work, so much so, a row of quarrymens' cottages were built. The quarry cut into a hill became known as Bell's Hill from which, it's said, the name derived. There was also a small weaving industry which would grow in time.

*B*y 1846, Bellshill had transformed somewhat, more weavers were employed and coal pits began to open and soon more people were arriving and, in time, the village's population grew to just over 1,000. There were now two shops, a post office, a Relief Church and two schools in Bellshill which would continue to grow throughout the 19th century. Towards the end of the century, more coal pits were opened, the rolls at the two schools had increased dramatically, the post office now

Bellshill War Memorial
Stevie Spiers© 2009
Geograph/1311313

had telegraph and savings bank facilities and two banks, Bank of Scotland and the Clydesdale had set up business. By 1894, the population had soared to over 3,300. Nowadays the population is around 20.000 making Bellshill the 38th largest town in the country.

*T*he 20th century saw Bellshill continue to grow and prosper and was soon attracting many incomers eager to find work and homes meaning, of course, as the town and population grew, there was now a dire need for new, affordable homes to be built. For some strange reason, in times gone by, Bellshill attracted many Lithuanian workers for decades before the formation of the European Union. So many people arrived from that country that Bellshill soon acquired the nickname *Little Lithuania.* During the 19th century, coal and steel industries grew rapidly but now, in the 20th it got really serious. Sadly the boom has gone but it doesn't seem to have affected the drift of people moving in to the town, in fact, for some years in the first decade of the 21st century, house prices rose higher in Bellshill than any where else in Scotland. There is still industry in the town including steel manufacture and many service industries.

*T*he town has suffered like most towns have done, with the recent downturn in the fortunes of local shops and many have closed their doors. The fact, Bellshill is smaller then its neighbours, Motherwell, Wishaw and Hamilton, makes the downturn appear to have affected Bellshill a little more than the larger centres but it is all pro rata really. Still, no one need travel for any of their needs and requirements from a town where there are still some good shops, inns, clubs, restaurants, cafés and hotels. Bellshill is no backwater town as some would say after the loss of so many jobs over the course of the last 50 years when the last of the pits closed and the powerful steel industries took heavy hits in terms of employment. The people of the town are, if nothing else, resilient, proud and adamant, theirs is a bright future.

North Lanarkshire towns are especially well endowed with sports and leisure facilities and Bellshill possesses its fair share. The Sir Matt Busby Sports Complex in the town caters for health, fitness, swimming and many other pitch sports with special attention paid to the youngsters. This large complex is popular within the town and surrounding areas and as I have been informed, is well supported. Of course the centre was named in honour of one of the town's most famous sons, Sir Matt Busby, the legendary footballer who went on to manage the Scotland International team and the almost mythical *Busby Babes,* the much lamented Manchester United team of the 1950s which was tragically decimated in an air crash in Munich in 1958. Of the 23 fatalities, nine of them were members of the wonderful team. Sir Matt himself was seriously injured but after a long stay in hospital and recuperating at home, he returned to the dugout. Here was a man, so full of the grit associated with the men of the steel and coal mining towns of Lanarkshire, just as Jock Stein and Bill Shankly were.

There are three bowling clubs in the town, Mossend, Bellshill and Orbiston, a popular cycling club, a boxing club and karate club at the John McKay centre, another fine facility at Orbiston where also exists a good par 71 parkland golf course and is home to Bellshill Golf Club which was founded in 1905. Football is represented by Bellshill Athletic, an old institution which was founded in 1897 and has competed at junior level since 1899. The Athletic now ground share with Glasgow club, Vale of Clyde who play at Fullarton Park in the east end of the city.

Bellshill Cultural Centre is another wonderful building offering so much to the community. The versatile centre can be adapted to accommodate a relaxed, cabaret style show or, if required, be realigned to host a theatre show with an atmosphere to match. Other space is available for meetings, clubs and groups including toddler groups and a fine library, yet another fine venue offering the whole community a choice within their own town; another popular destination is the Michael Sherry Centre. There is so much grassland in and around the town joining some lovely gardens meaning folk are spoiled for choice when thinking of where to go and relax.

Churches too, play an important role in any community and the people of Bellshill are well served with their houses of God including, St. Andrews United Free Church, The West Church, Holy Family Roman Catholic Church, St. Gerards, Sacred Heart and the Macdonald Memorial Church. In recent times, a lovely Mosque has been built at Mossend to serve the local Muslims and is home to the Lanarkshire Muslim Welfare Society whose website bids us all

Industry

Asalamu-Alaikum – Peace be upon you. As all towns, the most important facility of all is schools, Bellshill contains five primary schools and two secondary, Bellshill Academy and Cardinal Newman High School.

A small reminder of the 'Killing Times' can be seen in the town near the rail track at Orbiston. Mary Rae's Well, the site of duty of Mary Rae and her love for her sweetheart, William Thomson, who was wounded at the Covenanting Battle of Bothwell. Mary cared and nursed him where he fell but failed to save his life. The heartbroken girl could not face life without her fiancé and was later found dead near his body.

*B*ellshill which, like all all parts of this county, is fortunate to be near good road and rail networks making travel so much easier, not forgetting Glasgow Airport which is just a short drive away.

*M*any locals have made their names in the wider world including the afore mentioned legend Sir Matt Busby. It is such a long list and I shall tell you, if I may, of a but a few. Football comes high on the list with men such as Derek and Barry Ferguson, Billy McNeil, Ally McCoist, Phil O'Donnell and Brian McClair. Architect, David Shaw Nicholls, Paul McGuigan, a film director; boxing champion Scott Harrison was also born in the town as were politicians Dr. John Reid and Douglas Cameron. Another noted Bellshill lad was Tom Birney who was a place kicker in American Football and from the world of music, Sheena Easton and Ashley Collins. It really is a long list and I must apologise for those not included.

*M*any other communities exist in this, so busy area, like Holytown, Newarthill and Carfin but we really must push on and get back to the River Clyde as soon as possible. Time to double back a little and head for Hamilton to the south-west.

*M*odern Hamilton really is a town for all, at all times, whether leisure, sport, dining, exploring history or shopping, it can all be found there. Though long in history, the town is not so well endowed with ancient buildings as some other towns in Scotland, but there is still much to see and do.

*I*n recent times, the town has been realigned with one way traffic systems and more out of town shopping. There is even a new town square, away from the town centre, at the Hamilton Palace Grounds which has been so heavily endowed with shopping areas, fabulous sporting facilities and new homes. My first thoughts on the new town square was, wonderment. Is this a novel way of creating a town centre, outwith the town? I wondered but decided to have a look and was not disappointed.

*I*n the old town, there are several shopping centres including pedestrian only malls, rows of independents offering a vast array of goods, all coping well with the influx of the national retailers who find their way in to every main thoroughfare in the country. Street side cafés abound and, in the better weather, a continental 'feel' envelopes the Lanarkshire air giving out a sense of well being, of gay abandon as others continue on with their own daily business. Coffee shops are many as are hotels and restaurants enclosed on every street corner by beautiful buildings. Walking along Duke Street, Quarry Street, John and Avon Streets, I noticed, on almost every corner, a pinnacled or towered building was waiting as if in welcome and encouragement to walk down the street to which it lay guard. Even the more simple crow stepped turret seemed to say, "This way sir"

Medical services are first class with so many health centres and clinics, residential and care homes for the elderly, sick and infirm and hospitals in the shape of Hamilton General Hospital, Udston Hospital and Caird House.

Of course many other streets offer good shopping, like Townhead Street, Keith Street and Cadzow Street where the wonderful theatre is situated in the grandest and most sublime building within the town, the town house (above) which has been tastefully converted to a concert hall and theatre offering top quality entertainment all year round. The great building was erected in stages and initially, the library was opened in 1907 by the philanthropic Scot, Andrew Carnegie, the administration section was unveiled by King George V in 1914 then the town hall completed the building we now see, in 1928. The modern council headquarters is not to be outdone however and, though lacking the sublime architecture of the old town house, the multi storey structure is an awesome and eyecatching feature.

The oldest building in the town is Portland, built in 1696 in the Low Parks, part of the Duke of Hamilton's parklands. It was originally used as the home of the 3rd duke's secretary and lawyer, David Crawford before being used as a coaching inn but now forms part of Low Parks Museum. The other building, in Muir Street, is the former Palace Riding School built by Alexander, 10th duke, in 1837. Collectively, the buildings play host to one of the top museums in Lanarkshire and are also home to the Regimental Museum of the Cameronians Scottish Rifles or as some proudly call them, *Lanarkshire's Own.*

Hamilton Palace, the former home of the Dukes of Hamilton and Brandon, was built in the late 17th century for William, 3rd Duke and his duchess, Anne, though the final building works, as the palace was continually being added to or altered, were not complete until the earlier part of the 19th century by Alexander, 10th Duke. The finished product left the most elaborate, ornate and beautiful building in the realm, it was also the largest, privately owned, lived-in house, in Western Europe. Sadly, in the 1920s, the palace began to subside, subsidence caused by the extensive mine workings below, all Hamilton owned. Soon the house was demolished and much of the artwork inside sold.

Before it was realised of the dangers to the stability of the palace, Alexander had began work on the the nearby Hamilton Palace Mausoleum (below) to replace the 'humble' family burial ground at the nearby collegiate church which was now in a state of ruin. Alexander wanted to make his new 'burial vault' the grandest in Christendom. The building, of colossal magnitude, was built in a Roman style,

domed building, of panelled masonry. Among other things, it contained a chapel where Alexander would be buried, inside an Egyptian sarcophagus which, as it happened, was a little too small for him and was not realised until he died in August, 1852. He was even fascinated by mummification to the point, he wanted to be mummified when he died and his wish came true. His ancestors were removed from the old burial ground and buried in the crypt of the mausoleum. As it happened, it was all in vain. The mausoleum later began to subside, like the nearby palace, but luckily, did not need to be demolished even though it subsided by some 20 feet and was beginning to lean, 'Pisa style' This caused the family to remove all their deceased predecessors to a new burial ground in the town's Bent Cemetery. Incidentally, the mausoleum has the longest echo of any building in the world and the domed masterpiece, one of Hamilton's top attractions, stands to an astonishing height of 37 metres.

*A*lexander's biggest problem was his untold wealth, brought about by the mines the family owned. While men, women and children toiled in that dark place, fit only for prince of darkness and his fiendish followers. Men died, women died and poor mites of children died to 'feed' the extravagance of a man who did nothing to earn his inheritance, other than be born to the right person at the right time. It is so true, never can we appreciate what we have until we have earned it, and earned in an honest way. Take a look at that man's ego, and compare it with the Colvilles of Motherwell and with Dale and Owen, who all had great business interests as did the 10th Duke of Hamilton but somehow managed to give something back. That is not to say, the duke did not do anything, he probably provided homes but really that was merely a means to an end. In his own time, he was said to have '*a great predisposition to overestimate the importance of his ancient birth*' He was a British politician, served as a Member of Parliament but was said to be a supporter of Napoleon Boneparte. He also held many ceremonial duties around the royal family. I suppose in a sense, the duke knew nothing other than wealth and probably did not really appreciate what he had since he was born in to it, so I must give him some leeway on his spendthrift behaviour, I don't think for a second, he was an evil man though he appears to have been very arrogant.

*O*n the subject of coal pits; many towns and villages of Lanarkshire suffered by the unholy happenings in the dark underworld. So many men were killed in what were totally avoidable accidents and Hamilton was no different. On Saturday, 28th May, 1887, 73 miners perished after a huge explosion caused by fire damp. Men from all the surrounding villages died in what was one of the darkest days in the region. The tragedy simply added to the misery of the miners and their families which had been going on for years. The people were working hard to cope with previous disasters in the area, most particularly at Blantyre, but some would never recover from the loss of their loved ones.

*H*aving said all that, it would be untrue to say all the Hamiltons acted as the 10th duke did and some were known to be benevolent lairds. When they finally found a new house in which to live, Lennoxlove in Haddington after spell at one of their hunting lodges, Dungavel House, they were known to do so much work for and in a community which truly treasured their great imput. In fact so many of the ducal family of Hamilton were known for their benevolence to others.

*T*he lands of the Hamilton family, particularly, the Low Parks are now the site of a world class sports facility with so many sports supported, including the ice palace, bowls, tennis, cricket, rugby, football, cycling, swimming and curling, it really is a sight to behold and yet another great venue for sport and leisure. Add that to a fine museum and a cinema complex, a nearby golf course and, of course, Strathclyde Park and it is easy to see why Hamilton is such a good place to be. The site of an ancient motte stands in that area which is very much one of the greatest regenerations in Scottish history. The beautiful Hamilton Park race course, with adjoining lochs, is nearby and they are all joined by so many other parks, recreation grounds, community and leisure centres scattered all around the town and still we haven't seen the buildings and sublime gardens and walks at Chatelherault to the south-east of the town. Before we head to the old hunting lodge of the Hamilton family, I must mention a couple of good achieving clubs in the town.

*F*irst of all Hamilton Academical Football Club is one of the oldest in Scotland having been founded in 1874. It is also the only club in the country which began life as a school team representing Hamilton Academy (now the Grammar School) The team played at Douglas Park for many years but in 2001, moved to their new home, New Douglas Park, after seven years of ground sharing. Their colours are red and white hoops and white shorts. They have have won the

First Division (second tier) once and have lifted the Challenge Cup twice but lost twice in the Scottish Cup Final. As I write, the team are top of the newly created Championship and making a strong challenge for promotion to the Premiership. Their most notable players are Jamie Fairlie, their all time top goal scorer, Stan Anderson who played for the club in three different periods, John Blackley, international defender, Andy Goram, international goalkeeper, James McArthur and James McArthy both home reared internationalists and Rikki Ferguson who played more games, 485, for the club than any other.

*H*amilton Rugby Club was founded in 1927 and currently play in the RBS Chamionship A league. When the league system was introduced in Scotland, Hamilton, Lanarkshire's top team had to work their way through the system until they reached the national leagues. They were later relegated back to the district leagues but in recent. times they have fought their way back to the top.

*N*ow to Chatelherault (above) where existed one of the Hamiltons' Hunting Lodges, another was thought to exist at Barncluith in the town. In 1548, when James Hamilton, 2nd Earl of Arran was acting as Regent to Princess Mary, he negotiated the Treaty of Haddington which allowed the princess to travel to France and become the wife of the Dauphin, heir to the French Throne. James was a great grandson of James II and, as such was a second cousin to the future Queen of Scots. During this process, he was created the Duc de Châtellherault in the French aristocracy. For some time, that title remained with the Hamiltons and James, 5th Duke of Hamilton, commissioned William Adam, eminent architect of the day to design and build a hunting lodge and *'Dogg Kennells'* with a view to providing a place of rest, relaxation and revelling for his family and guests. The magnificent building and outlying lands we see today, are a credit to the duke and his architect. The buildings consists of two pavilions providing, a banqueting hall, relaxation space and bed chambers for the lord, his lady and their guests with other quarters at the back for the 'do fors' Of course space had to be found too for horse and hound. The magnificent gardens were laid out including the parterre garden to the rear and a simply awesome avenue consisting of grasslands and two rows of lime trees leading right through, what is now the town, to Hamilton Palace, a line stretching from south-west to north-east. Chatelherault is now a free to see attraction in the town, providing the story of the pavilion, of the motte-like mound viewing point, of the wildlife, gardens, the Cadzow Burn and Cadzow Castle which we shall hear of soon. Foot bridges take us over the burn providing views of other, older bridges and beautiful woodlands. So, the Low Parks, and the High Parks, which once belonged to Scotland's premier duke, Keeper of the Palace of Holyroodhouse and Bearer of the Crown, now belong to the people which were given in lieu of death duties incurred on the death of Douglas, the 14th Duke in 1973. Interestingly Douglas Douglas-Hamilton, 14th Duke of Hamilton, was the man Rudolf Hess wanted to meet to discuss peace when he parachuted in to Scotland in 1942. It is thought the duke met the deputy-fuhrer when he attended the Olympic Games in Berlin in 1936.

A visit to Chatelherault is a must when in the area. See how the aristocrats spent their relaxation time and how they entertained their guests, where they hunted and how they ate. This truly, is a world class destination in our own backyard. The surrounding woodlands provide wonderful and educational walks where time is never lost on the flora of the park. Take to the viewing mound and look over old Cadzow and marvel the steeples of the churches in town. Parking at the park is plentiful and even if disabled, there is still so much to see and do.

*I*n Hamilton at the present time, there are some 18 places of worship covering all denominations and where warm welcomes are always given and solace offered. The Old Parish Church, a wonderful building, of 1734 in the Georgian style, is the oldest of them and descendant of the original Catholic and Collegiate Churches though some believe the church may go back to the Culdee worship of the early Celtic peoples and saints. The old parish was the only church ever designed by William Adam who used timber, full of lead shot, from an old warship. Schools too are plentiful and local children never have too much further than walk 'round the corner' for their education. In total there are around 20 places of education serving the town including university, college, independent, primary, secondary and a fine school for the deaf. Many of the schools are non denominational and all are co-educational.

*T*he town of today is a truly wonderful and 'switched on' place, a real credit to the people and council, but where did it all begin, let's step back two thousand years or so and find out.

*I*t is more than certain, the area we are now visiting was populated by ancient tribes before and after the coming of the Romans, and there is some tell of the kings of the ancient kingdom of *Ystrad Clywd* (Strathclyde) one of whom was Rhydderch Hael, who ruled the region from c580-c614AD, visiting Cadihou.

Industry

There is a legend of St. Kentigern (Mungo) finding a ring inside a salmon which belonged to the Queen of Strathclyde after her husband wrongly accused her of betraying him with another man. When Mungo found the ring in the Cadzow Burn, her husband forgave her and later, both converted and were baptised in the waters, by Kentigern. Since Kentigern died on the 13th January 614, the story could only have applied to Rhydderch Hael. That king did a lot of travelling around his kingdom and would definitely have visited his queen who is said to have owned a palace at Cadihou, perhaps on the site of old Cadzow Castle.

Some other moments of early history are known to us including the fact that by 1150, David I had granted the church at Cadihou to the cathedral at Glasgow and raised the barony to that of Royal status. The church was then in the Deanery of Rutherglen and intermittently known as Cadlihou, Cadyhow, Cadiou and Cadzow. Cadihou, was soon a prebend of the cathedral and was served by a perpetual vicar. While that is the earliest, known mention of the area, the legend of Kentigern and the queen lingers. That legend further tells us, Kentigern founded a church at Cadzow, the first in that area.

During the days of David I's grant of church to Glasgow, he too resided at Cadzow as did his grandsons, Malcolm IV and William I, who granted the barony to his illegitimate son, Robert de Londres or Londonis. Robert, a generous man, made several grants in the late 12th century to Glasgow, Paisley Abbey and Kelso Abbey and was known to visit the mother church of the deanery at Rutherglen.

The 'modern' history of Hamilton began during the reign of King Robert Bruce who granted the Barony to Walter Fitz Gilbert, the son of Gilbert Fitz William of Hambeldone in southern England. Walter had earlier sworn fealty to Edward at Berwick in 1296 in the name 'de Hambledon'. Another who bent at the English king's feet during what became known as the *'Ragmans Rolls',* was Adame de Cadiou. In 1368, during the reign of Robert's son David II, the king granted the Barony and lands of Edlewood to Walter's son David Fitz Walter. At that point, the family resided at Cadzow Castle but soon that would need reparation. The castle was finally repaired in 1445, around the same time as the name Hamilton came in to popular use. By that time of course, the main branch of the family had moved to a new home on the High Parks known as the *The Orcharde* or *Pomarium*. The village, at that point, was huddled around the apple orchard (Pomarium) and church. That is where the Hamiltons would build their new seat, the palace, in the knowledge they still possessed Cadzow Castle and another at Barncluith at what became known as Castle Hill. The ruins of Cadzow Castle which we now see, are of the new castle built in 1530 by James Hamilton of Finnart, an expert on artillery forts and who also, as we know, built the mighty castle at Craignethan. Cadzow Castle, broken as it is, looks to have been in a particularly, defensively strong situation, hanging as it does, over the Cadzow Burn just SSW of Chatelherault.

The old medieval church at the Orchards was largely re-built in the 15th century but not much is known of that early church or its fabric. What we do know is, John Malklenere of Castle Hill, was bound, in 1367, to contribute two wax candles to the church each weighing at least one pound, to light up the altar of the Virgin within and that Henry the vicar of the church had bought some land from Patrick Fitz Adam another of the Hambledone (Hamilton) family. Others mentioned as granting to the old church were, Hugh de Seviland of the *Terre de Pomarios* (Lands of the Orchard) David Fitz Walter (son of Walter Fitz Gilbert) and Agnes de John. It is also believed, a chapel, in the dependency of Cadzow Church, was built on the lands of Eddlewood.

*I*n 1452, the church of Cadihou was 'raised' to Collegiate status by Lord James Hamilton after being granted permission by the Bishop of Glasgow, William Turnbull and Pope Nicholas V; the church was granted the right to employ a provost and eight prebendaries. James Hamilton then granted the provost and two former chaplains and the other six prebendaries, a manse, a yard and glebe on the haugh of Hamilton while further lands and properties at Stonehouse and Dalserf were granted to them in order to make their lives more comfortable. In 1548, Queen Mary (de Guise) wife of the late James V, granted the patronage of the church to the aforementioned Duke of Chatelherault in recognition of his dukedom in the French aristocracy. The old church was finally abandoned on the opening of the new church, the present kirk, in 1732. (now known as Hamilton Old Parish Church)

*F*rom, the mid 15th century, while Cadzow and Dalserf or Machan were still a united parish, the Knights Templar were busy in the area and during their tenure, a hospital was founded in the name of St. Mary of Bethlehem by Pope Pius II. The only other reference we have to the hospital is of John Hamilton of Edston bequeathing *"to the puir there, twa hundred merks to be devetit by my lord and ladie how it sould be yasit"*

*A*s for the family themselves, they went on to create a larger, grander house, as we have seen and, in 1643, they were raised further up the peerage ladder, by being bestowed with the Dukedom of Hamilton. The present Duke, the 16th is Alexander Douglas Douglas-Hamilton who was born in 1978, the son of Angus, who died in 2010. The late duke and his duchess were a very much respected couple in East Lothian, as is the dowager duchess still is today.

South Lanarkshire Council Headquarters in Hamilton

A list of notables with association is extensive and would take reams but I shall attempt to give a balanced list as follows, William Cullen, an 18th century doctor & chemist,

Industry

Charles Aston, a botanist in the 18th century, John Roberton was a doctor and social reformer in the 19th century while Sir Alexander Cairncross was an economist of the 20th century. The world of football is represented by Jock Stein, legendary manager, the late Davie Cooper who played for Motherwell, Rangers and Scotland, and the late Phil O'Donnell of Motherwell, Celtic and Scotland. The world of entertainment is represented by Mark McManus of Taggart fame, Laura Brett an Eastenders star, musician, Brian Connolly and actor, Nicol Williamson. Other sports stars are, Walter McGowan, World Champion boxer, Helen Orr Gordon, international swimmer, and Jamie Burnett from the world of snooker. Others are broadcasters, Jackie Bird and Alison Walker, and William Logan, founder of the Scottish Temperance League in 1844. James Keir Hardie, better known as Keir Hardie spent part of his childhood years in the town before going on to 'immortality' as the man who, more than any other, who founded the Labour Party in Scotland and was the first independent Labour Member of Parliament when he entered the House of Commons in 1892. His party have came a long way since those early beginnings.

*H*amilton is a delight and surprising in so many ways. It has changed so much since I last visited many, many years ago. It exudes a confidence seldom seen but that confidence is tempered, by down to earth, friendly folk with welcoming words, but sadly it is time to leave and there is another benefit, the roads have improved beyond recognition. As like everywhere else round about the town, road travel is easy and quick, there are abundant buses, and trains from Hamilton West, Chatelherault and Central providing a faster alternative but... I have decided to make my way to the Avon Water at Chatelherault and track my way from there and where we instantly flow under a footbridge within the park. Then it's past the High Parks farm before the famous Cadzow Oaks just south of the site of an ancient fort. On the opposite, the right bank, is lovely Hamilton Golf Course before swinging left, we pass the ruins of the old Cadzow Castle. Now it's on a course to pass the old house and gardens of old Barncluith Tower before heading to a section of bridges, the rail bridge, *the auld brig* then the road bridge and the Avon Bridge, carrying the A72 trunk road. Near the old Cadzow Bridge, in 1650, a battle, the Battle of Hieton, was fought between the Covenanting soldiers under Colonel Kerr and the invading *'roundhead'* forces led by General Lambert. On this occasion, the invaders won the day with Colonel Kerr being killed along with many of his followers.

*S*winging left, the river is almost hidden from sight by the heavily wooded banks as she passes nearby South Haugh then under the M74 motorway, she is eager to move on her to her destiny and has now arrived, her time is here and now as she embraces the Clyde before, suddenly, the waters are forced left and under the bridge carrying the A723. Now together, the Clyde and Avon waltz hand in hand in the arms of beauty, heading north in the company of Strathclyde Loch where another sharp bend awaits. Suddenly the quiet waters loop left below the M74 and A723 bridges before encountering the old Bothwell Bridge. Bothwell is on the right bank as the river heads between that town and Blantyre, birthplace of David Livingstone, the ground breaking missionary to Africa, but not before saying "Hi, climb on board" to the Gow's Linn, the latest tributary to sign up for the Clyde adventure.

*D*avid Livingstone was born in 1813 and went on to be educated at Blantyre school before working in a local textile mill for many years. He was influenced by local ministers and evangelists and soon he began saving in order to attend Anderson's College, though he also attended Glasgow University studying Theology. His mission in life had began, and, while he originally wished to go to China, that changed when he met Robert Moffat, a missionary to Africa, his mind was set. Later he married Moffat's daughter Mary and together, they spent a lifetime as missionaries on the 'Dark Continent' and were staunch and vociferous anti-slavery campaigners. Memorials to Livingstone are many including several in Zambia. Other countries with monuments to one of the world's great humanitarians are, Zimbabwe, Uganda, Malawi, Tanzania, Congo, Burundi, Botswana, Zanzibar and South Africa. Cities, towns, streets and so many other institutions across the globe, have been named in his honour including of course, in Scotland, England, USA, Australia, Canada and New Zealand. There is absolutely no doubt, he is one of the most cherished men the world has ever known and one of his favourite lines came from another 'colossus' of mankind, Robert Burns, those words *"When man to man, the world o'er, shall brothers be for a' that"* which were forever on his mind. He died in 1873 in what is now Zambia and local people buried his heart under a tree before his body was returned to Britain where it was buried in Westminster Abbey.

*D*avid Livingstone's birthplace provides one of the top attractions in the region. The famous man was born in Shuttle Row (right) which still exists and is home to a museum containing so much memorabilia of his life and times. The centre is based within 20 acres of beautiful parklands including  gardens and wonderful walks along the river where is situated the David Livingstone Bridge allowing you to cross the Clyde without getting your feet wet. So many lovely views are to be had nearby including the awesome ruins of mighty Bothwell Castle. There is another bridge nearby but that is used simply to carry piping across the waters. The town of old was made up of a series of villages and, in a sense, still is, with Blantyre village, now High Blantyre in the south-west and Low Blantyre, formerly Blantyre Works to the north-east facing Bothwell over a deep, heavily wooded gorge. Other areas include, Calderglen, Craigknowe, Wheatlands, Stonefield, Whitehill, Springwells, Auchentibber and Auchinraith,

There are several theories put forward as to the meaning of Blantyre but the one most suited perhaps, relates to the first known mention of the area, the old Augustinian Priory on the banks of the Clyde near Low Blantyre suggesting *The land of the holy men* or Rev. McKenzie's theory in the Third Statistical Account of 1952 when he suggests it is so called in the name of holy missionary, Blane, thus making it the *Land of Blane.* St. Blane, who died in 590AD, was born in Bute and later buried there. He was a missionary monk who travelled the length of Scotland and now sanctified, his feast day is 10th of August. Another theory was of Blantyre being a *Land of warm retreat,* and certainly, it was a relatively safe and warm retreat for the medieval canons who left Jedburgh, in fear of their lives because of continuous English incursions on that town and others in the borders or debatable lands which separated England and Scotland.

From very early times, the barony of Blantyre was in the hands of the Earls of Dunbar, the first of whom, Gospatric, fled his earldom of Northumbria soon after William of Normandy invaded England. He was granted lands by Malcolm III particularly in south-east Scotland and from those early beginnings, they spread across the country. The earliest mention of the church came when it was said to be part of Blantyre Priory, which was founded in the 13th century, and remained as part of that foundation until the Reformation. The priory itself is said to have been founded during the reign of Alexander II, 1214-1249 and was populated by Augustinian canons from Jedburgh Abbey, before being granted to that abbey in the Borders, though some say it was to Holyrude Abbey in Edinburgh; both sides of that argument could be true since both were houses of the Augustinian Order. The prior of Blantyre was present at the treaty of Birgham in 1286, when commissioners of Scotland and England attempted to 'put to bed' the claims of the de Baliols and the de Brus' in their quest to become king of Scotland. Another prior swore fealty to Edward at Berwick and was designated *Frere William, priour de Blauntyr.* Walter the prior, was one of the commissioners who went to London to negotiate the ransom for the release of David II of Scots who was kept captive at the Tower of London after his capture at the Battle of Neville's Cross in 1346. Not too much is known of the buildings of the priory but it was noted in the mid 18th century, scant remains of the ancient, red granite divine, including two gables, were still standing and they made, over the deep gorge created by the river, a dramatic scene.

The first known prior at Blantyre was William de Cokeburne who reigned from 1296 until 1304, the last being William of Chirnside who reigned from 1552 until 1577 when the first commendator, Sir Walter Stewart, 1st Lord Blantyre was elected. Presumably William was also the first minister of the reformed faith but since most monastic houses were allowed to stay open until the last man died, it is possible he was prior there until his death. The last but one prior was John Hamilton of Bothwellhaugh, a relation of David Hamilton who was some form of chancellor to the church after the Reformation, since he was given some nine score and 17 merks to distribute, forty merks for 'ane meenister', 20 merks for his pension, thirteen merks to Robert Lindsay of Dunrod for his legal fees with the remainder going to the commendator of the priory. A grand daughter of Walter of Blantyre, Frances Theresa Stuart, was said to be a lover of King Charles II who made her the model for the Britannia figure which appeared on the reverse of so many coins in Great Britain over the centuries.

*I*t is quite a coincidence, that the Lord Blantyre who was the commendator of Blantyre Priory, was the first in a line of 12 Lords Blantyre ending in 1900 with the death of Charles Stuart who lived, like many of his forebears, at Lennoxlove House at Haddington, the present seat of the Dukes of Hamilton. For many years, Gilbert Burns, brother of the bard, was factor to the Blantyres where he remained until his death in 1827. Burns' mother, Agnes went to live with Gilbert and both are buried in nearby Bolton Kirkyard near Haddington. Many Lords Blantyre are interred at Blantyre old kirkyard while the later ones are buried in their own mausoleum in Bolton kirkyard.

*A*part from David Livingstone and the Stuarts of Blantyre, other notables include, the late, Jim Cornfield, Bill Sim and Andy Paterson, keepers of the town's heritage, Anna Fotheringham who could not do enough for the village especially the elderly, Fraser Wallace, kart racing champion, Ryan McCann, John Cushley, John Fallon all from the fields of football, actor, Ryan Fletcher, Andra McAnulty whom we shall read of later and Philip Murray, born in the town and who went on to be one of America's greatest trade unionists of the 20th century. Philip had followed a similar path to a slightly earlier man of the workers, William Wilson, again of Blantyre. Margo McDonald, a Member of the Scottish Parliament was a land lady at the Hoolet's Nest Inn for some years.

*O*thers, of 'noble' status, have passed through Blantyre even if only to visit Bothwell Castle. The Hepburns, Earls of Bothwell passed many times, including the dastardly James, 4th earl who, as we know, married Mary Stuart, Queen of Scots. Mary herself travelled through the village when visiting the great castle across the river but, more poignantly, she rode through Blantyre on her way to the Battle of Langside which would take place the following day, 13th May, 1568. Mary and her followers made their way up Pathfoot, locally known as *Pech Brae,* (because of the effort used in tackling that hill causing one to 'pech' or pant on the way). Mary stopped at Dysholm Well to refresh herself, and her horses before continuing on her dark journey to oblivion. Mary's forces were defeated but she escaped to England hoping for support from Elizabeth I but was imprisoned instead, the rest is history and Mary became known as the most tragically betrayed woman in history. My beliefs are simple, Mary was a child when she left Catholic Scotland to become the young queen of Catholic France. When she returned, the Reformation had arrived meaning she was stuck between a rock and hard place. In her case, some leeway should be given, many she believed in, let her down. She

Industry

was ultimately executed but she died with the dignity, not of a confused girl but as a queen, one of the most famous ladies ever to grace the planet. Another Stewart known to have walked the lands of Blantyre was Charles, the *Bonnie Prince,* during his brief sojourn to Scotland in an effort to restore his father to the throne.

The present, wonderful old parish church (below) with its magnificent spire was opened in 1863 replacing a church on the same site which was probably built around the time of the Reformation. The exact site of the original church is unknown but was thought to be a little to the south of the old priory and overlooking the river Clyde. The kirk underwent some 'remedial surgery' in recent times when a section of the great spire was worked on, keeping it safe and sound for future generations to see and admire. Today Blantyre, contains nine churches,

one in memory of David Livingstone which stands near St. Joseph's, which all serve the townsfolk covering all denominations. Blantyre's schools, and there are six of them, including Calderside High, are renowned for their academic excellence thanks to their hard working pupils and teachers which really is the residue of what has always been a diligent and hard working community.

The town is, like all the neighbouring communities, proud of its facilities of which there are as many as you would expect in a town of Blantyre's size with a population of well over 17,000 though it still retains a 'villagey' feel. Hotels, cafés and restaurants cater for all tastebuds and shops are plentiful, local independents, national stores and a fine shopping centre, the Clydeview. Of course inns too, are plentiful which reminds us of one notable family of inn keepers. Captain McNeil and his family, for over 70 years, were well known around the town since taking up the reins of the Caledonian in 1925 after Joseph McNeil and his wife Elizabeth left their home on the Isle of Barra for a new life; as a form of endearment, the locals renamed the pub, *'The Heilandman's'* The McNeils then purchased the West End Bar in 1929 and, from that time until recently, they were still pulling the pints and holding out a hand of welcome to their customers but sadly that remarkable era has come to an end.

River Clyde

*T*here is a good leisure and sports centre, and so many other halls, which can accommodate most functions while most sports have a base in the town, if not the leisure centre, golf course or skatepark, then at the many well used venues catering for boxing, judo, karate, cricket, rugby, football, swimming, squash, badminton, bowling and tennis. Other groups are the toddlers, fitness, health, dance and walking plus older folks' groups. Many of the above meet in or are organised by the Blantyre Miners Welfare and Social Club, the legacy of the coal mining industry on which the town grew and flourished, a simply wonderful facility which reminds us all of the town's great heritage.

*S*o many former mining towns have institutes, bowling clubs, golf courses and so on, all under the umbrella of CISWO, the Coal Industry Social and Welfare Organisation, but rarely do they boast such a venue that exists in this South Lanarkshire town. It has so many activities therein and is easily the most popular of all meeting places in the town. So many men worked so hard over the years to establish a miners' club, which they achieved, but when the new Blantyre Miners Resource Centre opened in 2008, the final result of so much effort, all their dreams had come true. Now they have something which goes a long way to reminding us all of the sacrifice made by men, women and children over the centuries, working in the most horrifying and dangerous of all occupations, and for a pittance. The sacrifice at Blantyre was dire with the town suffering pit disasters in three consecutive years, 1877, 1878 and 1879.

*F*or some years leading up to the tragic events, miners were forever urging the pit owners, Dixons, to take precautions to make safe the pits. When the Dixons refused, the men decided they needed extra money if they were to continue working in such hazardous conditions but again the bosses refused, which resulted in a strike and the inevitable, some of the miners were sacked and removed from their tied homes. On 22nd October, 1879, the miners' worst fears came to pass, in pits 2 & 3, an almighty explosion occurred, killing 215 miners, the youngest being a wee boy of eleven. The tragedy left more than 90 widows and 250 children who would never see their dads again, but more tragedy was to come. A year later, at the direct instructions of greedy, unsympathetic owners, widows and their children were evicted from their pit homes, surely one of the worst of so many uncaring actions ever seen in Scotland. That cruel act came barely a month after another accident when a pit cage overturned throwing the occupants 900 feet down the shaft, another six poor souls died, more sorrow for an already grief stricken community but yet, even more was to come. In July 1879, there was another explosion, this time killing 28 men bringing the total to 249 dead in less than two years. If you add that to many of those who died of related illnesses, the total is horrifying and too high a price to pay in order to heat our homes.

I have often harped on about man's inhumanity to man and the Blantyre disaster era is one of the worst examples I have known. Everywhere we look, we see so many examples of how the wealthy land owners, pit owners and farmers have treated their workers, over the years, with less respect than they would treat a sheep, or a cow, or a lump of coal, Not only were the workers treated with less respect than the product with which they worked, they were also treated with less value. As I have said before, the working man was simply a means to an end, nothing more, but sometimes a lot less. Soon though, things would change and men of courage would arrive and stand tall for the working folk and help to change all that. In time a movement would grow which would stand for a form of equality and more would join their ranks and help change the world in which we live.

Anyone who ever walks through a cemetery in a former coal mining town, cannot help notice the ages of many of the men who lie in a sweet repose they never enjoyed in life, working in an environment which cost them their health and life. *Satan's Hell Hole* has a lot to answer for, as have the greedy, uncaring men who owned the pits, they should have been held more responsible for giving the townspeople of Blantyre the facilities they now have and deserve but had to work hard for themselves. Men like Andra McAnulty and others, who worked so hard all their lives in the pits and fighting for the creation of the fine welfare club, are the real heroes. Forget lords, earls, dukes and priors of old, Andra and his colleagues are among most noble of all with association to Blantyre. Andra also served as President of Lanarkshire Minworkers Union, Chairman of the Parish Council and School Board and was also a Justice of the Peace. He was a friend,

Andra McAnulty
photograph courtesy of his grandson, Andrew McAnulty Paterson

colleague and secretary to Keir Hardie, another of the great men who made this country a little more bearable, a little more like home for the common folk. The park at Blantyre has been renamed in Andra's honour and I am sure he will smile down in appreciation, though a little embarrassed no doubt. The legacy left by Andra will live always in the hearts of the right minded and he must surely be the one of people of Blantyre's greatest heroes. Having grown up in a mining town, and hearing of Andra, it has been my pleasure, writing just a few words of tribute to a humble man who did so much for his fellow man.

From the beginning, man has trundled this route heading in all directions looking for a suitable place in which to settle and there are many clues to their being, all around. The Romans certainly visited the little 'island' and local hills, particularly Camp Knowe, where ancient activity has been found, which provided useful lookout points for the Latin invaders. Many artefacts have been found over the years including Roman urns and other pottery items. Many more have visited Blantyre over the years and not all with conquest on their minds. Local people have been joined from the beginning by people wishing to live and work in a lovely location surrounded by water, and still the population grows.

The parish, as a whole, is a peninsula or virtually even, an island, surrounded by water, the Clyde, to the east and north, and the exciting waters and falls of the Rotten Calder to the west, yet no matter where you enter, you must cross water at some point. Of course, the rivers contributed greatly in the old days, to turning the many wheels of the mills of Blantyre with cotton production, the main industry. With that production followed by the spinning and weaving of the textiles, more than 1,000 people were employed as early as the mid 19th century. During that early period, neat cottages were built for the workers, many of whom had travelled from Ireland, the Highlands and as far away as Lithuania, in search of work and a roof over their heads. The new church of 1863 was built with 400 sittings to accommodate the growing population, shops opened as did small service industries, like smiddys, carpenters and stone masons, all of which blossomed. A Free Kirk arrived and there were two schools, the parish school and a school for the children of the mills which utilised the church building.

All the old industry has gone but there is still work to be found in the town at the nearby industrial and business parks and the technology park, all just a little cleaner and so much safer than the old pits. Anyone who works outside of the town have the choice of a good road network, excellent bus services and a railway station and if using that station, look out for some fine pavement artwork.

There is a confidence about the town and the future looks secure. After work and at the weekends, there is so much to do, as we have seen, but there is also large parks and fine walks on the two rivers and perhaps adventurous kids will still learn to swim at the Lido near Bothwell Bridge just as their forebears used to do. Saturdays is busy for the local football minded people as they head down to see their local junior team Blantyre Victoria who play in the West Region of Scottish Junior Football. The Vics, as they are known, were founded in 1890 and play at Castle Hill. The team, who play in blue and white vertical stripes have produced many fine players including Jock Stein, Joe Jordan and Billy McNeill who were all associated with the Scottish International team and Charlie Johnstone who went on to play for Motherwell. Andy Paterson, a top grade referee, was another who represented the town's football heritage but wearing the all black attire of officialdom.

Industry

*B*lantyre is a fine town with ever so friendly people, many differing areas, giving a good balance between town centre living, housing estates, rural and waterside locations. Speaking of waterside, let's get back to Bothwell Bridge before heading across to Bothwell and Uddingston. At Craighead, we can view the pillars of an old railway viaduct which was built by the same company, Sir William Arrol & Sons, who built the Forth Bridge. Now we have reached Bothwell Bridge, originally built in the 17th century but has been strengthened and widened to cope with modern day traffic but another kind of traffic of yesteryear gained the bridge immortality, or notoriety if you like, for a very different reason.

*O*n 22nd June, 1679, the forces of 'rebel' Covenanters, commanded by Robert Hamilton of Preston (Prestonpans) faced, from the south bank of the Clyde, a Government army led by James Scott, (originally Fitzroy or Crofts) Duke of Monmouth, an illegitimate son of Charles II. The Covenanters were in good spirits after their recent victory at Drumclog but Monmouth, an ancestor of the Dukes of Buccleuch, had been commissioned to lead the Royalists after the defeat of Graham of Claverhouse a few weeks earlier. After some initial success, the Covenanters were pushed back and many fled the field heading for shelter in the grounds

Weir between Blantyre and Bothwell where two mills stood

of Hamilton Palace. Differing figures are banded about how many died but, what is known, 1200 were taken prisoner and dragged to Edinburgh. Some were executed while most were imprisoned in the Covenanters' jail adjacent to Greyfriars Kirk before being shipped to the colonies. Covenanters' Field, on the north side of the bridge, was the scene of many Coventicles (open air services or Blanket Sermons) in later years in remembrance of the men who died or imprisoned because of their defence of their national church.

*B*othwell, ecclesiastical and secular, is indeed a place of ancient roots and of 'heady' importance. While, the Romans and the ancient tribes of Cluywd walked the road and the miles of this remarkable neighbourhood, long before the coming of the so called middle ages, and where the kings of Strathclyde would party and rejoice in one of their greatest estates, the real importance came with the church and early fortification of Bothwell Castle. It seems the fortunes of both have tread the same winding route at the same time but the church and men of peace have stayed the full course just as the ways of battle and warring men have, hopefully, gone forever.

While it is difficult to put exact times on the foundation of the manor, it would appear one of the Olifard (Oliver) family, who were Justiciars of Lothian from the days of David I in the 12th century until the death of Walter de Olifard in 1242 were, without doubt, responsible for erecting the first church but which one and when? It would seem, Walter, baron from 1215 until 1242, was the man responsible for the first divine on the site of an old Celtic kirk dedicated to St. Bride, but who built the earliest castle? Well that would appear to have been the work of Walter's son-in-law, Walter de Moravia (Murray or Moray) who became the proprietor of the lands after Oliver's death. De Moravia was a member of a powerful family who gained much importance and lands across Scotland.

From the beginning, the church of Bothwell (below) was a free rectory and

was in the hands of the local barons and their were a few, until the elevation to College status on 10th October, 1398 by Alexander, the Earl of Douglas, a man often referred to as the 'Grim'. The earliest known parson at the church was David de Moravia who also paid homage to Edward I in 1296 along with Sir William de Moravia, possibly the priest's brother. Not much is known of that earlier church, though Orbynistun (Orbiston) Chapel as we have already seen, was in its care from those early days as was Shotts but we do know the church was cared for by a provost and eight prebendaries and almost certainly boy choristers. The first provost at the church was Thomas Barry, a canon of Glasgow Cathedral.

In time, the prebends of the church included Orbiston, Bertram Shotts, Hawick and Hasseldean in Roxburghshire. Newton, Cathkin, Stonhouse and Overtowne. It became a very important and wealthy church and was soon known as the Cathedral of Lanarkshire. Today, many of the old names are remembered such as the Vicars yard and the Prebend yard bearing in mind all the prebends had their very own houses around the great church. So much is left of the old kirk including a section of the choir within the chancel and some magnificent medieval carvings and ancient grave slabs. There were thoughts of a nunnery standing on the site of the old church but that appears to be not the case.

Today's church, a beautiful monument on the Main Street, set in the most serene setting at the heart of the small town, is testimony to the architects and master masons, who designed, built then maintained their high standards through the centuries. The residue of their works is there for all to see and admire; a magnificent red sandstone edifice which is a match for any church in the country but then, this is not just any old church, Bothwell Old Parish Church, is one of oldest collegiate churches still 'working'. Other churches in the town are St. Bride's Roman Catholic Church and the Evangelical Church. There is also a monastery of the Poor Clares.

Of the castle, well we have seen the Murrays were the first builders but it was added to so often over the years to form the colossal building we now see, the largest castle ruin in Scotland. While a ruin, so much is left to be seen with wonderment and admiration. The great castle with its remarkable towers is now in the care of Historic Scotland. Over the centuries, the castle changed hands so often through marriage, forfeiture and conquest, and several times was in the hands of the English who, quite often, placed it in the stewardship of 'loyal' Scots.

During the years of the competitors for the Scottish Crown and the ensuing Wars of Independence, Bothwell Castle (pictured below) played a pivotal roll. Edward I seized the castle, taking the governor, William Murray of Bothwell prisoner in the process which resulted in a Scottish attack, besieging the castle for over a year until they triumphed in mid 1299. However, two years later, Edward was back, regaining the castle and installing the 2nd Earl of Pembroke. Aylme de Valence, as governor where he remained until long after the crowning of Robert

Bruce at Scone in 1306. By the time of the Battle of Bannockburn in 1314, Walter FitzGilbert was governor at the castle and he provided shelter for those English generals fleeing west from the Stirlingshire battlefield. However, he soon surrendered the castle to Bruce's army

Courtesy of M.J. Richardson ©2012

whether by threat or collaboration, and was soon granted the Earldom of Cadzow. The rest as they say, is history but that was not the end of English possession of Bothwell Castle. In 1336, they, under Edward III retook the castle and, though much damaged, he made it his headquarters for at least a month when he was in residence. The castle then changed hands several times, including many branches of the Douglas family before coming in to the ownership of the Douglas-Home family, the Earls of Home. That family gifted the castle to the people in 1936, first the Ministry of Works cared for the old fortalice before passing to Historic Scotland. A new castle mansion was built in the 18th century but that was demolished in 1928 and is now lost and gone forever, buried under new housing. It was in that house of Bothwell Castle in 1808, where *Young Lochinvar* was penned by Sir Walter Scott.

Old Bothwell town, or the parish as a whole, was deeply involved in all the sectors of the farming industry, pastoral, sheep and cows, and arable with potatoes and turnips the main crops. There were quarries scattered in all areas of the parish as were large coal workings, pig iron and steel - the villagers and farmers were kept extremely busy. Flax growing and large scale weaving was busy at various times but that seemed to evaporate in the early 20th century. Nowadays things are so much different. Bothwell is no longer part of the great industrial estate that was Lanarkshire but now a very up market locale where in the 19th century, Glasgow business magnates arrived in numbers to occupy their 'away from it all' mansions and villas most of which were built in a very desirable red sandstone and so many of those wonderful homes can still be seen. Furthermore, Bothwell is still a very desirable place, whether to raise families or to spend their retirement years.

Leafy lanes and roads lead to the Main Street where most, though not all, of the shops are situated. The street has a rather old world charm with many local independents, inns, cafés and other meeting places where old friends meet, 'whiling' away some time and putting the world to right. Bothwell also contains hotels, a library, two primary schools, the community hall, the Russell Memorial hall and church halls. Kirklands Hospital is also based in the small town which is home to a bowling club and a very fine golf club, Bothwell Castle.

There are many groups in the town including a youth group, cubs and brownies plus many others including the Organic Growers of Bothwell, a group who care for the lovely gardens, conventional and organic, plus the new but very popular Scarecrow Festival which began in August 2011 and is now well established. Everyone is welcome to witness the fabulous displays of hilarious scarecrows all over the town in late Summer, and, of course, the beautiful Community Organic Gardens.

There have been many notable, or otherwise, people associated with Bothwell some of whom have already been mentioned. Others include Joanna Baillie, a 17th - 18th century poet and dramatist. She was born a daughter of Bothwell Manse in 1762 and, after a lifetime of literary genius, died at the age of 88 in Hampstead. Gordon Strachan, footballer, and present manager of the Scottish international

Industry

football team, lived in the town and the not so noble, James Hepburn, 4th Earl of Bothwell who was said to have raped Mary of Scots at Hailes Castle, before marrying her. Finally, he deserted his wife at Carberry Hill before escaping to Norway where he was arrested on suspicion of rape. He spent the rest of his life in a Danish prison where he died and his mummified body remains, on show and being depicted as the *King of Scotland.*

Once again we head to back to our 'guide', the River Clyde, which flows, and glows, gracefully, in the setting sun as she trickles onwards, deep in her 'leafy lane' below Bothwell Castle on the right bank and Blantyreferme on the left. Uddingston is now in sight as the great lady, her silky gown creating ripples in the gentle waters, reaches ever closer to Glasgow. This little section of the river, gentle as it is, reminds us of a little 'fairy dean' where pixies play amidst the tiny whirlpools sending out a heavenly scene to us mere mortals who can only stand and watch, in awe and admiration.

Old Uddingston town, and its sister districts like Tannochside, Viewpark, Birkenshaw, Spindlehowe, Kylepark and Calderbraes, is something of an enigma, Uddingston being part of South Lanarkshire council and the rest being part of North Lanarkshire even though, to all intents and purposes, are all part of the one community. Uddingston itself, was for long in the parish of Bothwell and not much more than a satellite of that town, but that all changed when industry arrived in the area.

In the 18th century, weaving was productive if small but the 19th century saw a great upturn in that industry, flax growing and the manufacture of fine linen joined by several collieries which opened, though only one, Maryville, was situated in the village itself. Iron foundries flourished, and they provided the raw material for, among other things, the Wilkie Plough which was produced and exported all over the world. The industry of today includes the production of good quality clothes and electrical goods though warehouses provide employment to many. Warehouse type showrooms and national chain stores are popular in the town and have provided much employment for the local people over the years. Various service industries provide more employment though many commute to Glasgow via an excellent road system or from the local railway station. I have of course, left to last, Uddingston's greatest claim to industrial fame, Tunnocks, the 'local' bakers.

Thomas Tunnock Limited was formed as a family bakery by Thomas Tunnock in 1890. The bakery has jogged along since those hazy days and still has a shop in the town centre but in post war Britain, Tunnocks began to roll out mass produced products which took the 'culinary' world by storm. Sweet treats such as Caramel Wafers, Caramel Logs and Tea Cakes are now recognised and enjoyed the world over and Tunnocks is now a byword in the Scottish language. Nothing quite tastes like a Tunnocks Caramel Wafer particularly when it is washed down with a glass of Barr's Irn Bru, another Scottish institution. More importantly to Uddingston, and the Scottish economy, Tunnocks employs more than 700 people, very large in any terms, gigantic in Uddingston terms, and still it grows.

River Clyde

*O*f course other jobs are provided around the town, in shops, of which there is an excellent choice, banks, various offices and council departments. Other shops exist in the 'suburbs' of the town ensuring no one needs to go far for their everyday needs, in fact no one need leave the Uddingston area for anything at all. More work is to be found in local inns, clubs, hotels, cafés and restaurants not forgetting the many leisure and sporting facilities in the town including Calderbraes Golf Club, though the nearby Glasgow Zoo at Calderpark has long since gone. Many sports are active in the town too, including rugby, football, cricket, tennis, bowling and so much more. All in all, Uddingston is a busy and thoroughly committed community. Many gardens provide good walking and leisure destinations including Viewpark Gardens, a real mouth opener and well worthy of a visit particularly during the fantastic Summer Festival when authentic Highlands and Japanese gardens can be viewed and admired before viewing the formal gardens in Kylepark Park.

*S*chools came early to the area and now there are six primaries and one high school, the well known and respected Uddingston Grammar. Churches were a bit later in arriving though since, as mentioned, the village was part of Bothwell. In modern times there are churches of all the Christian denominations providing, not only for the spiritual needs of the community but much of the town's social life too as does so many groups for both young and old, held in the various halls and centres provided.

*N*otable folk with association include, actress Gay Hamilton, footballers, Jimmy (Jinky) Johnstone, George McCluskey both of Celtic, Tommy McQueen of Clyde and Aberdeen, John Robertson of Nottingham Forest and Lindsay Hamilton, a goalkeeper who played for Rangers; Jinky Johnstone and John Robertson were both celebrated Scottish international players. Finally, James Black who went on to win a Nobel Prize for his discovery of Propranolol and Cimetidine. The eminent doctor and pharmacologist who was born in Uddingston in 1924, died in 2010.

The Green Bridge
Courtesy of Lairich Rig
©2005

*O*nce again, more walking needs to be done along the Clyde Walkway on our way to pastures new and though the river still cuts a deep furrow, the hills of Lanarkshire are all but memories. Under the emerald green bridge carrying the walkway, then the rail bridge where the trains from Glasgow come and go. On past Kylepark on the right bank and Haughhead golf driving range on the left as the river heads for Haughhead Bridge carrying the B758 to and from the A74. On past Maryville where the North Calder Water is welcomed to Clyde's family as the

 river loops hard left below Chuckle Hill near Daldowie Crematorium, a beautiful, domed building which contains two chapels and is surrounded by a stunning garden of remembrance. Now we are heading south to shake hands with the Rotten Calder river which has just

River Clyde near Uddingston – Courtesy of G. Laird©2012

crashed in to Clyde from her exciting waterfalls spraying gushing waters on to a river island, or should I say what was once a river island, now split in to three, mainly due to the power of the waters at this particular confluence. Now the river takes a severe twist to the right and is now heading in a north-westerly direction to Newton Farm on the left and works on the right just below Broomhouse, the most south-easterly community of the council area of the great city of Glasgow. Leaving the river for a moment we head across the waste lands of old Daldowie Colliery and the former Mount Vernon greyhound race track before reaching the lovely little community where history lies long in the past, with Daldowie House and Calderpark House, both the centres of large estates and the history of that area on the north bank.

Calderpark Estate has had a chequered career throughout the years and was once a domain of the eminent Stewart family of Minto. In time they sold out to James McNair, head of a Glasgow family of sugar refiners and it was he who built the great house which was later demolished due to the subsidence of coal workings on the site, such an endemic problem of Lanarkshire. Happily that was not the end of Calderpark, far from it, The Glasgow and West of Scotland Zoological Society bought the lands and proceeded to build up one of Britain's great zoological parks, Calderpark or Glasgow Zoo. It was a celebrated and highly respected institution but sadly the park closed in 2003 meaning one of the most wonderful days out in Scotland had closed its doors for the last time, such a pity.

The aforementioned Stewart family also lived at nearby Daldowie from the 16th century and several of their own acted as Lord Provost of Glasgow many times from the late 15th century and throughout the 16th.. The estate was sold to the

River Clyde

Bogles in 1724 and it was one of theirs, George, who built the house we know, then, in 1745. he also constructed the most wonderful doo'cot. In the earlier part of the 19th century, the house was sold on to the Dixons of iron and coal mining fame but they sold it again after only five years of ownership. This time Daldowie

Estate went to James McCall, yet another of the wealthy Glasgow merchants. The house was, as many others, built atop extensive coal workings and, inevitably, its days were numbered. When it was finally demolished, the site lay bare for a while before the magnificent Daldowie Crematorium was built on the site of the old mansion, though the old doo'cot (right) still remains.

George Bogle Snr. of Daldowie, was one of Glasgow's wealthiest merchants and carried on much trade in the West Indies and America, trading in tobacco, tan and sugar; he was, three times, Rector of Glasgow University. His son, George, was a diplomat who attempted to open an embassy in India before creating diplomatic relations with Tibet while attempting to do the same with the mysterious empire of old

Courtesy of Lairich Rig ©2005

China. His name is still mentioned 'in dispatches' to this day when those subjects are discussed.

In the meantime, many small tributaries have joined the river but as the hills become lower in height, so does the tributaries in volume, though the Tollcross Burn bucks the trend as she enters Clyde south of the east end of London Road in the city. Now, before we look at Glasgow as a whole, let's make our way to Rutherglen via Cambuslang, the *village on the long bend.*

Clyde once again, loops to the left on passing the lands of Newton Farm heading for a weir which once powered the mills at Carmyle and the former railway bridge between Cambuslang and the city. There is a road bridge and, further down stream, a footbridge in the company of the old Cambuslang Road Bridge which now serves as another footbridge (see opposite) The Newton Burn is the latest 'bairn' to join Mother Clyde near the Westburn and Newton district of 'Cumlang' as the town is sometimes known locally. Another, the Kirk Burn drains into the river just a few yards to the west passing, as the name suggests, the old kirk on the way. Let's look at Cambuslang, where did it all begin?

The earliest known activity was of local tribes celebrating the God of Fire, Baal, every year on what became 1st May. The people would ascend the top of the nearest hill, take their animals with them, and light great fires. The celebrations would begin by walking over the fires, barefoot, taking their unsuspecting animals, like sheep, with them as a form of performing fealty to their god who rewarded them, and their animals, with greater fertility. It is a celebration which

Industry

was carried out all over the known world and in some places is still celebrated, including Peebles in the Scottish Borders, who still mark the feast of Beltane every year but in a less dramatic and less dangerous fashion. The annual fire-walking took place on Dechmont Hill which was later used a lookout fort by the Romans and even later by more 'modern' men, who built a fort. Other fortifications of old included, Drumsargart (or Drumsagart) and Gilbertfield Castles with Gilbertfield built on the slopes of Dechmont. Another old motte type castle existed to the south of the town at Kirkhill. That castle is widely believed to have been constructed by the Olifurds but was later in the hands of, as was so often the case, the Murrays.

The manor, then known as Drumsargart, was granted, like several other parts of Lanarkshire, to the Olifards, Justiciars of Lothian in the early 13th century during the reign of Alexander II but the history of the church goes back much further. Cambuslang Church was well established during the 12th century in the Deanery of Rutherglen and we are so fortunate to know some of the parsons from that time, in the shape of William, who witnessed several charters of Jocelin,

 Bishop of Glasgow and of Conall who, in the latter part of the 13th century, swore fealty to Edward of England in the company of Hugh Crockett of Cambuslang. William Moneypeny was another rector who was responsible for founding a chaplainry dedicated to Our Lady of Kirkburn in 1390 and granted the feu of lands from the ferme of 'Ruthirglen' to that chapel. The rector of the church in 1394, John of Mertoun in Berwickshre, claimed lands from Rutherglen but was unsuccessful while John Cameron, yet another rector, later became the Bishop of Glasgow when Roul succeeded him at Cambuslang. Cameron later created Cambuslang a prebend of Glasgow. Sir John Millar was chaplain of the chapel of Our Lady around the time of the Reformation while another of some note, even if for the wrong reasons, was David Beaton, a Rector of Cambuslang Church who went on to be a cardinal and Archbishop of St. Andrews. He was a dreaded man who spent the latter part of his life seeking out reformists of the church in Scotland. Even though there was a powerful surge

away from the Catholic Church, Cardinal Beaton was responsible for the executions of several reforming preachers including George Wishart in 1546. Beaton was later assassinated at St. Andrews in 1548 by some of the very people he attempted to stamp out.

*O*ne famous event of ecclesiastical importance was the *Cambuslang Wark or Work* which took place over a ten month period in 1742 when the local minister organised an outdoor service, as was happening elsewhere in the country. It was a way of renewing our faith and finding oneself, a form of *Blanket Sermon* which were being held during the days of the king's episcopacy. This particular meeting held on the lands below the old kirk, lasted for nine incredible months when more than 30,000 people of all persuasions gathered to hear many thousands of speakers in what was thought to be 'a special outpouring of the Divine Spirit' a gathering of its kind or magnitude had never been held in Scotland before that time.

*C*hristianity is thought to have arrived even earlier however when Cadocus, a Welsh monk, is said to have founded a monastery at Drumsargart in the 6th century. Cadocus came as a missionary and wandered the hills of Lanarkshire before his foundation came to pass at Cambuslang. That venerable man became the patron saint of Cambuslang in the name of St. Cadoc. His monastery is said to have been situated on the site of the first church in the village, the site where the Old Parish Church now stands in Cairns Road. An holy hospital was founded at an unknown date and was situated near Spittal Farm to the east of Flemington House.

*T*he remains of St. Cadoc were thought to be removed from the medieval kirk to the William Moneypeny foundation at Our Lady's Chapel but that chapel has long since disappeared; some locals

Victoria Jubilee Fountain
Courtesy of Thomas Nugent

believe however, that today's St. Bride's Church is built on the spot and the remains of the holy man lie below that church which in turn, receives many pilgrims eager to pray near the relics of the saint. History seems to tell us, the chapel founded by Moneypeny was at Sauchiebog, and not on the site St. Bride's but, as we know, history is not always as dependable as it could be.

*I*n the modern day, holy worship is still alive and kicking with many churches covering all denominations, including Church of Scotland, Roman Catholic, Scottish Episcopal, Scottish Free Church Outreach and a Baptist Church meaning no one need travel far for their particular service. There is also a Nurture Education and Multicultural Society in the old Trinity St. Paul's building, a Salvation Army Citadel and last but certainly not least, a Kingdom Hall of the Jehovah's Witnesses.

Industry

*S*chools too, arrived early and there has been education offered since before the Reformation and nowadays, the town can boast of an impressive eight primary schools and two secondary schools. There is also South Lanarkshire College which has links with the West of Scotland University. The original school building is now a care home for the elderly and infirm.

*T*he town has many impressive buildings but none more so than the Cambuslang Institute. The institute was originally built between 1892 and 1898 before additions were added in the early 20th century. The purpose of the institute was for the relaxation and education of miners and weavers of whom many missed out on education as children because they were required to help their hard pressed families by finding work. In recent years it has been totally revamped, though the exterior is as magnificent as ever. The great building now comprises a large hall which can host anything from weddings to concerts, two lesser halls, meeting places, bars and toilets, in other words, a facility to host any occasion at any time, a facility of the people, for the people, and which the people are so proud of; many other halls in the town are more than able to cater for various occasions whether they be social or business.

*I*ndustry of old consisted, initially of weaving from mediaeval times, of mills and agriculture of all crops but more particularly of oats, joined by livestock in the form of goats, cows and sheep. Of course the residue of those industries was the production of food, meat and dairy providing for local needs as well as exporting further afield. That industry would one day lead to one of the parish's great days, the annual Cattle Show attracting visitors from near and far but more importantly, giving local workers a well deserved break from everyday life. Coal mining too arrived early and by the close of the 15th century, there were dozens of coal heughs being wrought. A coal heugh is where coal is extracted from the surface digging deep through the seam. Many of them can still be seen in many former mining areas and now provide, believe it or not, some peaceful walkways. As the centuries wore on, coal mining increased and developed in to larger pits being opened meaning more men and machinery thus the population increased accordingly. By the end of 18th century, steel was becoming a large employer as several new works opened, powered of course by the abundance of local coal supplies. Local quarries, some producing high quality 'Cambuslang Marble', were productive and another provider of jobs.

Abundant coal and steel would soon lead to other industries arriving and that was the case at Cambuslang with the arrival of companies like Mitchell and Hoover, with the latter ultimately providing over 1,000 jobs. When we think of Hoover, we think of household appliances but during the Second World War, the company was producing implements for fighter planes and bombers. Mitchells was not all about heavy industry, they too made little works of art from their metal works and even opened a shop to sell their wares. There is still some steel manufacture in the town but not nearly in the scale it once was. While there is still work to be had at the industrial estates and business parks, the vast majority must

River Clyde

travel for work with only memories of the great Clyde built ships which were put together with the steel of Cambuslang. *Clyde Built* would in time, become the two most important words applied to industry, 'Clyde built' meant simply, works of the highest order. At least good communications, road and rail help commuters on their to way to the city to earn a living. Services, council,

Railway at Cambuslang
Courtesy of Thomas Nugent ©2010

inns and restaurants and hotels are now the main providers of work but that same, sad scenario, is applicable to so many towns these days. Some good news though, is the impressive plans for development of the old Hoover site with a large national superstore, shopping complex and up to 250 new homes planned for the near future. That would be a dramatic 'shot in the arm' for the town's economy.

Many social clubs too provide good facilities for relaxation and fun when work is over for another week. Other places to rest, relax or play are the superb public parks and gardens in the town. Sports clubs too, thrive in Cambuslang including Cambuslang Rangers Football Club which was founded in 1889, blue and white are their colours and they play at Somervell Park in the town. Former players are Tommy Tait and Bobby Murdoch who both played for Scotland in different eras and Brian Ahern who played at Shawfield for a total of 14 years with Clyde Football Club in two different spells at the club. Cambuslang Rugby Club, founded in 1903 play at Coats Park. Other sports like golf, bowling, athletics, kuk sool won and tennis are popular and well supported. We can look at some of the other facilities when we reach Rutherglen since the 'twin towns' share so many of the nearby centres of which there are many.

Apart from those already mentioned, some other notables were involved with this, one of Scotland's great industrial towns include, William de Cambuslang, Bishop of Dunblane in the 14th century, David Dale the great 19th century industrialist, James Meek the parish minister in the 18th century who enthused and waxed lyrical of Cambuslang, Robert Wilson, the great singer, Mick McGahey, the rabble rousing trades unionist, Midge Ure, singer and songwriter and world champion boxer, Scott Harrison.

Industry

*G*racious Clyde flows below Clydeford Bridge which, as the name suggests was a ford over the river before the coming of the bridge. Then it is the turn of old Cambuslang railway bridge, which is now disused, before sweeping at right angles to the north and passing a Carmyle industrial estate as she heads for more bridges, road and rail, on the flow past Rutherglen. Even more bridges await including the one carrying the M74, the Dalmarnock Bridge, the Bridgeton Bank railway bridge and Rutherglen Bridge itself which heads in to the town at the southern edges of Bridgeton.

Main Street, Rutherglen – Courtesy of Thomas Nugent ©2013

*R*utherglen, old Rutherglen, was, in former times, the single most important town and parish in the west of Scotland and that includes the great city of Glasgow. While Glasgow was home to the chief church of the old Diocese of Glasgow, the town and churches were in the oversee of the proud Deanery of Rutherglen where lay most of the commerce. The history of *Ruglen* however, goes back long before the coming of the Catholic Church or even the old Celtic Church, stretching deep in to the mists of time. In fact many believe the town was named in honour of Reutherus, or Reuther who was said to be the fifth in line after Fergus I 'founded' Scotland in 330BC. Fergus was mentioned in the fictional chronology of Boece and Buchanan and as such, his place in the history of Scotland is deemed, at best, debatable, since Scotland as a country and nation was still a long way off. However, King Rhydderch Hael, King of Strathclyde in the late 6th and early 7th century and whom we know much more of, is as likely a candidate as any to have given name to the town. The king's name was probably pronounced in form of 'ruther' bearing in mind the 'dd' element in Welsh is pronounced as 'th' as in 'other'.

*R*utherglen in those far off days, was indeed an important stopping point, and a place of river crossing, ford and ferry, for the invading Romans and the later kings of the day, travelling along the length of their kingdom of Strathclyde from Cumbria, to their capital *Alt Clut* or Dumbarton Rock from whence they reigned until beyond the coming of Kenneth McAlpin, the King of Picts, and, some say, the first King of Scots. We must remember however, the Scots, originally from Ireland, were a tribe who had settled in, mainly Argyllshire and Lochaber in the 7th century and 'christened' the area Dál Riata or Dalriada. Of course those lands of Dalriada were situated well above the Forth and Clyde basins, whereas below that line was the Kingdom of Strathclyde which stretched from the Clyde at Dumbarton down towards Cumbria while the old kingdom of first, Northumbria then Bernicia, ruled the south-east including Edinburgh, Lothians and Borders.

Created a Royal Burgh by David I in 1126, a creation which was confirmed by every King of Scots thereafter, Rutherglen was one of Scotland's most important and indeed, one of the most historic towns. It is a town which has embraced everything that is good about Scottish character and culture. The old days of heady importance have, of course, long since gone but that is not to say they should be forgotten.

From the beginning, we have talked about the river, great castles, local culture, like Lanark's Lanimer Fair, the riding of the marches, great food producers, orchards, important churches and great mansion houses, important men and monuments to the past. We have also seen the great industries from farming, arable and pastoral, iron and steel, quarrying and coal mining, all creating a productive environment. Many towns and villages have or had much of those traditions and industries, but Rutherglen has embraced them all and yet it is so sad, all of those things, which make much of what the town is justifiably proud of, is not being promoted to the good of the burgh, the county, the country but most of all, the people.

Sometimes it is worthwhile looking at our past, learn from it, and use it to help our future. So many towns have made their heritage work for them and so can Rutherglen. Work has already began at Farme Cross, to remind us of the boundary stones of the burgh which were periodically checked in case of unwanted encroachment but much more can be done. The history and proud heritage of such an important burgh and parish in Scotland should never be allowed to drift down the river, it should be saved for future generations, and the visitors who may arrive would give a big helping hand to the local economy and may even participate in the resurrection of the old St. Luke's Fair, once held in October every year for centuries.

My latest visit to the town drew

Rutherglen Town Hall

Industry

immediate thought of, "Gosh, it's so busy" and so it was, appearing to thrive, at least on the Main Street. I also witnessed some very prosperous looking and busy industrial sites and business parks. I saw too an old church which is crying out "Come and see me, I am ancient and I sit on the corner of Main Street and Queen Street, next to the most wonderful town hall and not far from the town cross which was erected in 1926 to replace an ancient cross which just withered away so long ago" There really is so much to see in Rutherglen not excluding the river.

I also learned of shopping malls which have more recently joined forces with a wide and varied array of local and national shops on the main thoroughfare. It does appear that no one really need cross a bridge to go to Glasgow unless for a day out, or work. The wee harbour would make a different and special way of crossing if you could tempt one of the boat owners in to 'doing the honours'. If you need a rest for some sustenance, there are many restaurants, cafés and inns around and, if you want to stay awhile, many local and nearby hotels are willing and able to accommodate. A new complex, soon to open, will contain more facilities like shops and cinema and should be in business before the Commonwealth Games get underway. In fact, there is so much going on in Rutherglen and Cambuslang in preparation for the great sporting event. Other places of relaxation are the many gardens and parks in and around the old town which provide peace for fine relaxing walks with the odd bench ready and willing to help ease the older legs.

*T*he old church we mentioned, is actually a section of gable and the tower of St. Mary's which stands in the kirkyard of today's parish church. The old tower was added early in the 16th century as part of a renewal of a 12th century church which was the church where, in 1297, the Patriot, William Wallace declared that peace now prevailed between Scotland and England, a wonderful oratory marking the end of hostilities but was it? Well history tells us that was not the case and fighting was to go on for nearly another 400 years and the end of the Covenanting, *'Killing Times'.* The old church was also the scene of a despicable episode some time later when Sir John Menteith learned of the hiding place of William Wallace, then met with a group of English officers and contracted to hand Wallace over to them no doubt for the bounty on the great man's head. The betrayal was concluded on 5th August when Wallace was captured at Robroyston by English soldiers, taken to London, 'tried' then executed. That betrayal became a crucial turning point in the history of Scotland, causing a great outpouring of nationalism and a greater defiance to English domination. The people no longer had Wallace to follow but they did follow his spirit, his ideals and his fight for freedom.

*T*he church Wallace knew was the second church on the site following on from a chapel founded in the early 7th century by a disciple of St. Kentigern, St. Conval, who is sometimes recognised as Conal of Strathclyde or the Confessor but even that church is believed not to have been the first place of worship on that divine site. A grove circle of trees which still stood in the late 17th century was thought to have been a circle for Druid worship but then why not? We have already heard of Reutherus, the king who is said to have lived nearly 300 years before the birth of Christ, so why not Druids in this area too - there is no doubt, whoever walked the paths along this stretch of Clyde in those mystical times, be it Reutherus or Druid priests, they would carry out some form of pre-Christian worship. A third church was built in 1794 and served the congregation until 1902 when the present church was built.

As we have seen, Ruglen was a Royal town from the days of King David and there is very little doubt the church was in place at that time as was St. Luke's Fair. Those were the days when David's Norman followers were being granted lands and putting in place, forms of local government and law and, since Rutherglen was the first of David's royal domains, it would seem logical, the town would stretch out to form a larger parish. When David's grandson William I came to the throne he granted the spiritual side of the parish to the Bishops of Glasgow. The bishop's sole responsibility was his own cathedral and to provide parsons or chaplains to various churches within their diocese but not to Rutherglen since that was not only a parish in its own right, but also a deanery and of course, a Royal Burgh and would provide its own chaplain, the first of whom we know of, was the Dean of Rutherglen, Phillip de Perthee in 1227, and Thomas, who was vicar in 1272. While the kirk was dedicated to the Virgin and the fair to St. Luke, their were altars within, dedicated to St. Nicholas and the

Old Rutherglen Church

Holy Trinity. To mark the importance of the church, the focal point of the Deanery of Rutherglen, a great stone cross was erected at nearby Cross Hill, signifying to travellers that they were entering a place of, not only great ecclesiastical power, but as the trading and commercial heart of Clydeside. By this time, William the Lion had granted the church (not the deanery) to Paisley Abbey and in that way, the great wealth of the parish was given, in part, to that holy institution. That grant followed a similar grant William's brother, Malcolm, had made to Kelso Abbey.

Alexander III, the last king before the disruptive Wars of Succession, followed the Lion's piety in granting money to Glasgow Cathedral for the lighting up of St. Mungo's Altar and the lighting of the old kirk at Ruglen. During those wars and the later Wars of Independence, Edward of England arrived in Berwick in 1291 and again 1296 demanding landowners and churchmen to attend him, pay homage and swear fealty to the power mad monarch. In 1296, two men of Rutherglen had the 'honour' of bending over to kiss the king's feet, they were Adame fiz Matheu de Ruglen and John de Legun of Rutherglen.

*W*ithin the area of Rutherglen's power, was the Bishop's city of Glasgow meaning, quite simply, the place of the deanery was indeed the place most destined to be the great city Glasgow has become – even the churches of Glasgow were in the Deanery of Rutherglen though Bishop Jocelin of Glasgow did 'cut a deal' with the powers in Rutherglen, that Glasgow should enjoy free trade, though Rutherglen would remain the power house of the west of Scotland and though Alexander II curtailed some of its influence over Glasgow, in general the parish on the south bank remained dominant. At one point the royal jurisdiction of Rutherglen covered the entire area of Glasgow, such was its power and importance. This was the chief trading and commercial centre and even when Lanarkshire was divided in to two wards in1402, Rutherglen was created the chief town of the Lower Ward. However, around this point, the town's importance (and prosperity) began to wane until, eventually, in 1692, virtually all the trade and commerce was transferred to Glasgow – history shows, Glasgow has never looked back.

*T*here were some necessary conditions Royal Burghs had to adhere to, it was not all sun and light without the usual 'catch'. The burgh had to erect a castle home for the king, which Rutherglen did, presumably small during the days of David and Malcolm IV but greatly enlarged during the dying days of William's reign and in to the reign of Alexander II. It must have been a favoured place of residence for William since he issued most of his charters from his power house at Rutherglen. The burgh also had to pay great fees and gift the income of tithes to the crown, a form of annual rent if you like, all for the privilege of being a burgh of great standing, though the benefits would be even greater.

*R*uglen Castle was taken by Edward I's army before, finally, Edward Bruce, brother of Robert, regained the bastion. The castle changed hands so often over the centuries including another spell in the hands of the English, but was finally destroyed by James Stewart of Moray as punishment to the owners, the Hamiltons of Shawfield. for their support of Queen Mary. Another castle existed in the town, Farme Castle which was built, or at least enlarged in the 15th century on lands which had been gifted to the Steward of the Isles by Robert I. The lands later passed, during the reign of David II, to the Douglases then the Crawfords. In the early part of the 20th century, plaster was removed revealing a painted wooden ceiling of the 13th century. Sadly, the old fortification was demolished in the 1960s. Another royal charter arrived during the reign of Robert III, when the king granted the lands of Castle Vallie of Rutherglen and the King's Isles to one, Robert Hall.`

*O*ther more 'recent' history of the town came in 1679 when Robert Hamilton of Preston near Prestonpans, with a posse of well armed cavalry rode to Glasgow to declare the true religion of Scotland as Presbyterian and that he was head of the Presbyterian party. As it happened, Glasgow was bustling with a large Royalist army forcing Hamilton and his Covenanters back to Rutherglen. The date was significant, 29th May, not only the birth date of Charles II, but also the anniversary of his Restoration to the English throne. The people of Rutherglen were busy, as was every other town in the kingdom, celebrating the holiday with merriment and dancing round great bonfires, enjoying the occasion with locally brewed ale. The Covenanters decided to make their declaration at Rutherglen Cross but only after the celebrations had come to a halt and the bonfires extinguished. The following day, the Royalists visited the town though none of the local people were implicated but that incident led directly to the battles at Drumclog and Bothwell Bridge.

Fast forward to the 19th century and we learn, education was now well established as was the library and reading rooms while local industries were booming around the town and its suburbs. Burgh chambers were built as was a new court house and the simply majestic town house, one of the most magnificent in the land, complete with its elaborate clock tower. More schools opened with the parents under the threat of court action if their children were not sent to school without good reason. Housing was built apace with many new streets being added and the more upmarket suburb of Burnside growing with the completion of many fine new villas.

New churches arrived after the Disruption of 1843 with Free Kirks sprouting up in every town in the country. Soon there were United Presbyterian, Free, Congregational and United Reformed and so on. In 1853, the first Catholic Church since the Reformation of 1560, St. Columbkille's, opened and is still in use; of course, in 1902, the new parish church opened in a town where all Christian denominations are served. There is also a Mosque, Minhaj-Ul-Qurab serving the Islamic community, the Hindu Temple of Scotland, a Church of Jesus Christ of Latter Day Saints and a Kingdom Hall of Jehovah's Witness all joining other groups in their holy worship. There are a total of nine primary schools, four high schools and a private school providing all the educational needs of the children of Rutherglen and Cathkin areas.

Many sports are catered for in the town including skate boarding, cycling, cricket, indoor and lawn bowls, swimming, rugby, golf, athletics and football. The most famous of local football teams is the junior team, Rutherglen Glencairn, who play at the Clyde Gateway Stadium in the town. The black and white hoops are a famous sight, they are the colours which have won the Scottish Junior Cup three times. They were founded in 1896, in the jail! Well that was the only meeting place at the time, so it was used to discuss the club's formation. The Glens, who currently play in the Western Regions of the Scottish Junior Football Association, have produced many fine players including, Sam Baird, Joe Donnachie, Archie Robertson of Clyde and Scotland, Bernie Slaven and Rob McKinnon.

Another club featured at Rutherglen from 1898 until 1986 when, outwith their control, they had to leave the town...forever? Clyde Football Club were founded in 1877, originally a sports club including rowing, but slowly began to re-emerge solely, as an association football club. Originally they played across the river at Barrowfield Park in the Bridgeton area of the city before moving to Shawfield Stadium in 1898. The club, who play in white shirts, black shorts and red

Industry

stockings have been, considering their size, very successful over the years and have won the Scottish Football Association Challenge Cup on no less than three occasions. In 1939, they beat Motherwell 4-0 in the final and held the cup for eight years! As it happened, war had broken out and the competition lay dormant during hostilities. Again in 1955 when the club beat Celtic 1-0 in a replay after the first game ended 1-1 and finally Hibs were the victims when they lost 0-1 to the Bully Wee (Clyde's nickname) in 1958. The club has also finished as runners-up on another three occasions. Clyde qualified for the Inter Cities Cup in 1967 but a crazy rule would only allow one team from any one city to participate in that competition. Clyde argued they were a Rutherglen team but the powers that be insisted they were a Glasgow team, meaning Rangers were in and Clyde were out with Hibernian of Edinburgh taking their place. Clyde did play a tie in the Friendship Cup in 1962 when the beat Lens of France by 4-0 in France and by 2-1 at Shawfield. They have also won nine league championships in the lower leagues, a truly incredible achievement for the old club.

*T*he club have produced many players for the international team like Harry Haddock, George Herd, Archie Robertson & Tommy Ring to name but a few while others who made the breakthrough on their senior careers at the club went on to win international honours while playing elsewhere including Stevie Archibald, born in Rutherglen, who left Clyde for Aberdeen before playing for Tottenham Hotspur, Barcelona and, of course, Scotland. Another, Pat Nevin, a wizard of the wing, went on to play for Chelsea, Everton and Scotland. The club have been  blessed with many other fine servants such as Brian Ahern, who played 420 games for the club in two stints, Tommy McCulloch, the longest serving goalkeeper, Other celebrated players include Alex Linwood, Billy McPhail, Harry Hood, Danny McGrain (the Celtic player's cousin) Neil Hood and Johnny Coyle who scored the winning goal in the 1958 cup final against Hibernian. Great managers include, Paddy Travers, Johnny Haddow, John Prentice, Davie White, Craig Brown and Alan Kernaghan though the present management duo of Jim Duffy and Chic Charnley are doing an amazing job under difficult circumstances but pride of place must go to the club's greatest ever servant, Mattha Gemmell, *Mr Clyde.*

*M*attha Gemmell, 'the wee man frae Brigton', started work for the club from the time they arrived at Shawfield in 1898. From that time until 1945, he served the club faithfully as groundsman, assistant trainer and trainer. He was simply Clyde. Clyde, Clyde, in every bone and drop of blood in his body. To the extent that when he was offered a really good job with Queens Park, for more money, his answer was immediate "Yes I'll take the job with you...as long as I get every Saturday off to go and watch the Clyde" In later life, long after he retired from the game, he became disabled and unable to leave his home. On the evening of the cup win in 1958, the players arrived outside his home in Main Street, Bridgeton, parading the Scottish Cup to a Clyde institution. I can only imagine the players were meaning they won the cup for Mattha while I am equally sure he cried his proudest ever tears of joy for his beloved Bully Wee who were, at least for that day of days if not every day, his *Kings of Scottish football.* It is interesting to note, Mattha worked under trainer, Bill Struth for a time and that man went to be one of Rangers' great managers. Clyde currently play at Cumbernauld but are set to move, with East Kilbride a possibility though many fans have not given up on a return to their spiritual homelands in Rutherglen. As I write, the club are enjoying their best season for some years having reached the 4th round of the cup and at the top of the league but best of all, with some promising young players in their ranks.

As mentioned at Cambuslang we shall discuss facilities in both towns since the people of both Cambuslang and Rutherglen do share each other's facilities First of all there is a skate park, four fine golf courses in the the area, all are very popular and well used. There are several leisure centres, swimming pools, sports fields and community halls to suit everyone and for all occasions, from small intimate meetings to concerts and weddings, all are taken care of. Both have hotels and social clubs meaning weekends are busy times around the towns. Daytime walks are everywhere, whether in the many gardens, parks, riverside or nearby woodlands; there are walks to suit all ages and abilities. Adding to the many venues, are the clubs, groups and societies embracing all ages including

babies, older kids, young adults and the elderly. Social clubs, reading groups, walking clubs, old folks, bingo heads, religious and charitable groups indeed, something for everyone; they all help to fill the needs and enjoyment for all.

Health services are good, but the loss of the maternity hospital probably meant some job losses in the town. Transport is excellent, within easy reach

Section of industrial area at Rutherglen

of the M74 and M8 motorways joining with the most wonderful bus and rail services.

We covered the old industries earlier but most of that is, sadly, part of local history now but there are many industrial and business parks around the area where so many are employed. Local government also provides employment in many mediums across the town but the local people are fairly lucky considering their proximity to Glasgow where most travel for work and, of course travel is quick and relatively easy meaning journey times are short, allowing more relaxation time at the end of the day. I still feel though, Rutherglen has lost out so much on tourism and, with such glorious history around a town, so prominent in the development of Scotland as a whole, something seems to be getting overlooked somewhere.

*N*otable people include, first and foremost, Dr. James Gorman who treated the people, day and night for free, long before the coming of the National Health Service. He was a devoted man who gave of his time to the people of the town and was always on hand in case of emergency at the pits and God knows there were many of them. A statue of the great man occupies the corner of Queen Street and Main Street near the parish kirk. Others including Australian cricketer, Archie Jackson who was born in Ruglen as were the rugby players, Duncan Weir, Richie and Johny Gray; also born in the town, was comedian, Robbie Coltrane but there are many good folk with association or were born in Rutherglen.

*R*utherglen has many districts, most of which were villages in their own right, and include Burnside and High Burnside, Cathkin, Gallowflat, Stonelaw, Burnhill, Springhill, Spittal where a holy hospital once stood, Clincarthill, Overtoun, Bankhead, High Crosshill, Shawfield and Cunnigar Loop, Fern Hill, Blairbeth, Farme Cross and of course the actual burgh. Most of the areas have their own shops and halls with some sporting facilities including Cathkin Braes where exists a mountain biking track and a fine golf course in such a

Entrance to Cathkin Braes Park
Courtesy of Lairich Rig ©2007

wonderful park while Overtoun can also boast a fine park, and at Blairbeth, a golf course of some note. Whatever the districts have to offer, it all adds to the making of a very fine parish and town.

A quick look now at a couple of nearby Glasgow suburbs before we head back to the river at Carmyle. For decades, the Gorbals was tagged as virtually a slum area and one of the 'bad boys' of the city but the people of the Gorbals I knew, were lovely, gentle folk who just got on with their everyday lives without fuss. In more recent times there has been so much regeneration of the city including Gorbals and Hutchesontown. The places are as good as many and contain everything they need from day to day. There are parks, bowling clubs and a church of ancient foundation. While in the area, let's have a look at the atmospheric and historic Southern Necropolis, an old burial place for the suburb, which was opened in 1840 to ease the pressure on the older cemetery in the area. So many fine memorials, and the graves of some well known people can be viewed within the hallowed walls of the graveyard which is entered by the most wonderful entrance gates. Men like Sir Thomas Lipton, the tea merchant and grocer, Alexander 'Greek' Thomson, a great architect, George Rodgers a proud recipient of the Victoria Cross and John Robertson, the Labour politician, are all buried there as is Agnes Reston a celebrated nurse during the Crimean War.

River Clyde

Carmunnock, another small suburb, is a little to the south-east of Ruglen and is a conservation village within the City of Glasgow, a rare bird indeed. The remarkable growth of Glasgow over the centuries has meant so many small villages have been caught up and engulfed in the path of urban confusion, losing their olde worlde atmosphere but not Carmunnock. It is quite simply, a beautiful village with many lovely homes dotted all around, from very large, to smart upmarket villas, lovely old cottages, a fine primary school, and a wonderful old kirk in the village centre. The village shop is near the church and surrounded by a sea of white buildings including houses and the popular Mitchell's

Stables at old Castlemilk House
Courtesy of Graeme Yuill ©2013

restaurant. Small greens and colourful flowers are everywhere, setting a most desirable and reassuring scene giving us a little piece of heaven before we enter one of the great cosmopolitan cities of the world. Castlemilk in the parish of Carmunnock, contained the celebrated 18th century Castlemilk House which contained an earlier, 15th century tower. The lands in that section of Carmunnock were purchased by the Stuart family of Castilmilk in Dumfriesshire in the 13th century and it was they who built a tower in what became know as Castleton, a place where Mary, Queen of Scots slept on the evening before the Battle of Langside, meaning that evening at Castilmilk was the queen's last 'bed time' as a free woman in her own kingdom. The name was later changed and a large mansion house was built around the tower. In time the house was purchased by Glasgow Corporation and was used to house evacuees during the Second World War then later as a children's home. The house was demolished in 1969 but still some scant remains can be seen including the most inspiring fireplace. The stable block has recently been restored and gives a great insight in to the past and the life of old Castlemilk which has, in much more recent times, been the recipient of a vast housing estate.

Carmunnock Kirk sometimes known as the Kirk o' the Braes, is an ancient foundation dating back to the 12th century when Henry, the son of Aselm, and his wife Joanna, granted the tithes to the Church of St. Mirin at Paisley, (Paisley Abbey) a grant which was confirmed by William I. In those days Carmunnock and Gorbals were both in the Deanery of Rutherglen and both received chaplains in to their respective churches from the Dean. In later times, the

Industry

churches had to provide their own preachers and we know of two of the early chaplains, Stephen and Peter in the 13th century.

Now it is time to head back to the northern banks of the river at Carmyle and travel through the city with the eternal flow. Carmyle too is a former mining and weaving community but like all the other surrounding, industrials villages, it has gone down the same road to nigh industrial oblivion. Some remnants of the old industry can still be seen on the riverside near one of the most exciting if unusual, weirs on the river taking the form of 'V' shape as it cuts past a river island and remnants of the old mill.

Entrance to Carmunnock Church with the church building beyond
Courtesy of Iain Thompson ©2005 Geograph/60169

Something old in Glasgow..............

**The semi ruinous
Caledonia Road
United Presbyterian Church**

Section Four

Glasgow

*D*avid I granted lands at Carmyle in the 12th century to the monks of Newbattle, a satellite house of Melrose Abbey and a monastery was founded in that area on the north bank of Clyde at the place once cleared of trees creating Carmyle, *the bare, rich, lands.*

*C*armyle is a lovely little place containing everything it needs for everyday living including an assortment of shops, community centre, primary school, leisure facilities and good open parkland, especially Orchard and New Carmyle Parks, providing for peaceful, flat walking in the village and near the river. There

 are two churches, the parish church and St. Joachim's Roman Catholic and two primary schools, one non denominational and the other, St. Joachim's Roman Catholic. Two bowling clubs exist providing more outlets for relaxation and fun while golf courses are aplenty situated mainly to the north of the village but provide even more sporting alternatives for the local people. There were two inns, both closed but there does seem to be some activity at the Auld Hoose on the river side near Carmyle Bowling Club and the river weir (pictured above) suggesting it may be preparing to open again. Carmyle really is a lovely place and many hours can pass discovering the surrounding area but the great river awaits and it is time to move on, there is so much still to see. Let's discover more of the river and the riverside amenities, but also visit some of the more ancient burghs which were annexed to Glasgow over the years even though some are not situated on the riverbanks.

*C*lyde, now flowing south of Dalbeth, Braidfauld and Auchenshuggle, suddenly loops north before swinging back to the south. On the right bank at the east end of the city, is old Parkhead, in the old days, a place of great industry with weaving, coal mines and a huge steel industry joining the ever present agriculture, both livestock and arable. From those times, the old weaving village grew in to a busy work house, attracting workers from all over Britain and Ireland with many more arriving from mainland Europe. Now of course, virtually all the industry has gone but a great shopping village has emerged on the site of the old Parkhead Forge Iron works. The shopping complex, the Parkhead Forge, is made up of a huge mall, an indoor market and another large retail park, attracting shoppers from all over Scotland and the north of England. The old place is also home to

River Clyde

Celtic Football Club, one of the city's institutions, and the Emirates Sports Arena and Velodrome, all ready and waiting to play a vital role in the 2014 Commonwealth Games. Just north of Parkhead is Carntyne, another old mining village where a steam engine for clearing water from the pit, was installed at the local colliery in 1768, a first in the west of Scotland. Yet another serious loop from south to north brings us to Dalmarnock and Bridgeton as the river reaches ever nearer to the city. It is a pleasure to be in the company of the imperious waters at Rutherglen Bridge on the southern reaches of old Bridgeton, where, once again, the beautiful Clyde walkway can be seen heading for Glasgow Green with the picturesque Richmond Park on the south bank. That park was purchased in 1898 by Glasgow Corporation from William Dixon for the staggering sum of over £41,000 which would equate to many millions of pounds in today's currency. The park, with two lochs, has recently been undergoing much refurbishment giving the people of Oatlands a facility to be truly proud of. Model boating is very popular much to the annoyance of the ducks and swans who frequent the pond but is great fun for the enthusiasts. It is a peaceful place for walks and picnics and is well used by the whole community. Jenny's or Polmadie Burn, which runs through to the river, has recently had the footbridge renewed making access a whole lot easier for everyone on both sides. Directly opposite is Brigton or Bridgeton on the eastern fringes of the city centre. Bridgeton was originally created within the Goosefield Estate owned by the Walkinshaw family, as a weaving village, but on the opening of Rutherglen Bridge in 1775, became known as the village or town near the bridge, thus the name. The weaving has of course died out but there is much work around and, being so close to the city centre, no one need travel far for employment. Nearby is Calton, yet another interesting locale with a turbulent history as we shall soon see.

Left : Richmond Park
Lynn M. Reid ©2008
geograph/723778

Having crossed the Polmadie Bridge, we have reached the Polmadie sports grounds, containing pitches for nearly every pitch sport and is home to the West of Scotland indoor bowling centre while, some distance to the south at this point, is the Toryglen national football centre and the headquarters of Scottish football,

Glasgow

Hampden Park, currently being restructured to accommodate the 2014 Commonwealth Games. The stadium once housed just a little less than 150,000 spectators for the 1937 Scotland v England international, which remains a European record attendance for a sporting event.

*P*olmadie itself was home to a shipyard with a difference. Being some distance from the river, the ships were built in parts then 'shipped' to wherever they were going and assembled. The suburb, in medieval times was home to an early church and a Knights Templar foundation, the Hospital of St. John. That hospital and chapel were confirmed to the parish of Govan and the deanery of Rutherglen by no less a man than Robert I (the Bruce) and existed through the later parts of the Middle Ages providing for the infirm and weary, rich and poor.

*N*ow looping sharply to the right, Clyde is hemmed in between Gorbals, Hutchesonstown and the world famous Glasgow Green. Immediately on the apex of the bend, on the left bank, are the premises of the ever popular Glasgow Rowing Club one of the oldest such clubs in Britain.

*H*utchesontown and Gorbals form a type of twin community, with the former the proud owner of one of the very first Carnegie libraries and the latter having the distinction of being one of the earliest areas in what became Glasgow. Indeed there has been a church at Gorbals in the care of the parish of Govan from mediaeval times. A church too was thought to have been sited in, what became Hutchesontown, from early times, in league with an ancient leper hospital. In recent times both areas have been subject to a great deal of regeneration and renewal in an attempt to rid them of the so called slum areas which existed, resulting in many of the people being relocated to one of the many new towns which were built to house, what became known as the Glasgow 'overspill'.

*G*lasgow Green is one of the best, one the most famous, one of the most alluring, parklands, and probably one of the oldest parks in the world, having been gifted to Bishop Turnbull of Glasgow Cathedral in 1450. Every suburb and the City of Glasgow, have many fine parks but there is no doubt this, more than any, is the people's Dear Green Place which, incidentally is said to be the meaning of the word 'Glasgow' or 'Glaschu' I don't think any Glaswegian hasn't a soft spot for this famous green, nor spent happy times at the wonderful park. Originally the lands on which the Green stands were thought to be marshy and uneven, probably caused by the overflowing of the burns, the Molendinar and the Camlachie, both heading towards their great drain, the River Clyde. From the 18th century, culverts and other drainage systems were put in place and the lands levelled in to much of what we see today. The flat lands would have been beneficial for Bonnie Prince Charlie and his generals to camp their troops on the Green in late December, 1745 while the prince demanded the people of Glasgow, clothe, feed and re-equip his army, during his retreat to Culloden, if they failed to comply, he threatened to place the city under siege, much to the annoyance of the local folk. Sadly for Charlie, the people of Glasgow showed no festive spirit nor goodwill. In those days, the people of Glasgow would have no more in common, as with so many

Downstream from
the Kings Bridge
adjacent to Glasgow Green

Courtesy of David Dixon
©2010

The
Doulton
Fountain
with the old Templeton
Carpet Factory
beyond.

Patrick Lee ©2005
geograph/51957

The Winter Gardens and Peoples' Palace, courtesy of Thomas Nugent ©2008

left:

High Kirk of Glasgow

**St. Mungo's Cathedral
and statue of David Livingstone**

Courtesy of Carol Walker ©2007

Right :

St. Andrews Roman Catholic Cathedral

**Courtesy of Thomas Nugent
©2009**

Left :

**Glasgow
Central Mosque**

**Courtesy
of
Thomas Nugent
©2013**

109

others in lowland and border Scotland, with the Highlanders as they would with the English. The masses took to the streets in protest at the presence of the Jacobite troops 'invading' their territory, the people of the city were never frightened to demonstrate their feelings at anything they thought wrong, as we shall see later. By this time of course, Glasgow was beginning to become one of the world's richest cities and on its way to becoming one of the greatest seaports, and the people would want nothing too much to do with the upstart of Italian birth who came to retrieve what his ancestors, because of their own arrogance and stupidity, had thrown away.

*T*he river has just flowed under the King's Bridge carrying the A74 to and from the city, and still the great park looms large. Soon Clyde will reach the wonderfully constructed St. Andrews Suspension footbridge linking Hutchesonstown with the Green. That bridge is only one of several memorable land marks on a green which also contains many sporting facilities including the Scottish National Hockey Centre. Other magnificent landmarks include the People's Palace incorporating the great glass construction of the Winter Gardens, the former Templeton Carpet Factory building, redesigned in the 19th century, along the lines of the Doge's Palace in Venice, the Doulton Fountain which is the largest terra cotta building in the world, the Nelson Column, William Collins Fountain, the Watt Stone and the sublime MacLennan Arch. So much exists on the great park which was originally created to provide a peaceful play area for the people at the east end of the city but is now, not only a city treasure, but a city icon, envied the world over as arguably the most meaningful of people's parks in existence. The wonderful home to museums, galleries and scenic walkways, with even a section of water forming a type of lade through the grounds, attracts people from across the world, helping make Glasgow one of the world's more interesting tourist destinations; such a long way from what was the 'dismal' east end yet, it is only one of many fine parks in the city, though the most historic. The wonderful Green is hemmed in, on the east by Polmadie, to the north-east by Bridgeton and the north by another old burgh which became part of the city, Calton.

*C*alton, from the Gaelic *A'Challtainn,* meaning the *'the hazel wood'* is a more than interesting place, being home to the most famous of all markets, *The Barras,* and the wonderful old Barrowland Ballroom which is renowned the world over but it owes its 'fame' to more seriously tragic events of the 18th century. The old village of Calton was, originally, very much a weaving village from the 17th century but, a meeting of the weavers on Glasgow Green in 1787 changed the British social and industrial landscape forever. They met to share their worries over cheap imports coming in to the country thus threatening their livelihoods, but what could they do? Their decision was to go on strike, a strike and protest which led to a split in the workforce, some continuing to work, some staying out on strike. Three months later, on 3rd September, a detachment of the 39th Regiment of Foot (the Dorsetshire Regiment) where sent in to quell violence when striking workers attacked others who had decided to stay at work, even for lower wages. Ultimately the soldiers were ordered to open fire which resulted in many injured and six dead, one of the blackest days in the history of the city and, as we shall learn in later paragraphs, was not the first nor last time the military would be ordered on to the streets of the city. Calton was later created, in 1817, a Burgh of Barony but that lasted only until 1846 when it was annexed in to the city.

Clyde now sweeps left between the park and Gorbals. tripping over an old weir before passing under the Albert and Victoria Bridges carrying the A8 between the city and Gorbals and Lauriston, as she heads for the Upper Harbour. In the next few moments she will pass under several other bridges including the railway bridge as she flows triumphantly through the centre of the city, passing the Florence Street campus of the Glasgow Metropolitan College and the Adelphi Centre as she reaches ever nearer her destiny. At this point, the river is also, in a sense, flowing through the togetherness of peoples and their beliefs. She is directly between three great houses of worship, the Glasgow Central Mosque on the left bank and a little further on the right, St. Andrews Roman Catholic Cathedral with the High Kirk of Glasgow (St. Mungo's Cathedral) hovering to the north. The great Mosque with the most wonderful dome, was opened in 1984 and receives at least 5,000 visitors every week, mainly for prayers but also many from other cultures eager to visit the beautiful place of worship. It is the largest mosque in Scotland and works very closely with all the other mosques in the city bringing peace and contentment to the many of the Islamic faith. St. Andrews Cathedral was built in 1816 but has recently been restored adding a lovely cloister garden which can be entered from Clyde Street. The building of the beautiful church, above all else, helped mark the return of the Catholic faith in Scotland; the present bishop is the Most Reverend Phillip Tartaglia. The High Kirk of Glasgow, or St. Mungo's Cathedral, has, since mediaeval times, been the principal place of worship for the people Glasgow, a city which came to be known as the Second City of the Empire. The present minister at the kirk is Revd. Dr. Laurence Whitley who has been in office since 2007. The city and the cathedral stretch back to the days of Kentigern when he was busy bringing the word of God to the people of south-west Scotland. It was he, by founding a small chapel here, who effectively founded the city. Incidentally, there are two other cathedrals in the city, St. Mary's Episcopal in Great Western Road and St. Luke's Greek Orthodox on Dundonald Road.

Kentigern was born to Thenew, daughter of the Northumbrian king of Lothian, Loth, who gave name to the district. Loth's capital was Dumpender Hill or Dyn Pelydr (Hill of Shafts) now better known as Traprain Law. When Thenew became pregnant out of wedlock, her father threw her over the rocks of the hill but remarkably, as if by divine intervention, Thenew survived and made her way to the coast of the Firth of Forth near the harbour of Aberlady. She scrambled in to a small craft without oar and pushed out to sea. She drifted for days until she landed on the rocky shores of the Isle of May but unhappily she was refused 'shore leave' and her feeble little craft was pushed away. As the viscous German Ocean (North Sea) stormed angrily in a terrible easterly gale, her craft was swept further and further west. Eventually her boat crashed on to the shore at what became Culross where monks from a local Culdee establishment met her. Within minutes, she gave birth to a son whom she named Kentigern. A few moments later, the leader of the local holy establishment, Serf or Servanus, came to her aid and, on receiving the baby boy in to his arms he called out *Mun goh*, meaning 'dear one'. That name, Mungo, remained with Kentigern for the rest of his life. After his young life was over, he entered the church of St. Serf at Culross before setting off on his travels bringing men to their knees and baptising all in to the Christian faith – he is even believed to have baptised the semi mythical Merlin the Wizard, in the River Tweed. He travelled to Wales for some time before returning home and founding Glasgow and the church from thence grew the great edifice we now see, where still the great man's relics lie in peaceful repose. The holy man's mother's name has, somehow over the centuries, been corrupted to Enoch and she is another patron saint of Glasgow where a church was said to have been founded early, in what is now St. Enoch's Square, a church in which Enoch was said to be buried.

*Q*uite apart from St. Andrews Cathedral and the Mosque, other buildings of note on this part of the river are the Nautical College building and the old fish market building, the Briggait. There, beyond the Albert and Victoria Bridges, the Clyde Walkway, adjacent to Clyde Street, is so peaceful and quite serene, surrounded with so much fine architecture. At this spot, for 44 years, the HMS Carrick, the world's oldest clipper, was berthed as an RNVR club house and was a major tourist attraction until she sank in 1991. The ship, formerly the 'City of Adelaide' was rescued and taken to the Maritime Museum at Irvine but, at this time, she is on her way to Adelaide to be restored and form the centre piece of a great project at Port Adelaide where, in days gone by, she shipped thousands of people hoping to start a new life in late 19th, early 20th century Australia.

*H*ere we are in the city centre which virtually made up the entire City of Glasgow until 1891 when six of the surrounding burghs, Maryhill, Govanhill, Crosshill, West and East Pollockshields and Hillhead were added by an Act of Parliament. Other non burghal districts also came under the umbrella of Glasgow at the same time including Alexandra Park, Kelvingrove Park, St. Rollox, Springburn, Sighthill, Keppoch Hill and Cowlairs all joining many residential areas in what was the first serious attempts to enlarge the city. At that stage, the burghs of Govan, Partick and Kinning Park resisted all attempt to annex them in to the bounds of the city but they, with so many other residential areas would, in time, come under the authority of Glasgow to form the great metropolis which now exists.

*G*lasgow Bridge, the railway bridge and the bridge carrying the A77 are the` next to be negotiated in one of the busiest stretches of the entire length of the Clyde Walkway, we are now on the Broomilaw with many fine buildings and ferry terminals, and perhaps one of the better known sections of the river within the city which is home too, to the sparkling Tradeston footbridge which traverses the river from Clyde Place. Bigger things, as they say, are still to come as Clyde prepares to flow between the Anderston and Springfield Quays, but before that, she flows under the busiest road bridge in Scotland, the awesome, ten lane, Kingston

Glasgow

Bridge which carries the busy M8 motorway in both directions. The M8 is the link between the country's two biggest cities, Edinburgh and Glasgow and is quite literally, a 24 hour thoroughfare. Now as the river approaches Lancefield and Finnieston Quays, we know that is the signal we are now in the ancient Burgh and Parish of Govan but before looking at that ancient place let's visit another of the old independent burghs which became part of the city, Anderston. Anderston, slightly to the west of the city, is an ancient town which was granted to the Bishopric of Glasgow in 1450 by the king, James II. In later times, the lands were feued to James Anderson, a major player in the textiles industries and who gave name to the town. Anderson built cottages for his army of weavers, creating one of the largest and most productive weaving communities of its kind in the country. The small town was becoming industrially important and it was no surprise when it was created a Burgh of Barony in 1824 by a Charter of the Crown. More industries in connection with weaving had already arrived including bleachfields and dyeing and soon, a print works would follow, as did other amenities like a school, church and shops, including Thomas Litpton's first ever premises. In time, the Lipton brand grew across the whole of Britain making him a household name. He was also world renowned as a yachtsman and competed in the Americas's Cup five times becoming a close friend of kings, Edward VIII and George V. The great man died in 1931 aged 83 and is buried across the river, as we have seen, at the Southern Necropolis. To the north of Anderston and on the 'confluence' of the River Kelvin and the Forth and Clyde Canal is, Maryhill.

The old suburb, formerly a burgh in its own right, is situated to the north-west of the city centre and is thought to have been home to a Roman fortlet on the Antonine Wall near where the Forth and Clyde Canal cuts through the old town. The suburb, named after Miss Mary Hill, a former owner of the great estate, was one of the earliest recipients of a Carnegie library, funded by the Andrew Carnegie Trust which built libraries in all corners of the United Kingdom and was also for several decades, the home to an army barracks. The old name for the area was Gairbraid but the husband of Mary Hill, Robert Graham was left specific instructions on the death of his wife, to have the village be known *in all times as the town of MaryHill.* Back down the road now to the river and to one of the most enduring and historic communities in Scotland, Govan.

Govan is believed to be among the very oldest of all the continuously settled sites on the entire length of the great river and is thought to reach back in to Neolithic times. Certainly Christian burials have been discovered which, after detailed examination, were from no later than the 5th century and the first church was founded no later than the 7th century by St. Constantine the Martyr. During his reign of the 12th century, David I granted the church to the Cathedral of Glasgow and was later placed as a prebend of the cathedral, in the Deanery of Rutherglen. The prebend status was placed on the shoulders of Helpe, clerk to the bishop before being dedicated to St. Constantine who came to Scotland with St. Columba when he founded the early church and abbey at Gouuen (an old name for the settlement) Govan was mother church to many others including Gorbals and the holy hospital at Polmadie. On February 14th 1440. Duncan, Earl of Lennox gave up all his rights at that hospital to the bishop of Glasgow, after a meeting at the West Chapel in Edinburgh Castle.

Other notes of interest regarding Govan Church included the church at Strathblane, which was united with Polmadie, and in the see of Govan Kirk until 1450, when it was taken as a prebend of the Collegiate Church of Dumbarton by Isabella, Duchess of Albany and Countess of Lennox. Govan too, was home to a Bishop's residence which was situated near the confluence with the River Kelvin, where the Bishop resided during his visitations to the town. We shall find shortly, that residence was in the village of Partick or Pertique as it was sometimes known, which was within the parish of Govan.

We do have some names of local dignitaries from mediaeval times including John of Govan, who was a baillie in Glasgow in 1283, William who witnessed a charter in 1289, Christiana, wife of Simon of Govan who granted lands to the church and Helia who was a canon at Govan and was witness to a charter of gift to Glasgow in 1161. William de Kirkintilloch was a master and parson of the hospital at Polmadie in the 13th century and was constantly in holy communion within Govan Church.

Beyond the Reformation, Govan was deemed to be the most populous single parish in Scotland, and the most valuable, giving some indication of the size and importance of both parish and burgh which was a very important agricultural, weaving and quarrying centre. It is unclear where the name, Govan came from but another old name was Gouan meaning *good ale,* so perhaps the breweries of the town were doing a good job. Old maps showing Gouan, indicate the river was wider at this point than it is now and there were several islands which no longer exist.

While Scotland had been freed from the English yoke, as we have seen elsewhere, both Edward II and Edward III have been noted, still making forays in to Scotland and the latter did have a of habit showing up at Govan. In 1319, he granted the parish to Johann de Lind and creating him prebendary for Govan at Glasgow Cathedral. By 1525, Walter Betune, or more recognisably, Beaton, was rector of Govan Kirk and was among the judges at St. Andrews for the trial of the grandson of James II, Patrick Hamilton, a rousing reformist who fought for the overthrow of the Church of Rome. He was executed at St. Andrews within an hour of his 'trial' starting. That man, who was born in Stonehouse in the Diocese of Glasgow, was the first protestant martyr in the quest for a national church. In the wake of the Reformation, Govan was fortunate to have many fine ministers including the celebrated William Melville.

Still the farming industry flourished as did weaving but in time, coal and iron took over with the companies of Dixons and Raes taking precedence over all others in moving industry forward. As industry progressed, wealthy families moved in and soon whole avenues of tree-lined streets emerged and, it appeared, the wealthy owners employed men to act as police to protect their properties. What those wealthy families brought with them, was more work and soon dyeing

Glasgow

and silk production factories were booming. Around that time, the Clyde was deepened, the old islands removed as commerce grew as did foreign trade. Factories of varying industries arrived and a new, enlarged quay, built of stone, was erected on the river. While the merchants of Clydeside were operating foreign trade, ship building was still in its infancy but that was soon to change and, as the 19th century wore on, shipbuilding had reached the 'big league' and that entire industry of the Clyde at that stage, was in the parish of Govan. In fact, nearing the end of that century, Govan still built at least half the tonnage of all ships built on the Clyde. Industry was thriving as never before...nor since. The roll call of industry was eye watering. Read this and see how prosperous Govan was and so, subsequently, was Glasgow as a whole.

There existed a huge bakery industry, iron works, foundries, boiler manufacture, tube works, steam crane manufacture, launching slip works, railway engineering, tool works, bolt and rivet manufactories, oil works, rope and twine manufacture, silk and cotton making with associated dyeing and bleaching, tile and brick manufacture, distilling and let us not forget brewing, the list just goes on and on. Of course, as industry grew, so did the population coming from all parts of Britain, Ulster, Ireland and eastern Europe meaning houses were needed as were churches and schools.

In 1891, the population of the entire parish of Govan was a remarkable 108,000 souls but then the parish contained, Govan, Abbotsford, Belahouston, Dean Park, Gorbals, Govanhill, Elder Park, Hillhead, Hutchesontown, Ibrox, Kingston, Kinning Park, Laurieston, Maxwell, Oatlands, Partick, Plantation, Pollockshields, Queen's Park, St. Bernards, St. Kiarans, St. Mary's, St. Ninian's Strathbungo and Whiteinch. There were also mission charges and wait for it, a total of 71 churches including Roman Catholic, Free, United Free, United Presbyterian, Reformed, Weselyan and so on; that figure did not include the 25 Churches of Scotland. Not only that though, every one of those towns and villages within the parish, had at least one school. There were some hospitals of sorts bearing in mind the National Health Service was still not a dream but there were several lunatic asylums, poorhouses, Halfway Houses, alm houses and charitable homes to so many very low paid workers.

The fine reputation earned at Govan, where some of the world's greatest ships were built, never dies but industries do, and now there is very little left of the old works, but one yard does remain and is, with the Yarrow yard at Scotstoun, part of BAE Systems Group which has been in the news in late 2013 with the announcement that the company is preparing to downsize its operations, either on the Clyde or at Portsmouth...or both. It would be a crying shame if shipbuilding ceased at a place where so many fine ships, both civil and military, have been been built before gracing the seas of the world.

There is still work in the area but like the rest of the region, is mainly associated with service industries, leisure and council though there still remains some manufacturing. There are still churches of all Christian denominations and a mosque, just as there are ample schools to meet the educational needs of the children. The area has many good leisure and sporting facilities and wonderful parks including, Pirie and Elder Parks on the south of the river and Mansfield, Yorkhill and Cross Parks on the north not forgetting Govan Nature Park. The old town has a lot of atmospheric places and landmarks, like Govan Cross at the town centre, a genuine Celtic Cross and so many pieces of ancient stones at the Old Kirk where Constantine the Martyr is said to be buried, a magnificent town hall, the William Pearce memorial and of course, much more. Moot or Doomster Hill was the site of a motte castle, where local justice was carried out and proclamations made, which existed in the town but sadly no clues as to the whereabouts have been discovered. Shopping is good and every thing you can buy can be bought in Govan. Inns and cafés abound and there are so many social and sports clubs for all ages with Rangers FC, the most famous of all Govan clubs, who play at Ibrox Stadium.

Many notables, particularly of the modern era, have association with Govan and the list is quite exhaustive but I shall give a few of the more recent, starting with Sir Alex Ferguson, Britain's greatest football manager, advocate Gordon Jackson QC., comedian, Jack Gilroy, and Mohammed Sarwar, MP.

Sometimes we tend to forget, the City of Glasgow consists of old Govan and so many of the other surrounding villages and towns, all with their own unique histories including Govan which has been quite a surprise for me, though I did know of its early ecclesiastical prominence. It really is a proud place and I am equally as happy to call it a town within a town if you like and when I asked some locals of their allegiances, the general answer was "I may be a Glaswegian but I come from Govan" That pride is actually well founded, when we bear in mind, at the downfall of Dumbarton at the hands of the Danes in the 9th century, Govan, for a while, was the capital of Strathclyde but it was important long before and after that notable event.

Many other ancient burghs exist around Govan including Cardonald, Carnwadric, Crookston at Pollock and, across the river, Partick.

Cardonald to the south-west of Glasgow, is an ancient village and was part of Renfrewshire until it became part of the city in 1925. It was, originally in the hands of the notable Normaville family until it passed, by marriage, in to the own of the Stewarts of Castlemilk in the early 16th century and, in time, a new line was created, the Stewarts of Cardonald, the first of whom was Allan, son of the 1st Earl of Lennox. That line ended when James Stewart, an officer in the Scots Guards, died in 1584 when serving the King of France thus leaving the estates of Cardonald to Walter, 1st Lord Blantyre.

Crookston, part of Pollock, is an ancient settlement which was owned and named after Robert de Croc who was gifted the lands by David I in the 12th century. Robert built a ring work defensive 'fort', but the magnificent remains we can still see today, were probably built by later owners, the Stewarts of Darnley. Croc also built a chapel in his old fort and probably granted it to the monks of St. Mirren at Paisley at the same time as his chapel at Neilston. One of the most 'notable' events at the old castle arrived in 1489 when the Earl of Lennox, the new lord of the castle, rose in rebellion against the king, James IV. The king, in no mood to be 'messed' around by rebellious lords, not least Lennox, responded with an artillery bombardment of the castle with his principal weapon, Mons Meg, destroying the west wall which culminated in the 'white flag' being raised above the parapets.

*A*nother ancient settlement in that area south of the river is Carnwadric which was a much sought after locale from the days of the Saxon invaders, through the Romans and the Scots of Dalriada who all gave the powers of Strathclyde continuing problems in how to retain one of the most fertile districts in the old kingdom which was,

Crookston Castle – Courtesy of Lairich Rig ©2005

in later times, in the personal own of the Stewart royal family. While part of Govan, the weavers and other textile workers at Carnwadric continued to remain fiercely independent in an attempt to uphold their village as a separate entity but, in time, that would all come to an end.

*N*ow we cross the river again and another place of great antiquity, Partick, a small but very important place since, at least the 6th century, and where the kings of Strathclyde lived from time to time probably at a hunting lodge considering the old Cynric name for Partick, *Thicket of woods*. When Strathclyde moved its headquarters to Govan in 870, there is the probability the kings spent more time at Partick since, at that point, that thicket was part of the old town. That situation would almost certainly exist until the 11th century and the final demise of the old kingdom.

*I*n 1136, David I granted the lands of *Perthick* (Partick) to the Bishopric of Glasgow who then proceeded to erect a Bishop's Palace, as we have seen, perhaps on the same site as the king's old residence. It was evident from those early times, Partick was very desirable place to live, even though, many would say, no settlement other than the kings' or bishops' residences existed but, it would appear, some form of community did indeed grow around the 'Thicket' and we do know of some notable people of Partick from medieval times. We find, Peter of Partick who was the son of Arnold, witnessing charters in 1177 before, in 1195, Phillip of Partick being appointed the Rector at Rutherglen. In 1296, Alexander Scott performed his Act of Fealty to Edward of England at Berwick on behalf of

River Clyde

Partick. There are several others, all designated 'of Partick' who achieved much during their lifetimes with the most notable being Elias, a canon and clerk at Glasgow in the late 12th century, Jocelin who was a canon of Glasgow Cathedral for many years in the earlier part of the 13th century and William who appeared to be a clerk to the eminent High Stewards of Scotland. This all lends to there being a settled community before the end of the 12th century. It would also be logical to believe, a chapel in the see of Govan would exist at that time.

Following the Reformation in 1560, and the retreat of the Catholic Church, the bishop's palace fell in to ruin but the site was soon utilised to build, what became known as Partick Castle, by George Hutcheson, founder of Hutcheson's Hospital. The house later passed to the Crawfords of Milton but sadly, the great edifice has long passed in to the history books buried under a supermarket in modern day Partick. On that historic site, where once stood the residence of kings and bishops and where men like King Rydderich Hael, St. Mungo, King David and so many greats of the early church, walked, is now lost and virtually forgotten. What is better known is, what community existed, was but small and even in to the early years of the 19th century was still a tiny village even though industries like farming, quarrying, some potteries and a tile and brickworks existed. Around that time, Partick was described as being *a rural village nestling amidst thickets of umbrageous trees and standing by the side of limpid and a gurgling stream.* The village consisted of a few large houses, not much more than twenty cottages and a very popular inn, the Bun and Yill House which even offered food on Saturday evenings when the whole village and many from the surrounding areas arrived to enjoy an evening of 'song and joviality'.

By 1834, Partick Church was elevated to Quoad Sacra status by which time, the working classes moved in to be near their work, the shipyards and boilermaking works, and with them, shops and a school opened. In 1852, the village was created a Burgh which acted as a magnet, attracting the wealthier among us who built their fine villas which in turn, attracted banks, a post office and more varied shops. Partick had arrived on the scene and was now much more than a mere 'speck' on the local map. Leisure facilities and parklands were still confined to people's dreams but things took a turn for the better when the Victoria Park opened n 1887 to celebrate the Queen's Jubilee.

Nowadays, the old industries have, more or less departed the scene and what remains is confined to Scotstoun but Partick, the old woodland thicket, has branched out and thrived, just to the west of the city on the north bank of the river which, as it happens, is where we now head back to the point we left at the east end of Govan.

We are sailing again having just passed the headquarters of Scottish Television, the BBC Scotland premises and Glasgow Science Centre on the Pacific Quay off Govan Road with a great crane on the opposite bank. The amazing sight of the Scottish Exhibition and Conference Centre just beyond on the starboard side, comes in to view and is a place where so many conferences and concerts have been held, featuring some of the world's top stars and attractions. If that was not enough, the recently opened SSE Arena, a huge bowl like structure, has joined the list of impressive buildings in the area with yet another traversing the river. The Clyde Arc, also known as the *'squinty or squiggly'* bridge, is fast becoming one of the most recognisable sights on the the famous waters. In to the lower docks we sail past the large Prince's Dock on the port side before reaching the Clyde heliport opposite some launching slides. We really are in the heart of the river's flow through Govan, and she is in upbeat mood as she heads for her confluence with another of Glasgow's rivers, the River Kelvin which, like Clyde, gives name, and life, to so much in the city. Near the confluence is the Tall Ship, a world class attraction which was built on the Clyde and launched in 1896 before going on to have a 'world' career sailing round Cape Horn 15 times. She was sold to the Spanish Navy in 1922 as a training ship but returned to the Clyde in 1990 and, after much refurbishment and renovation, she now stands in all her glory, not only as an attraction but as a memorial to the greatest ship building river in the world. Also situated at the meeting place of Clyde and Kelvin, is yet another world class attraction, the Riverside Museum, featuring the history of transport in Glasgow since the beginning to the present. The futuristic building is yet another eye catcher on the river with its 'zig zag' design and reflective mirrored walls, an amazing sight indeed.

A gentle sweep to the left take us to Linthouse on the south and Whiteinch on the north then over the Clyde Tunnel which carries many, many thousands of vehicles, travelling north and south every day. More cranes fill the skies on the left bank hovering over the small ferry boat which is as busy with locals as it is with tourists. Incidentally Whiteinch was, what it suggests, a white inch or island which is no more. Linthouse was an entirely separate community until 1901, with its own thriving shipbuilding yard, when it became part of Govan. Now the river flows gracefully past Shieldhill as if in tribute to the proud home of the great George V dock, now virtually redundant.

*B*efore we travel further downstream, and I keep on saying this, the Clyde Walkway through the city is quite splendid. Magnificent buildings are everywhere, overlooking the gracious river and the many flower beds. During the summer months, it is so colourful and, with so many benches dotted along the way, where we can sit, relax and savour the surroundings. Glasgow was the scene of sparkling flower displays when it was the first Scottish city to host the Garden Festival in 1988 and it would appear that great honour still lingers, at this beautiful stretch of the Clyde. It is so different from the country walks with hills looming above but as just as peaceful and exhilarating in its very own way. Being chosen as the host of the 1988 Garden Festival was really just another 'feather in Glasgow's cap' having already been recognised as the European City of Culture in 1952 and subsequently being designated city of Architecture and Design in 1999.

*A*t Scotstoun where we now are, there is always something going on mainly due to the BAE Systems yard at this, still industrial section of the river. There is too, on the left bank, the great Braehead shopping centre with the Muslim, Marhaba Welcome Centre and Mosque almost directly opposite. Great cranes are

River Clyde

everywhere as if to remind us of what the River Clyde has meant to us all over the years. The flow becomes slightly sluggish as we reach the point between Garscadden and Yoker looking over towards Renfrew. Docks are everywhere, small craft scurry on their way and the city centre has gone. Now we must wait for the oldest river ferry service in Britain and while it now only carries foot passengers, the Renfrew Ferry is still a delight. Clydebank is in sight as the great waters of the Clyde prepare to leave Glasgow behind, for the time being at least. While this drift of water sprouted in the southern hills and heads to the open seas of the world, no one ever thinks of the River Clyde without thinking of Glasgow. Almost since the first settlement grew at this dear green place, the words, Glasgow and Clyde have become synonymous with each other so, before venturing in to Renfrew, let us take look at the great city as whole.

From the dawn of history as we know it, and looking back deep in to the mists of time, man has walked the route we have just travelled. Through the hills they came as they spread across the moorlands and heavily afforested plains. They were in search of food and shelter and found the rich pickings of the Clyde Valley to their liking but, before venturing further, I must ask, what does the name 'clyde' mean? Well it appears to derive from the Brythonic word *Clwwyd* meaning 'loud, loudly, noisy from a distance' therefore it would seem Clyde is the noisy or loud waters which can be heard from afar. Another definition of the word is 'muddy' which could also apply, so the final definition may be 'muddy waters which can be heard from afar' Some areas can get muddy especially the estuary when the seas have receded but for most of the trip, the waters can best be described as sparkling. The old Celtic word *Clywd* meaning 'strong' is probably nearer the mark.

While the general course of the river and its estuary are much the same as it was during the occupation of the Romans, it appears, it has not always been quite as it is. In much earlier times, but after the coming of man to populate the area, it is thought, the mouth of the Clyde was actually nearer to where Rutherglen now is and, from that point, spread out to form a wide estuary. So many finds, which suggest a wider stretch of water, have been made over a long course of time. In areas of the present city such as Stockwell Street near its junction with the Trongate, near St. Enoch's Old Kirk, at Drygate near the Necropolis and Clydehaugh, all of which indicate quite positively, those sections were indeed under marine water. Various finds included the natural, like sea shells and the man made, dugout boats and other ancient craft. Dugouts are the earliest type of boats ever found, having been made out of tree trunks during the Neolithic period some 6,000 – 3,500 years ago. It is even suggested the estuary at one time in the lost and distant past, embraced Loch Lomond. From that period, but before the coming of the Romans, there appears to have been a great land shift, lifting many areas along the course of the river several metres higher. This had the effect of reducing the width of the Clyde between Rutherglen and perhaps as far as Renfrew, taking the estuary westward and further down from its original position. Some say the original estuary began at the west end of Govan while others refer, in the present day, to Greenock. My own feeling is, the estuary of any river is at the point where the tidal waters of the sea are more dominant (in control if you like) than the out flowing waters of the river, even in flood. That would appear to me to be at Cardross on the north bank and Port Glasgow on the south and that is where my journey will end. Greenock and Gourock must wait for another day.

As time passed, the population of Glasgow grew but so did the dangers, there were always others who wanted what was not theirs to take. The powers shifted constantly until the Romans arrived and marched their way northwards. When they reached what became Glasgow, they would use many sections of the waters to ford but the furthest downstream point for fording at that time, was near the mouth of the Molendar Burn at the point where Glasgow Green was created. Other fords, Marlin Ford near Renfrew and the 'to-be built' causeway at Langbank were also available to pedestrians but only at very low tide. As with many other fords, communities settled nearby for one reason or another but the fact, they had easier, quicker access to areas on the other side of the water made a lot of sense. At that section, on the city side of the Albert Bridge, at the Saltmarket, I believe the first settlement was established, and from that time, what became the great city of Glasgow, began to grow. That settlement was very likely to have been created, or at least enlarged by a Roman presence at a nearby fort of Antonine's Wall which was in the Roman province of Valentia. The settlement probably grew to the south where the Gorbals now exists and, perhaps as far north at what is now Wishart Street where the first church may have been built. The name Molendar itself, refers to a mill or mill settlement.

After the departure of the Romans and of St. Ninian arriving in the area in 380AD to establish a burial ground, not so much is known until the coming of Kentigern in the late 6th century. Kentigern would certainly arrive at a place where a community was already established, small though it may have been but the simple fact is, the holy man needed people to whom he could pass his beliefs.

For some time. Mungo, as Kentigern was better known in Scotland, was spreading the word in Wales, where he founded a church at St. Aspath. He founded a college of secular or Culdee monks but, in time, was encouraged to come home by the King of Strathclyde, Ryhdderch Hael. One of Mungo's first tasks was to baptise Ryhdderch and spread the holy word throughout the king's lands. He ultimately settled in that tiny cell on the Clyde which would become known as Glasghu where he founded a church believed to be on or near the site of the present day High Kirk. He is notionally regarded as the first bishop of Glasgow who lived very much a private life and like other Celtic missionaries who spread the word of God, it would not all be by direct preaching to a congregation but much by action and deed. He was a hermit and during Lent would disappear in to the hills then, at Easter, he would return and 'live' the crucifixion before rejoicing at the rising of Christ. His examples were passed to the people of the area and his church grew. As the church grew, so did the community and because of that foundation of the church and the growing congregation which settled around it, he is generally accredited with the honour of

Rowing on the river with the Peoples Palace in the background
Courtesy of Thomas Nugent ©2011

Scottish Exhibition & Conference Centre or the so called 'Armadillo'
Courtesy of Carol Walker ©2007

Works at Anderston Quay
Courtesy of M.J. Richardson ©2013

Glasgow

founding Glasgow. The deeply pious Mungo died in 613 or 614AD and was interred within the church he built and, since that time, during every renewal or renovation of his church, his tomb has been treated with the greatest reverence and, to this day, still lies in the crypt of the great church.

In time, the church and town became prey to the many in those ever changing days, with Picts, Scots, Danes, Britons and Saxons attacking, destroying and taking possession. When Kenneth Mac Alpin 'united' the kingdom of the Scots and Picts in the 9th century, some peace and order overtook the constant violence but that is not to say it was entirely peaceful and it was not until the reign of Alexander I in the early 12th century before some kind of order was established. Alexander, like his brother, Edgar, followed in his father's, Malcolm Canmore, footsteps, inviting many nobles, quite often of Norman descent, to settle in Scotland where they were granted lands and title. That mode of thinking grew apace when Alexander's younger brother, David, titular King of Strathclyde and Prince of the Cumbrians, arrived from the English court in 1116. From that point, and during his reign as David I, he introduced a system of parishes and local government which directly led to what we now have. During those days, the Roman Catholic Church arrived in a big way and the philanthropic David was eager to see the Scottish Church grow and match other foundations in England and beyond. One of his very first 'special interests' was Glasgow or Cathures as it was sometimes known.

From the death of Mungo until the arrival of Prince David, there is little mention of Glasgow but that was all about to change. David established the great church as the centre and headquarters of all churches in the *City, Barony and Parishes of Glasgow* which became known as *St. Mungo's Freedom.* David instigated a great inquest in to the church, parish, barony and now burgh, an investigation which would last until 1136 when the Cathedral Church was consecrated on July 7th of that year and the bishopric re-installed. John, the first bishop after the restoration of the church, was largely instrumental in the building of the wonderful edifice. That is a significant date in the history, not only of the church but of the town. That date 7th July, 1136 can, with confidence, be known as the day Glasgow became a cathedral city. The consecration was conducted in the presence of the king who promptly assigned the church to the town of *Deschu* which, it is said, is the same as Glas Chu or Glasgow. David did however, grant Glasgow special status but no one really knows if he was creating a Royal Burgh at that time or a King's Burgh as David mentioned. David's interventions of 1136, when he created the bishop, Chancellor of Scotland, was a short lived affair but it was indication of how much importance he placed on the city. Before 1214, Glasgow was created a Burgh of Regality by the king, William I, but to be controlled by local lords (in Glasgow's case, the bishop)

While a city, as we have seen, it would take a few centuries to overtake Rutherglen in terms of trade and commerce. The church was largely rebuilt a few years later during the tenure of Herbert before being reconsecrated by Bishop Joceline in 1197. During the early periods of renewal, the town was still growing, its importance and growth were really quite in tandem with the cathedral's increasing importance within the Scottish Church. William I signed a charter erecting Glasgow, this time to the status of Free Burgh with the ability to hold eight fairs every year under the auspices of the Bishop. Now indeed a Bishop's City but, in a political sense, that would more hinder than help since the Bishop alone had the power to install the provost and baillies of the town.

With the death of Margaret, the so called, *Maid of Norway,* who died on her journey from Norway, to take the Scottish Crown following the death of her grandfather, Alexander III, Scotland descended in to chaos. So much infighting, especially between the families of de Brus, de Baliol and the Comyns, broke out with the country quickly descending in to anarchy. Edward of England saw his opportunity to wield some power and influence on his northern neighbours igniting a flame of war which would last for centuries. After much 'noble' infighting, Edward chose John de Baliol to be king but he was no more than Edward's puppet or a *Toom Tabard (an empty coat)* as his fellow Scots so named him. The arguments did not stop there and the Wars of Independence were soon upon us. Glasgow was seen as a great prize for Edward who installed his men Anthony Beck to the see of Glasgow and Earl Percy as his commander-in-chief in the West of Scotland with his headquarters at the Bishop's Palace or castle in Glasgow. While lordly Scots stood back, William Wallace, the victor at Stirling in 1297, decided to take action. He formed his troops in to two divisions, one marched straight to Percy's HQ and the other, under the Laird of Auchenleck, filtered off, taking a 'back' route. Wallace's force engaged the English and more than holding their own when Auchenleck's forces attacked the opponents from the rear and helped rout the invaders in what was the first of several battles in the city. That battle of 1300 near the High Street, became known as the *Bell o' the Brae* but warring men would return in the centuries ahead.

Noble men, in time, were gaining more sway in the development of the city but the church continued in power and even grew stronger. The all powerful church was raised from status of Bishopric to Archbishopric in 1492 during the reign of Bishop Robert Blackadder. This was only 40 years after Bishop William Turnbull, Keeper of the Privy Seal, founded Glasgow University in 1451 after consultation with the Pope. During that period, the late 15th century, Glasgow was growing in importance as a centre of ecclesiastical matters, trade, commerce and now, education, but as you may have guessed, the church was still very much in control and, if truth be told, that was the case right up to the Reformation in 1560.

As indicated, other battles were enacted in Glasgow thereafter and in 1544, two serious skirmishes took place. The first, on 16th March was a fight concerning some lords wishing the infant queen, Mary of Scots, marry the son of Henry VIII, Edward. On the 'pro marry' side stood Matthew Stewart, 4th Earl of Lennox and on the 'anti marry' side was James Hamilton, 2nd Earl of Arran who was Regent of Scotland during Mary's minority. Hamilton wished Mary to marry the Dauphin, heir to the French throne. With the help of Robert Boyd of Kilmarnock, Arran won that day at the Butts of Gallowmuir before his troops were allowed to sack the

Glasgow

town including the taking of the Bishop's Castle which Lennox had held before the battle, a battle which became known as the *Battle of the Butts*. The next battle, in May, was largely inconsequential with all parties 'ridding' themselves of the scene after some English intervention. The marauding English under Edward Seymour, Earl of Hertford, had just burnt Edinburgh and created havoc throughout the central belt during those wars of the Rough Wooing, and Glasgow was not spared.

Yet another 'battle' occurred during the year of the Reformation, 1560, when the rule of the Regent, Mary of Guise was challenged by the Lords of the Congregation. Mary received the support of her native France who sent soldiers to her aid. Another skirmish took place in Glasgow, but depending on which chronicle you read, both sides won the battle but, bearing in mind the Reformation did indeed come to pass in actual fact, suggests the reforming Lords were victorious. The previously mentioned Battle of Langside in 1568 was another turning point in Scottish history and the last battle at the city.

In the aftermath of the Reformation, the roof of the cathedral was removed before the destruction of the great church was ordered but when all the trades of the town arrived to take the church down, they suddenly turned, obviously pre-planned, and issued an ultimatum that any man, who would remove even but one stone of the old divine, their proudest, *'treasured ornament'*, would do so at the peril of his life, the church was saved and still stands proud to this day, with the relics of the saintly Mungo still safe and unhindered. However the treasures, the relics and precious records and anything else of value, were removed, stolen if you like, by Archbishop James Beaton who removed them to the Bishop's Castle before taking everything with him when he later retired to France.

Some time later, in 1611, and as if to end any argument and controversy, James VI officially created the town a Royal Burgh which almost certainly was the case since the days of King David.

During his Commonwealth from 1650, Oliver Cromwell was not the most wanted visitor but in actual fact he was very impressed with the town. Though not as pretty nor as large as Edinburgh, Cromwell commented he was very endeared to the warmer, friendlier people. Strange isn't it? I have heard that so often during my own lifetime and here we are, more than 360 years later, reading of Cromwell's thoughts whether he was right is a matter for conjecture.

All this time, the city was growing and by the time of the last battle in Glasgow at Langside, Gallowgate was the latest street to have been built. More and more churches were being built meaning more houses for the ever expanding congregations who had embraced the new faith. Part of the terms of the reformed church was the building of schools for all children and that was the case but initially in the larger communities, like Glasgow, where schools were opened in every sector of the town. With churches and schools sprouting all over the district, smaller, separate communities grew, one day to be suburbs of the city. Of course the growing population needed jobs.

Since the Reformation, the provost and baillies of the town, men of means, decided who would govern the city and, though not ideal, it was a step towards democracy. In time, the principal trades of the town put forward candidates for office and those trade associations give a better insight in to the industries contained within. They included, hammermen, fleshers, tailors, cordiners, maltmen, weavers, baxters, skinners, wrights, coopers, masons, candle makers, carpenters, gardeners, barbers, souters, bonnet makers, foundries and colliers. Democracy was progressing but it wasn't until 1918 before all men over 21 and women over 30 could vote; It would be another 10 years after that however, before women had the same rights. Then, and only then, did the people of Glasgow, as every where else, gain the right of self determination.

During the conversations leading to the Treaty of Union with England, Glasgow was strongly represented and, from a commercial point of view, the burghers and merchants of the city were in full agreement of joining with our neighbours, which would lift a lot of trade restrictions on the Scottish merchants, particularly on the continent of Europe. In 1706, Hugh Montgomery, Lord Provost of Glasgow, was one of the Scots Commissioners who left for London to thrash out the proposed treaty which, of course, came to pass the following year. While the Treaty was welcomed by the rich merchants, it was not so welcome with the common people who had absolutely no say in the proceedings, once again, the common man was placed in the corner, to sit tight and stay silent. The people of Glasgow, in keeping with the rest of the country, were totally in disagreement with their beloved country joining forces with the country which, for centuries, had put a yoke around the Scots' necks. Remember, the cruel and evil occupation of Cromwell, which ended in 1660, was still fresh in some people's mind. On 7th November, 1706, Reverend James Clark of the Tron Kirk, encouraged protest during a fast day sermon and, within two hours of his sermon, the streets of the city were full of angry protesters. Led by the city drummers, they marched on the council offices and the home of the provost and attacked them with a fervour which would have made Bannockburn look tame in comparison, so angry were the proud Glaswegians, adamant their homeland should never be sold to English authority. They disarmed the militia and continued to ravage through the streets. Further protests were enacted when the Treaty became fact but the union did help the economy...and added a few noughts to the end of the merchants' bank balances. As we shall see, the union did help industry, though industry was already growing by that stage in any case but generally, it was not the most lucrative financial deal for the common masses. Perhaps the words of Burns sounded loud in the ears of the people when he describes *"Such a parcel of rogues in a nation"*. Changes came but some things were not to everyone's liking, the ordinary folk were not at all amused and took to the streets again to try and show their utter discontent.

Industries like agriculture were already busy as, of course, was house building all being subsidised by local coal mines and quarries. Fishing was growing and so too was the curing of salmon which became a very large industry by the middle of the 17th century. The fish were exported to the low countries of Europe and France

Glasgow

and in return, fine brandies and wines made the opposite journey. Herring fishing was another productive business, so important was that fare, groups of fishers took a small, armed privateer to sea with them for security and protection. However, Glasgow's industrial greatness did not really arrive however until the Treaty of Union in 1707. That single act opened up so many new markets, the Americas and the West Indies, then the far eastern trade loomed large and Glasgow businessmen were not slow to act. Previously the city imported much iron from the Baltic countries but with the local steel and iron industries growing on their own door step, the wealthy merchants had a heaven sent trade ready and willing to supply everything needed for ship building. While the American Wars of Independence and Civil War interrupted trade severely, the merchants of Glasgow soon won new markets on the continent of Europe. Ship building had become the biggest single industry and that attracted more industry and trade. Coal, steel, iron, leather, tobacco, fine silks, linen, cotton and so on. Perhaps the biggest import at that time was tobacco but many wealthy men did get involved in another very lucrative trade, slaves, the slaves who worked the tobacco and cotton fields, two of Glasgow's most important, prolific and profit making imports. Tobacco, snuff and cotton created large scale trade, producing profitable industries within the city, joining ship building, potteries, production of some of the finest tableware in the world while printing too was blossoming. Soon financial institutions arrived with just about every man and his dog desperate to get in 'on the action'. Glasgow was now Britain's most industrious town and the seeds of finance had been sown with every bank in Britain opening branches. By the end of the 18th century, there were in excess of 500 ships registered in Glasgow and regularly using the local docks. It was not all full of roses though, the Union did bring more business but it also brought more taxation. In 1725, when the malt tax was introduced, it hit the poorest most. The men of Glasgow enjoyed their beer and whisky but when the tax was added, meaning higher prices, many demonstrations took place in the city centre. Bearing in mind too, Scotland, unlike England, never held a standing army therefore, even more taxes were introduced north of the border for the upkeep of the new British Army meaning more riots and, once again, troops were ordered in to the city after the rioters had destroyed the home of their Member of Parliament, Daniel Campbell of Shawfield. During the ensuing fight, the troops killed nine of the rioting townsfolk. In time, General Wade was sent to 'police' the city with his dragoons. More riots were to follow in the years ahead including a huge demonstration against the new tobacco tax. All this new, extra taxation had a profound effect on the ordinary peoples' wealth or, more correctly, lack of it.

At the onset of the two Jacobite uprisings in 1715 and 1745, Glasgow formed a militia to contest any trouble which may have arisen on the arrival of the tartan clad men in the town, meaning many of the citizens were patrolling the streets keeping a watchful eye over the Highland strangers if or when they arrived. Apart from the Highlands, there was never a great support for the rebellions in other parts of Scotland. I have mentioned the Royal Stewarts and their arrogance before but they never seemed to learn. They constantly let their own people, the Scots, down, but when they needed help, where did they come?...Scotland. In earlier years, for whatever reason, the people of Scotland decided on a new form of worship, what did the Stuarts do? they attempted to force the Episcopacy down their throats thus barbaric warfare – they did not seem prepared to listen to the will of the people, nor later, it seems, the people of England and that is why they are no longer. Yet if only they had presided over a changing nation with some grace and understanding, the Stuarts would still have been the ruling royals of the United Kingdom but then that is the history which they themselves created.

We have already seen the effect of the American War of Independence but it is more than interesting to note the precautions the merchants of Glasgow took on receiving the shock news of that war. Apart from supplying men for the British Army, the merchants of Glasgow raised a battalion of some 1,000 men and fitted out fourteen privateers of twelve and 22 guns for the protection of their trading ships and the security of the west coast. If you think of Scots born John Paul Jones who became known as the founder of both the American and Russian navies, then you may know that during the wars of American independence, he destroyed many British merchantmen and even had the audacity to attack the British coast. On the west, he attacked Whitehaven in Cumbria and on the east, Dunbar. Men were again deployed to defend the city and west coast at the onset of the French Revolution and beyond.

Having took to the streets so often, at the union, the malt tax, tobacco tax and war taxes, repelling the Jacobites and so on, you would have thought the people would have had their fill of of street riots but more were to come. More demonstrations and violence erupted when, towards the end of the 18th century and well in to the 19th when restrictions were being slackened on Catholic worship, resulting in the Relief Act of Catholic Emancipation. Then, in 1820, during the so called Radical War, three men were hanged then beheaded, two in Stirling, the other, James Wilson, in Glasgow, when they were found guilty of High Treason when their 'crime' was to lead a rally during a week of strikes, all that added to even more protests on the streets of Glasgow. That came four years after, at Glasgow Green, 40,000 gathered for a meeting, protesting against high unemployment in Glasgow following the end of the French Revolution when the British economy was in freefall. The authorities turned armed troops on the people again, but still that was not the end.

Many more confrontations would take place but the next serious meeting would not occur until the 20th century. On the 31st January 1919, several thousand Glaswegians took to the streets to protest against their employers because they were refused the opportunity to work less hours. People, for their own sakes, wished to work less hours but another, more noble reason was given. The end of the First World War meant many thousands of men were returning home in need of work and this was a chance to kill 'two birds with the stone', work less hours. for personal reasons and also help give the returning soldiers some work at a time when jobs were scarce. That was a wonderful gesture by the existing workers to the men who had helped, not only to keep the workers free and safe, but also the mill owners and would be a fresh start for our returning heroes. That is typical of the people of Glasgow, always willing to help others. However trouble did erupt for whatever reason and was getting out of hand. The huge police presence which awaited the demonstration were not there simply to make up the numbers and soon fighting broke out between, what became known as the *Red Clydesiders* and the police. The government called in the troops from all the garrisons in Scotland but no Glaswegian soldiers were sent in case of 'divided loyalties'.

Extremely heavily armed soldiers surrounded George Square blocking all the exits and fixing canon and howitzers on the rooftops surrounding the square. Tanks were deployed all around making the government's response to the riots akin to, as far as most sensible people would think, something of an overkill. This was not a large detachment of the Kaiser's army, this was a show of people fighting for rights they had been denied since the beginning of time. Many, including police were hurt, some seriously, in an action the government deemed to be Bolshevik in nature and reacted like they did because of 'similar' uprisings in Russia.

Subsequently, peaceable men, who had been in consultation over jobs, and the working week, in an effort to make things right for the workers, were arrested as they left the City Chambers, for causing a riot. It seems strange how men negotiating peace inside the chamber could possibly be arrested, tried and jailed for causing a riot? Perhaps they were perceived to have organised the riot beforehand but why then would they go in to the chambers to broker peace? It is frightening to think, had the trouble not stopped, would the Scots' troops have fired on their own people? especially some of their comrades-in-arms who, only a few months earlier, were in the hellish trenches with them but that situation never materialised, thank the good Lord for that.

Thankfully today, everyone is treated with a bit more respect, meaning the lives of our forebears, were not in vain and, poor as they were, they all played an important part in a greater team, which built the old city in to what it became, and still is. The three men arrested at the city chambers were Willie Gallacher, David Kirkwood and Emmanuel Shinwell who all went on to become Members of Parliament, a direct result of the common folk finally getting the vote. Emmanuel Shinwell, who was more commonly known as Manny, served in the House of Commons before entering the House of Lords as Baron Shinwell of Easington until shortly before he died in 1986 aged 101. He was the second longest serving member of parliament in history. All this after being jailed for inciting a riot, causing heavily armed troops to be mobilised against their own people.

If only more wealthy people, particularly the ones who owned factories and mills, had been just a little more thoughtful, a little more caring towards the people who helped create their wealth, the people would have been more willing to work diligently and indeed be happier at their place of work. After all, it was not a new concept, look at Owen at New Lanark, the Colville family at Motherwell and so many more men the length and breadth of Scotland who treated their employees as equal and with a bit of respect. Sadly that was not

River Clyde

always the case and, since the beginning of time, many wealthy men treated their slaves (workers) with absolutely no repect whatsoever. If nothing else, what that riot in Glasgow did achieve was, a wider spectrum of political belief, meaning no matter how wealthy or poor you were, each had the same right, to vote. The end result has made Britain a much more caring society and a much better place in which to live. The 1919 demonstrations changed the face of Britain forever and proved, the down to earth people of Glasgow over the centuries, were never slow to show their united strengths in the face of adversity, they were not always right but they were always, as one.

There were many wealthy men in Glasgow, particularly after the Union, but wealth alone does not produce great men though some were indeed great and benevolent people. What wealth did achieve however, was the means to provide for the building of magnificent buildings and that is an area where Glasgow is not found wanting. Bearing in mind, the ancient cathedral and the last great edifice to open, the SSE Arena, the wonderful architecture of Glasgow is the envy of many, if not most cities around the world. Other great buildings are littered all over the city including the cathedrals, the university, Trinity College, older hospitals, Govan Town Hall, the recently built Scottish Exhibition and Conference Centre and the Science Centre joining so many more wonderful constructions of the modern age. A walk around Glasgow can carry us safely in to the arms of eight centuries of fine architecture beginning with the Cathedral, the oldest building in the city with the atmospheric Provand's Lordship, the oldest house. Formerly part of St. Nicholas' Hospital, the Lordship is now embellished with period furniture donated by shipping magnate, Sir William Burrell. The Royal Exchange in Queen Street is a show topper as are the awesome towers of St. George's Tron Church and the Gallery of Modern Art. The City Chambers is amongst the very best public buildings anywhere while you would have to walk a long way to see the most dramatic contrasts of the church and tower of St. Vincent Street Church. Elgin Place, St. Aloysius Church, the Caledonia Street UP Church, Queen's Cross Church and the Cathedral of St. Andrews, are, all worthy of more than a second glance. Other, more commercial and arts buildings like St. Enoch and Glasgow Central stations, the Royal Exchange, Tower of Glasgow Herald Building, The Gallery of Modern Art, the School of Art, Mitchell Library, St. Andrews Halls, Clyde Port Authority building, Custom House and the Beresford Hotel are all deserving of a place in Glasgow buildings' 'Hall of Fame'. More beauty awaits at Kelvingrove Park, Tollcross House and Pollock House, three more of the great buildings of a great era. Within the grounds of Pollock Country Park is yet another wonderful building most of which is glass, where the great Burrell Collection is shown. The Burrell Collection, bequeathed to the city by Sir William Burrell is the greatest private collection in the world. Of course there are so many fine buildings in the city as we have seen during our trip on the river and Glasgow Green – the Broomielaw too is an area full of wonder, with buildings doing honour to the banks of Clyde. All around, buildings of the most exquisite architecture anywhere can be seen and a look round every corner brings another gasp of

Glasgow

amazement including George Square and its monuments. There really are supreme buildings all around as we swelter in the midst of stone, wood and glass building genius. The Merchant City too oozes beautiful buildings and even the most discerning would concede that, per square metre, of any modern city in the world, Glasgow must rank very high on the list of architectural treasures including so many of the great bridges crossing the river. It is little wonder Glasgow was designated the City of Architecture and Design in 1999. If only I could go on but perhaps a whole volume or two might be required to give a little more justice to the city than I have given. For architecture of a different variety, we could do worse than take a walk round the Necropolis, and view some of the most awesome...and beautiful memorials any where; see the graves of some very notable people and generally feel the peace and serenity of the whole experience. The Southern Necropolis in Gorbals as we have seen, is another unforgettable experience and is truly worth a visit.

The parks too, are unsurpassed anywhere with so much open space, greenery, gardens, woodlands all combining with Glasgow Green with its supreme buildings and the Clyde Walkway providing so many beautiful and atmospheric walks as well as being a paradise for joggers. Of course the parks have so many facilities built in for young and old, there is never a dull moment. There is no part of Glasgow or its suburbs where a park is not available within easy walking distance. Pollock, Kelvingrove, Alexandra, Botanic Gardens, Dawsholm and Hogganfield are all places in which peace is taken for granted and there are many more, adding to that impressive list. There are water features, fountains or other memorials in every park where ample seating is provided for rest or simply to take in colourful surroundings with good, clear air, all amidst a great cosmopolitan city.

Eating out is well catered for too, as are hotels providing for business and pleasure while clubs and inns abound in a town created for all occasions. In recent times, numbers visiting the city has increased dramatically making this one of the most visited cities in Britain with, apart from shopping etc. there are so many attractions not least the many museums and galleries. It is often said, Glasgow is not as pretty as some other cities in Scotland, it does not possess for instance, the beautiful panorama of Edinburgh where dramatic is the most used word to describe the Castle and Calton Hills. Stirling too possesses dramatic contrasts from the castle and Abbey Craig to the mesmerising windings of the Forth but the attractions on offer in Glasgow including the majestic river, more than make up for its geographical shortfalls.

Today's Glasgow in no longer the industrial powerhouse it once was but there is still so much diverse work, from finance to general manufacturing, from commerce to ship building and, of course council and services industries. The city, which is amongst the top financial service cities in Europe, also provides the greatest shopping and social experience in Scotland and that too employs several thousands of people in a city which supports more than 400,000 jobs. The city is, as we have seen, the headquarters of BBC Scotland just as it is home to the Scottish Television network. The press too have a great and historic foothold in

River
and
walkway
at
Clyde Street

A street scene
in Glasgow
with the Scottish
Exhibition and
Conference Centre
middle background
and the new arena
partly hidden on the
right

Magnificent
Govan Town Hall
reminding us
Govan was a large
town in its own
right

Glasgow University

Tom Morrison
©2009
geograph/2513535

Provand's Lordship

Courtesy of

Thomas Nugent

©2013

Kingston Bridge
at
sunset

Courtesy of

Patrick Mackie

©2012

the city with the Glasgow Herald, Daily Record and Evening Times the most popular.

*E*very social and leisure facility known to man, is provided in the city and its many suburbs. Sport facilities are second to none and the Glasgow is busy building, upgrading and improving in a great effort to make the 2014 Commonwealth Games in Glasgow, the best ever, all while the Commonwealth baton is making its way around the world to all the countries of the British Commonwealth in preparation for the great event.

*L*ocal services are well provided for, as are medical centres within easy reach of all. Hospitals abound covering everything from accident and emergency to all other branches of health and caring. The people of the city are justifiably proud of their hospitals and overall care which, of course also includes nursing and residential homes for the elderly.

*E*ducation is primary in every village, town or city and, of course, Glasgow is no exception, in fact Glasgow is widely acclaimed to be a world class centre of learning. Schools of all shapes, sizes and denominations provide education almost from 'cradle to grave' with everything in between. Nurseries for toddler, crèche for a little older, on to nursery, pre-school, primary, secondary and colleges providing for every educational need in both state and private sectors all adding to the universities catering for all things, there is nothing left out of the overall curriculum. From ancient times, the University of Glasgow as been churning out excellence almost on a conveyor belt scale and in more recent times has been joined by the University of Strathclyde and Glasgow Caledonian University. The many and varied colleges are a wonderful back up to the young folk of the area as they strive to find a better future for themselves and serve their city as their forefathers did before them.

*T*he people of Glasgow are very sports minded people, and have been since the beginning, with rowing, archery, boules and bowls the most popular of the earlier sports along with, would you believe, cricket and of course, quoits. Nowadays, golf is very popular and has been from an early time and is still a much supported sport in and around the city with dozens of golf clubs catering for all standards of golfer. Athletics is well supported and two fine stadiums at Scostoun and the indoor arena at the Kelvin Hall cater for that sport in track and field. Glasgow, from time to time, hosts top shinty matches particularly the final of the Camanachd Cup, the sport's *Holy Grail.* Speedway is supplied by the Glasgow Tigers who race at Saracen Park and, as you can imagine, waters ports have always been well supported, like swimming, fishing, yachting and rowing which, as we have seen, formed clubs in older times, some of which became involved in other sports including athletics and football. Other sports with popular followings, are ice hockey at Braehead, rugby league at Easterhouse, while basketball is represented by Glasgow Rocks. You can even ski all year round at Bellahouston Park or, if you prefer, indoor skiing on snow, at Braehead near Renfrew and the Snow Factor. Badminton and squash are very popular as is martial arts but boxing is a sport which has brought great success with some of its finest winning world titles including the legendary Benny Lynch and, more recently, Jim Watt to name but two.

The city is, most of all, a world renowned footballing centre and with good reason. As mentioned earlier, the greatest rivalry in football is based in the city between Rangers and Celtic Football Clubs. Those two clubs, until recently, have strove against each other, to win everything, Scottish football has to offer, every year. Both have played and won European competitions bringing praise and glory to Scotland so. let's, in alphabetical order, have a look at the two clubs.

Celtic were founded in 1887 and since that period have been crowned Scottish Champions on 44 occasions, won the Scottish FA Cup 36 times and the League Cup on 14 occasions. Their crowning glory came in 1967 when they won the European Cup in Lisbon by beating Inter Milan 2-1 earning their place in football folklore as the Lisbon Lions. That team was managed by a wonderful football manager and man, the irreplaceable Jock Stein. The club also reached the final three years later but lost after extra time to Feyenoord of Holland. In 2003, they reached the final of the EUFA Cup but lost out to Porto.

The club was founded at a meeting in the Calton area of the city by Brother Walfrid an Irish Marist priest in November 1887 and played their first game the following year. The club was founded to raise money for one of Walfrid's charities, the *Poor Children's Dinner Table* and has been a charitable club ever since. The name 'Celtic' was suggested by the founder to reflect both its Irish and Scottish roots and their nickname is the 'Buoys' or sometimes, '*The Hoops'.* They have always played at magnificent Celtic Park in the Parkhead area of the town which is now Scotland's largest football stadium. They play in green and white hooped jerseys and white shorts.

Over the course of their history, the club have produced literally hundreds of fine players but sadly I can only give a few. I must begin with the man who accepted the trophy after the historic first British win in the European Cup, Billy McNeil and I can only follow that with a Celtic legend who died playing for his club after a tragic accident against Rangers, goalkeeper, John Thomson who lies in his hometown cemetery at Bowhill in Fife. It is a much revered place and akin to a shrine to Celtic supporters. Having a stone from John's grave in your pocket is considered good luck and good health. By all accounts John was a good man taken, sadly, long before his time. Jimmy McGrory is a Celtic institution, the club's top goal scorer ever with an incredible 522 goals and one of their legendary managers and a Scottish internationalist. Henrik Larson is rated the club's greatest overseas player while Irish internationalist, Patsy Gallacher will live in the hearts of older fans forever. Other greats simply trip of the tongue, like Kenny Dalglish. most capped Scot of all time, and memories of Jimmy (Jinky) Johnstone will never fade. Roy Airken, Paul McStay, Bobby Evans and Danny McGrain, Tommy Gemmill, Bobby Lennox, Bertie Auld and Bobby Murdoch all deserve special mentions as do many, many others. They have had many wonderful managers but two come to mind who will always be sewn deep in the fabric of the club, the afore mentioned Jimmy McGrory and the inimitable, Jock Stein, their greatest ever manager.

Currently, Celtic are leading the Scottish Premiership but, for the second year running, without the challenge of their great rivals who went in to liquidation and had to start over in the bottom tier of Scottish football. While Celtic play to the east of the city, their rivals, Rangers play to the south-west, at Govan.

Rangers, who wear blue shirts and white shorts, play at Ibrox Stadium on the west side of the city. They were founded 1872 and were one of the founders of the Scottish League and, until recently, always played in the top tier of Scottish Football. In the early days, Rangers used several venues for their games with the first being Fletcher's Haugh. While using other grounds, they ended up playing at Kinning Park for ten years before they moved to Ibrox in 1889. Along with their great rivals, Celtic, they dominated Scottish Football throughout their history until 2012 when the club went in to liquidation. They were reinvented as a club but had to start anew in the bottom tier of Scottish Football. They won the Division 3 title in 2013 and, after league adjustment, were in League One for season 2013, still two tiers away from the Premiership. There is ongoing debate regarding the club's history and I have no intention whatsoever in entering in to the topic. All I can relate to is the great rivalry between the clubs before liquidation befell the Ibrox club. I can only talk of a club known as Rangers who played, and still do, at Ibrox Park in the Govan area of Glasgow, whether they are same club or not is something more to do with more learned men than me.

In the entire history of Rangers, they have finished top of the league on 54 occasions, won the Scottish Cup 33 times and the League Cup 27 times. They too have triumphed in Europe, winning the Cup Winners Cup in 1972 when, under the management of Willie Waddell, they beat Moscow Dynamo in the final 3-2 at the Nou Camp Stadium in Barcelona. The occasion was marred when thousands of fans, believing the game was over, invaded the pitch in celebration only to find out the game still a had a minute or two to go. The pitch invasion meant captain, John Greig was presented with the trophy indoors, a sad end to a great win. They have reached another three European finals but lost them all, in 1962 to Fiorintina of Italy then in 1967 when they lost to Bayern Munich. Finally they lost yet another final in 2008 at Manchester when they went down 0-2 to Zenit St. Petersburg.

Rangers have always been known as the 'Gers' or *'Teddy Bears'* and, despite their lowly position in the Scottish game, still play to near capacity crowds at Ibrox, another fine stadium. They currently lead the League One title race with a 100% record in the league as at November, 2013. They, like Celtic, have produced many fine players and managers, some of whom join their counterparts across the city, in football folklore.

Among their greatest players and top of my list, though by no means the most capped, is the genial Jim Baxter of the most sublime skills, captain marvel, John Greig, Davie Cooper, Richard Gough, Brian Laudrop, Paul Gascoigne, Terry Butcher, Graeme Souness and Willie Waddell, player and manager but like Celtic, it is so difficult too leave anyone out. They too have had great managers, like Scot

Glasgow

Symon, Walter Smith and Bill Struth. Another successful manager, Alex Ferguson, was a player with Rangers.

There are of course, other senior clubs in Glasgow at the present time, Partick Thistle and Queens Park, though many other clubs have competed but now, no more. Those teams included Third Lanark who could be associated with Rutherglen too, Vale of Leven, Linthouse, Northern, Johnstone and Carlairs. Queen's Park, or *the Spiders* as they are affectionately known, are Scotland's oldest, surviving football club and remain as they have always been, amateur, the only one in a professional league set up. They wear thin black and white hoops on their tops which, traditionally, are worn outside their black shorts Their home is one of the world's most famous football stadiums, Hampden Park, opened in 1903, and until 1950, the largest football stadium in the world and Hampden, as we have seen, still holds the record for an international match in Europe.

The club's honours include, four league championships from the lower tiers and Scottish Cup winners ten times. The club also competed in England's FA Cup and were twice beaten in the final. Notable players include, Ronnie Simpson who went on to play for Celtic and Scotland, Malky Mackay, Scottish internationalist, and manager of Cardiff City, Simon Donnelly, also of Celtic and Scotland, Alan Morton, legendary Rangers and Scotland winger, Jack Harkness, goalkeeper in the great *Wembley Wizards* team, Andy Roxburgh, a manager of Scotland, Bobby Brown, another manager of Scotland and Aiden McGeady who went on to play for Celtic and Ireland. Presently, the club are rooted to the foot of the lowest tier in Scottish football but, in fairness, so far, it is their poorest performance in recent years. Queen's Park really are a veritable Scottish treasure. Which brings us to the 'Jags', or, as they are better known, Partick Thistle; the *Maryhill Magyars or Jolly Jags* are other affectionate names for the club.

While known as Partick Thistle, and founded in 1876, the club left Partick in 1908 and have played ever since at their Firhill Stadium in the Maryhill region of Glasgow. They have always been considered as one of the most loveable clubs in the country but their fans' loyalty is fierce and committed. Their greatest rivals in the modern era are Clyde F.C. who, as we have seen, now play at Broadwood in Cumbernauld. Interestingly Clyde shared Firhill with the Jags for five years after leaving Shawfield Stadium in Rutherglen. The games between the derby rivals are always well supported and the atmosphere is electric. Thistle play in yellow, red and black shirts and black shorts; it is one of the most recognisable strips in Scotland and it was thought to be inspired by the club continually borrowing strips from the West of Scotland Rugby Club in the early years.

The club have never been champions of the top tier in football but they have won several titles in the lower leagues including the First Division in 2012-13 meaning that they now play in the Premiership. They won the Scottish Cup in 1921 when they beat Rangers 1-0 in the final then they triumphed in the League Cup in 1972 when they sensationally beat Celtic by four goals to one. They have also qualified to play in European competition three times.

River Clyde

*P*artick have given many players to the international scene either when they played for the club or at other times in their career; no less than 29 Thistle players have played at international level, most with Scotland but others for Ireland, Northern Ireland, Namibia and the Faroe Islands. I would really need to be a Thistle fan to pick out their most notable players but Alan Rough must be one while others would surely include the club's greatest ever goal scorer, Willie Sharp while Davie McParland nor Alan Archibald, who also managed the club, can be ignored. I must add, I do miss the regular Derby matches between Thistle and Clyde, and the great atmosphere it produces. Glasgow also plays host to many junior clubs and many more from amateur and under-age clubs.

*R*ugby Union football is also popular and, while there are many clubs from the area competing in the Scottish Leagues, Glasgow Warriors, formerly Glasgow then Glasgow Caledonian after a unification with another club, Caledonian Reds, are the city's professional club. In season 2006, the team played competitively as Glasgow Warriors for the first time when they competed in the Celtic League. Their first game was against Wales' Newport Gwent Tigers but lost out to a last minute penalty when the scores ended an agonising 23-24. Towards the end of the first season they won four games in a row but lost the last game, still it was an encouraging start finishing fifth which they repeated the following season. The next two seasons, the club reached the play offs so progress was still being made. As I write, they are placed second in the league, an absolutely fantastic position and have high hopes for the rest of the season. This season they have moved their ground to Scotstoun having previously spending some years at Thistle's Firhill Stadium.

*W*hether going to work, shopping, off to school, or simply visiting the city, Glasgow is not difficult to get around by foot or car. If heading out of the city in any direction, you are never far from one of the major motorways making travel to other parts so much quicker. Again, no matter what direction you are heading, there is a train for you just as there is the subway rail system, known affectionately as *clockwork orange.*

*N*otable people with association to Glasgow? Where do I begin? where do I finish? I have already mentioned some in the world of football, boxing and politics for instance but let me find one or two from other areas, sadly, it really is not possible to name them all. From the church of old, we have heard of Mungo, founder of the church and city, William Turnbull who founded the university and Robert Blackadder the first Archbishop. Charles Macintosh was a chemist who invented waterproof clothes, Charles Rennie Mackintosh, the great designer, Sir William Burrell, shipping magnate and philanthropist, David Hamilton, 18th century architect often referred to as the *father of the profession,* Major James Miller VC hero of the Indian Mutiny, Thomas Lipton of tea and grocery fame, George Rodgers VC, Indian Mutiny and George Thomson, shipbuilder. That is a very small list from literally several hundred worthy candidates.

*G*laswegians have possessed the ability to make us laugh over the years because of their wonderful sense of humour and have helped brighten our lives.

Glasgow

Men like Rikki Fulton, Jack Milroy and Stanley Baxter will long live in the hearts of most Scots as will the whole cast of *Chewin the Fat and Still Game,* depicting that great sense of humour at its finest. On the subject of laughing, Billy Connolly has never been found wanting when it comes to his Glasgow story lines gathered over his lifetime and putting a smile on all our faces.

Now the river is beginning to widen as she flows ever nearer the Firth as her time in Glasgow is coming to an end having transformed her country waters in to the single most important river in Scotland's history. Much more than half the country's industry has passed along her flow while so much of our wealth has sailed to and from the great docks. That is not so much the case in the present day but Glasgow still excels and is truly one of the great cities of the world. Now though, it is nearly time to salute Renfrew one the left bank, as Clyde's eternal quest goes on and on. Now passing Yoker on the right and some business buildings at Blythewood on the left, we are now opposite Renfrew and time to step ashore once again. Yoker has been the site of the famous Renfrew to Yoker ferry since the 14th century when the river was much wider, and in more recent times, was home to a strong ship building industry in company with a large motor car and tram car manufacturing plant.

The most prominent of ship builders at Yoker was Yarrows shipyard which was founded by a London engineer, Alfred Yarrow who was encouraged to move his business north to the Clyde. Part of his original business came by chance when he was asked to build a vessel which would sail Lake Nyasa, now known as Lake Malawi, to help curb the trade in African slaves and was funded by the David Livingstone Trust. Only problem was, the lake was inland and the craft had to be built in pieces in a way where it could transported to and assembled on site. Having solved that problem, he set about his task, built a 'jigsaw' ship and transported it to Africa where it was all fitted together. When he left his base on the Isle of Dogs for Yoker, he carried on building, fit it yourself ships, including a 260 footer for Lake Victoria in 1960. Yarrows became one of the principal developers of modern warships including torpedo boats and, much more recently, Type 23 destroyers. On a down note however, the famous yard closed in 1971.

Nowadays Yoker, meaning *river bank,* is probably better known as the Glasgow section of the crossing, foot passengers only ferry, which is about to be my means of transport in order to reach the old *Cradle of the Royal Stewarts,* Renfrew. The crossing is smooth over the calm waters of the Clyde and the captain of the 'ship' has delivered us all safely to the south bank near the King's Inch and the start of our visit to Renfrew, old county town of Renfrewshire, yet another county the river is about to visit. Renfrew Ferry is an ancient and well loved institution and was actually granted or at least confirmed by a Royal Charter to the burgh in 1614 at the hands of King James VI. At one point it was moved a little downstream to accommodate a mansion built at the King's Inch by tobacco merchant, Alexander Speirs but is now back in its original position.

......and
something
new.....

SSE Hydro Arena,

north of the river

Courtesy of William Starkey ©2013

Glasgow

Sadly as I write on this, December 1st 2013, news is still filtering through of a day, Friday, 29th November 2013, when a tragic disaster hit the City of Glasgow. A police helicopter, with two officers and the pilot on board, fell out of the sky and on to the the roof the Clutha Bar in Clyde Street on the right bank of the river. All three on board and five members of the public, enjoying a Friday evening of music in the bar, lost their lives with many more rushed to hospital with serious injuries. Two more members of the public, died of their injuries, in hospital, This dreadful incident arrived only six years after a terrorist attack at Glasgow Airport and the people could have been forgiven for keeping clear of the scene with, perhaps, terrorism on their minds, but not a bit of it. The survivors in the bar and other passers by put their own safety at risk to help the injured and assist the emergency services as best they could. In situations such as this, the people of the Glasgow all come together as one to help one another and others in distress. The city has always had that reputation, sticking together in times of need and helping others in need of assistance. The disaster struck the day before the Feast Day of Scotland's Patron Saint, St. Andrew, as people gathered together, happy and looking forward to another Festive Season and the City's hosting of the 2014 Commonwealth Games. All our hearts go out the those poor souls and to the loved ones left behind, they will never be forgotten. May they rest in peace and I pray their loved ones gain peace in their hearts in the days and years ahead. Glasgow cares for you and the thoughts of everyone in Scotland are with you in your time of need. God Bless you all.

Heading for the Kingston Bridge and Renfrew
Courtesy of Thomas Nugent ©2011

Renfrew Town Hall & Tolbooth
Built in 1872, replacing a 17th century building

Section Five

To the Estuary – Renfrew to the Firth

Renfrew, meaning a *'point of land at flowing water'*, is a truly ancient and important place in Scottish history. Its church was founded in 1136 by David I who then built a castle between the lands of the Clyde and Cart as protection against unwanted 'guests', like Somerled of the Isles then later, another castle was built on King's Inch, an island on the Clyde. David gave Renfrew, then known as *Arrenthrew,* all the dignities normally granted to Royal Burghs with the associated importance, commerce and trade. That situation would exist for centuries up to and beyond 1397 when Robert III of Scots granted the old burgh the official statutes of Royal Burgh but that came as no surprise to anyone since the king had much connection with the town as we shall see. Robert was grandson x 5, of Walter Fitzalan, who was granted the great hereditary title of High Steward of Scotland by David I in 1150. Walter was born at Oswestry in Shropshire to a noble family and was invited to Scotland by David as one of the many the king would bring north to 'clean up' Scottish life, laws and governance. Little did David know, Walter Fitzalan, High Steward of Scotland, would be the founding father of a future royal dynasty but let us look towards the church in the meantime.

The kirk was founded no later than 1136 as we have seen and was, notionally, in the hands of Paisley Abbey but after the interception of Pope Urban II, the church was placed in the see of Glasgow where it soon became a prebend and placed in the Deanery of Rutherglen in keeping with so many other churches in the region. While so many names of important people have been lost with the passing of time, we do know some of the men who made a big impression at Renfrew during mediaeval times. Men like Davide de Renfrew who confirmed a grant of a saltpan from Amlaib of Lennox in the late 12th century, Grieves who ensured payments were made to Paisley Abbey on time

Renfrew Parish Church

in the early 13th century, John Pride who was chief burgess of the town in 1274 and Adame de Reinfru who had the unfortunate task of swearing homage to Edward in 1296. We also know some of the names of the clergy at the church including Roger, Robert and Stephen who were chaplains in the latter part of the

12th century and another Roger who was deacon in 1270 while Robert Semple, a local dignitary, was a steward of the church in 1306.

Within the church, which was dedicated to St. James and patronised by the Stewards, were two chapels, one dedicated to St. Thomas the Apostle and the other to St. Thomas the Martyr. There were also six altars, dedicated to the Holy Cross, St. Mary, St. Christopher, St. Ninian, St. Andrew and St. Bartholomew; another chapel stood close to Renfrew Mill dedicated to St. Mary and in the own of Paisley Abbey. Soon after the granting of the church to Glasgow, the king gifted lands and tithes to the monks of Kelso and the Holy Rude in Edinburgh. In slightly later times, around 1163, Walter Fitzalan, the Steward, who had previously founded Paisley Abbey, granted more gifts including the mill and fishing rights of Renfrew to that abbey and two shillings every Easter to light up the cathedral at Glasgow. Walter had earlier settled a colony of Cluniac monks at Renfrew Abbey, probably near the castle on the King's Inch, before resettling them at Paisley; that priory of Cluniacs was dedicated to SS Mary and James. Other gifts were made by Walter's descendants, to the churches of Oswestry and Wenloc in Shropshire from whence his family came. At the same time, monies were gifted to the Chamberlain of Scotland in 1370, as the church's share in the repayment of the ransom which Scotland had to pay in instalments for the earlier release of David II.

After the Reformation, the first minister at the church, probably the third building on the site, was Andrew Hay of Renfield while the last minister before the wonderful divine closed after its final service in December, 2012 was Rev. Lilly Easton, who bid a fond but sad farewell to her parishioners. The old church which opened in 1862 contains the 16th century tomb of Sir John Ross of Hawkhead and his wife, Marjorie, within the chancel of a church located in one of the most historic kirkyards in old Renfrewshire. The church now stands behind the 'For Sale' signs, a tragic end to an ancient foundation and while there are other churches in the town, it is difficult to imagine Renfrew without the Old Parish Church.

Other places of worship in Renfrew in the present day include, the North Parish Church, Inchinnan Parish Church, Trinity Church, St. Columba's Roman Catholic, Masjid Darul Quran Islamic Centre, Baptist and Evangelical Churches, a Mission Station and a Christian Fellowship. Interestingly, the minister at Renfrew North, the Right Reverend, Lorna Hood, a Chaplain to the Queen, has made history as being the first serving female minister to be elected Moderator of the General Assembly of the Church of Scotland for 2013.

Renfrew, as we have seen, was a strategically important town, geographically and militarily, on the river, just to the west of the important settlements of Govan, Glasgow and Rutherglen. It was the route of pirates and warring men for countless decades, and the same route Somerled, King of Mann and Lord of the Isles took on his ill fated attack of 1164. His mission was to oust Malcolm IV from the throne of Scotland and replace him with a northern prince who was descended from the old Kings of Alba and the House of Dunkeld, the same royal house as

To the Estuary

Malcolm himself. Somerled headed his massive force up the Clyde on an armada of *birlinns*, wooden craft propelled by sail and oar. However the royal army, commanded by, the High Steward, Walter Fitzalan, lay in wait. When the armies came face to face, the forces of Somerled were no match for the soldiers of the king, armour suited knights and well trained archers. Fitzalan led them in true Norman fashion as they waded through the Norsemen and Islanders until they fled the field, back to their boats. Somerled and his son, Gilliecallum were killed and the isles of his kingdom were now up for 'grabs' and a further unification, in to the country we now know, was imminent. Walter's reward was the royal castle on the island of King's Inch though greater rewards awaited his descendants in the 14th century. The Stewards fought in many affrays, in the service of David, Malcolm, William, Alexander and Robert the Bruce, theirs was a family in waiting, Incidentally, when that attack occurred, the town, or most of it, was near or on, the King's Inch, and he river banks, much more so than today. Boat building was carried out, as was a healthy fishing trade but later changes and some alterations to the river's channels, mainly to support the building of large ships, resulted in a slightly different course in some areas causing the trades of Renfrew to decline to a great degree.

Walter, the latest patriarch of the High Stewards, had, because of the Battle of Renfrew, hurled his family, firmly in to the notice of kings and courtiers not to mention Scottish history. He later raised a monument to the battle but that was wrecked by a thoughtless farmer in the 19th century. Another lost memorial marked the birthplace of the 'to be' king, Robert Steward, grandson of Robert Bruce who was born in difficult and horrific circumstances. His mother, Marjorie, was out on horseback one day viewing the hunt while she was heavily pregnant. She was thrown from her horse and later died at Paisley Abbey where a hastily arranged *cæ*sarean section was carried out and the future king was delivered safely though one of the baby's eyes was damaged causing him to be known later in life as the *Blearie King;* Princess Margorie was interred at the Abbey. That birth was to become known as the *Cradle of the Royal Stewarts,* when Robert's uncle David died without issue, he became king as Robert II. A Memorial Cairn to the memory of Marjorie Bruce, daughter of the king, was raised in 1954 and unveiled by one of her descendants, Sir Guy Shaw Stewart, Baronet and, at that time, Lord Lieutenant of Renfrewshire.

More history, or legend? centred on the castle near the King's Inch, concerning a wrestling contest between the champions of the kings of Scotland and England, James IV and his father-in-law, Henry VII. John Ross of Hawkhead, was James' victorious champion but the identity of his opponent is unknown. It was all part of a 'family' get together when James and his queen, Margaret, invited Margaret's parents Henry and Elizabeth of York, to stay with them at the castle, the wrestling contest was all part of the celebrations. The end of the contest arrived when the English Champion raised his arms and asked Ross to 'palm mine arms' which the Scot did and proceeded to overthrow him. King James later nicknamed John, *'palm mine arms'* before granting his triumphant knight, the title, Constable of Renfrew Castle and later created him Lord Ross. Considering the date of John Ross' elevation to the aristocracy, 1501, if James did indeed have an English King as guest, it could only have been Henry VII.

*H*enry VII was by no means the first English King to visit Renfrew, two of the Edwards. I and II arrived with no good whatsoever on their minds, they were the sort of tourists, the town could well have done without. In 1301, during the Independence Wars, Edward I granted the town and manor to the Earl of Lincoln and, while that did not have a long future, Edward II, son of the 'Hammer' arrived in 1310 and was wined and dined at the castle before, as he left the next morning, he issued orders to his generals to burn the town, such gratitude. Another Edward, the short lived king of Scots, and son of *Toom Tabard,* took Renfrew away from the Stewards and awarded it to the Earl of Atholl but again, that was a temporary affair before the Stewart family won the barony back. Another monarch who visited in much later times was Queen Victoria who arrived in 1888.

*W*hile some monuments of old have been lost, others have been saved, or at least, part of them. Part of a stone to the 9th Earl of Argyll and a section of stone from an ancient healing well in memory of and dedicated to St. Conval, are laid side by side in a small enclosure near the Inchinnan Bascule Bridge in the old Blytheswood policies. One stone is said to be part of the stone which St. Conval is said to have 'walked, or floated on' across to Ireland and later was used in the building of his holy well which became known as *Conval's Chariot* while the other stone was built to mark the capture of Archibald Campbell, 9th Earl of Argyll who was in league with the Duke of Monmouth in an attempt to overthrow and hopefully, assassinate James VII & II. As we have seen earlier, Monmouth was an illegitimate son of Charles II who was executed in 1649, and who felt he should be king. In May, 1685, while Monmouth was invading the west coast of England, Argyll was attempting to break through to Glasgow. His troops, by in large, deserted him and he, with his son and a few friends, were captured near Inchinnan. Argyll was taken to Edinburgh, found guilty of treason and executed by beheading before being buried at Greyfriars Kirk in Edinburgh. St. Conval is said to be buried at Inchinnan but the exact spot is debatable.

*O*n a much more recent and sombre note, three brave Polish servicemen lost their lives in 1941 in an attempt to save St. James Church in the town which had been set alight by several explosions, heard for miles around. The men, without considering their own safety, went in to the church and, though they managed to save the building, lost their lives in so doing. A plaque was unveiled in their honour, blessed and dedicated by Bishop McGill, during a special mass held in 1982.

*R*enfrew truly has been a royal town since the days and the actions of the family of the High Stewards and, even to this day, their titles are still accorded the heir to the throne. All their titles, of Great Steward, Lord of the Isles and Baron of Renfrew are all Scottish titles held by Prince Charles, Duke of Rothesay and heir apparent to the throne of the United Kingdom. Charles is also the Earl of Carrick, a title emanating from the Bruce.

To the Estuary

*P*resent day Renfrew is a town with a strong 'backbone', a vibrant town centre with good and varied shopping facilities offering all the day to day needs with other nationals around the fringes including Blytheswood Park and the wonderful all singing, all dancing, Braehead Shopping Centre where virtually anything you could ever need or want can be found. Over 110 stores of the national kind simply spoil us all for choice, and with cafés, restaurants and leisure centre waiting with open arms to pamper us. There is also the Braehead Arena where first class entertainment is always on the menu to suit all tastes and genres. Why not take in a curling competition or even try it out yourself, or simply try waltzing around the ice, view ice dance competitions and exhibitions or marvel at the skills of the ice hockey players. Braehead is situated near the famous King's Inch so you can be assured there are some beautiful and refreshing walks along the hallowed lands on the side of the Clyde and where a new housing development known as the Ferry Village is nearing completion.

*T*he town and all its districts offer too, so many wonderful parklands like the King George V, Moorcroft, Robertson, Kirklandneuk, Knockhill, Clyde View and Paterson Parks all with fine facilities combining leisure and sport and all joining forces with local halls and community centres where much more is on offer. There is also the Renfrew Leisure Centre with facilities like a gym for exercise, various sports and dance or, if you prefer a dip, why not try the town's Victory Baths. Alternatively you can combine many sports in the one place, the David Lloyd Centre, for

King's Inch today, Housing and Clydeview Park
Courtesy of Thomas Nugent ©2010

gymwork, power fitness equipment like rowing machines or go for a swim in the pool. All the racquet sports are taken care off on full sized courts and have some professional coaching 'thrown in' if you wish. To help take your mind off everyday life, there is also a café, crechè and kiddies' play area to care for the wee ones. Strained? visit the physio, needing something sporty? then try the sports shop where so much is on offer.

*R*enfrew Football Club compete in the Western Region of the Scottish Junior Football Association and play at Western Park where they have been located since their formation in 1912. The have won the Scottish Cup once, in 2001 after losing in three previous finals. An older club, Renfrew Victoria also played at Western Park until they folded in 1910. Yet another Renfrew team competed in Scottish

River Clyde

Football in earlier times and appeared in the Scottish FA Cup. Rugby and bowls are also popular with the rugby club, only founded in 2007, playing in the west regional league with their home games at the the King George V fields. Renfrew Golf course is probably one of the busiest locations in the town at weekends. The club was founded in 1894 but now play on a sparkling new, parkland course which opened as recently as 1970.

The boat and dredger building businesses have gone I know but there is still a lot of work in Renfrew, mainly in retail and services but still, some industry remains at places like Hillington Park though most of the work is centred on council offices and facilities, banks, shops and so on. Rolls Royce Aviation have a plant in the area and don't forget nearby Glasgow Airport also provides many hundreds of jobs and, no doubt, many Renfrew people will be employed at the airport which began life as a military airbase at the outset of the Second World War. While there is strict security at the airport it could not prevent a terrorist attack in 2007 when two men drove a flaming motor vehicle in to the entrance of Terminal One, one of the men later died at the scene of of horror. Another incident, in 1999, saw a plane from Glasgow to Aberdeen carrying air crew staff, crashing soon after take off and sadly, eight people were killed. Glasgow Airport took over operations from the smaller Renfrew Airport, which also served as a military facility, in 1966. Sections of the old runways were later used to extend the M8 motorway and a build giant superstore meaning more jobs for the locals.

Schools too, provide employment for local folk and they are plentiful in the town including, nurseries, pre-schools, primaries and secondaries offering an excellent range of education for the children in the town and surrounding areas.

Renfrew boasts some fine structures but the elegant Town Hall with great clock tower must take pride of place and is best viewed from the beautiful High Street. The building, which was behind scaffolding for nearly three years as great renovations took place, is now back to its sparkling best. Though there has been a hall and tolbooth on the site for centuries, the present building opened in 1872. The Bascule Bridge is another structure of note as is the Princess Margorie Memorial Cairn. St. Columba's, North Parish and the Old Parish churches are all lovely buildings

Mercat Cross & War Memorial
Courtesy of Thomas Nugent ©2010

demanding a second look as is the War Memorial which is built in to a market cross structure which features the Scottish Uncorn at the top a tall shaft. That structure is very similar though smaller, to the ancient Mercat Cross in Preston

To the Estuary

Village, Prestonpans which is the oldest market cross in Scotland still on its original site. Brown's Institute, a museum building in Canal Street is also worthy of mention.

The old Renfrew ferry has gone down the same road as the old chain ferry did before but the little motor launch ferry we have just experienced, still provides a service to foot passengers, and though not quite the same as sailing up the Clyde on a great liner, it still provides a very useful service sailing as it does, across the river. Now we head along the A8, over the Bascule bridge across the White Cart Water before taking the conventional bridge over the Black Cart and in to the ancient district of Inchinnan.

Ferry to Yoker

The two bridges over the rivers, meet on the tiny peninsula only yards from the confluence forming one of the 'shortest' rivers, the Cart, in the country as it travels less than a kilometre on its way to joining the great River Clyde directly across the river from the docks near the Kilbowie area of Clydebank. Inchinnan is best remembered as the place where the British Airship industry was born and, indeed where the aviation industry still exists but more of that in a while, but why Inchinnan?

Well there are two trains of thought concerning the naming of the sparsely populated parish of old. One is, it is derived from the old Gaelic and means, *River Island,* which surely fits its situation, being locked in by the River Gryffe, the Black Cart and the Clyde but the other meaning is just as fitting. In times gone by, the parish was sometimes known as *Killinnan* with 'Kil' referring to the old, historic church dedicated to St. Conval, which stood only yards to the the west of the Inchinnan side of the bridge.

During the life and times of Kentigern, pilgrims followed the holy man, some of whom took up his mantel and carried the good word to other parts of the land, one of those was Convalus who was later sanctified as Conval, as he was locally known. He founded a chapel near the ferry at what became known as Ferrycroft on the Black Cart signifying a ferry existed in the days before the bridge was built. The present bridge was opened in 1812 replacing a previous bridge which had collapsed some 90 years earlier. Conval's chapel in time was replaced in 1100AD, before the coming of King David, by a larger, (50 feet x 18 feet) more 'congregation friendly' building, as opposed to the tiny chapel it replaced. More importantly however, St. Conval, it is thought, was interred within that chapel on the banks of the Black Cart in the area then known as Strathgryffe with reference to the River which confluenced with the Black Cart just a few yards upstream.

River Clyde

*T*he 'new' church was the one which David granted to the Knights Templar before Walter Fitzalan granted other churches in Strathgryffe to Paisley Abbey but expressly leaving out St. Conval's Church by the water. The old church, with so much reparation and renewal lasted until 1828 before a new kirk. All Hallows, was built in 1900 which, in turn, was demolished in 1965 to allow for extensions on the nearby airport. The older church was thought to be of considerable importance and was said to have had a status akin to that of a Minster church in England whereby it was used as a monastery while still providing priest led worship for the local people. When the site of the 1100 church was being cleared to build the new kirk in 1828, astonishing finds were made including a floor virtually paved with skulls and four stone coffins, thought to be of Knights Templar. Other finds, with markings of Christian and Maltese Crosses, were removed to the Hunterian Museum in Glasgow, while the coffins were left in situ and the skulls re-interred. So often, around the country, when old churches have been in the process of demolition, in order to build a new church, dozens of skulls have been found but no bodies; no one has ever came up with a good solid reason for that type of burial. The feast day of St. Conval is the 28th September.

*O*n the suppression of the Knights of Jerusalem in the early part of the 14th century, the church passed to the Knights of St. John and their preceptory of Torphicen in modern day West Lothian where the rectorship of the church remained, but within the Deanery of Rutherglen in the Diocese of Glasgow.

*I*n the early years, so many gifts of land and mill, were bestowed on Paisley Abbey by Walter Fitzalan and his son, Alexander Fitzwalter but nothing was forthcoming for the church of Conval. Those grants to the abbey were witnessed by some important men of the time, like Ralph, the King's Chaplain, William Lindsay, Dean of Glasgow Cathedral and Thomas, son of Ranulf (Randolph) Many of those grants contained the tithes of many churches in the Borders including Stichill, Hassendean, Legerwood and Birkenside. Lands at Stenton in East Lothian were also mentioned along with Partick and, of course, Inchinnan as providing the income from the local mills to the great foundation at Paisley.

*B*y this time, Alexander Fitzwalter, who was designated 'of Dundonald' was declared the Steward after his father's death, by Malcolm IV, David I's grandson. More gifts were made, by Alexander, to the Abbey including the King's Island near Renfrew Castle, ploughgates at Inchinnan and Innerwick in East Lothian along with that church and mill witnessed by Ada de Warrene, mother of Malcom IV and William the Lion and daughter-in-law of King David I. Ada lived at Haddington Palace with her husband, Prince Henry who would have been king had he not predeceased his father David.

*I*n later times, another Walter Stewart, 6th High Steward, gifted lands at Inchinnan to his Godson, Gilbert of Hamilton as a gesture of goodwill for the baby's future. It is thought that, in time, most of the lands which were owned by the Stewards, were left in the hands of their relations who inherited the title, Lord of Darnley.

*I*n time, the Darnleys demolished the old Steward fortalice and built a grand new dwelling, the Palace of Inchinnan which itself, fell in to ruin in the late 17th century and now, not a sign of it nor its associated mill, are to be seen. It is thought, St. Conval's Well stood within the policies of that palace. The Campbells of Blytheswood were the last proprietors of the lands.

From early times, agriculture with associated mlls, weaving and quarrying were the most productive industries but, in the early 20th century, things changed when Beardmore of Dalmuir arrived. The engineering company, based near Clydebank were busy developing aircraft or, in fact, anything that would fly. They ultimately opened at Inchinnan on what was to become Renfrew airport and began building airships which was seen as an extension to their well established aircraft business - the company had supplied many planes to the War Department, of which, most were engaged during the 1st World War. After the war, they began developing the R34 type airship with plans to fly it over the Atlantic, which would become the first crossing of its type using a very large scale machine though a couple of other crossings had been made using light aircraft. On July 2nd 1919, Major George Herbert Scott, his large crew and some passengers, took off from East Fortune Airfield in East Lothian en route to Mineola, New York, a distance of

Looking downstream from Renfrew Ferry. The Titan Crane and Clydebank College can be seen in the background

3,000 miles. The journey took four and half days before he made the return trip on the R34 to RNAS Pulham in 75 hours meaning this was the first return trans Atlantic air crossing. Sadly, history would show, the rigid airships would never compete with the much faster air travel of the future and the Beardmore company folded in 1921. Happily, as we know, aviation is still to the fore at Inchinnan with the great name of Rolls Royce Aviation Services, who produce gas turbine engines at their plant, one of many they own in Scotland. There is a lot of work to be had at the small place on the Gryffe, Cart and Clyde and the local business park is an extremely busy neighbourhood. The old Beardmore site was later taken up by the India Tyre Group offices and though it was later used in many guises, the Grade A listed building is now a thriving office for technology companies and also open for public use, for example meetings and conferences. An extension, which has been added in recent times, features a roof designed as a replica of the R34 airship, providing one of the finest landmarks in the area being as it is, very large, unusual...and white. More work is all around including as previously mentioned, the nearby airport.

There are some shops in the village, a post office, a large superstore nearby and more at Blytheswood Park though much more are available in Renfrew. There is still a Parish Church in Inchinnan and, while built in a modern style, is still the descendant of some wonderful old churches which were all situated on the banks of the Black Cart. Primary education and nurseries are provided but children must travel further for secondary learning.

India of Inchinnan building - Courtesy of Thomas Nugent ©2007

Before we move on, it is important, while not on our route, to mention the ancient Abbey of Paisley, founded in 1163 by Walter Fitzalan, the Steward, after he had signed a charter at Fotheringay in Yorkshire, to found a monastery of Cluniac monks on his lands south-west of Glasgow. In time, thirteen monks from Wenlock in Shropshire, spiritual home of the Steward, arrived in the area, now known as Paisley, to create their church on a site of an old church of the 6th century which was founded by the Patron Saint of Paisley, St. Mirin. The great foundation was dedicated, not only to Mirin but also St. Mary, St. James and St. Milburga, the Patron Saint of Wenlock. In 1316, perhaps the most notable event at the Abbey occurred, as we have seen, the birth of a king, Robert Stewart, son of the Steward and Princess Marjorie Bruce, daughter of the King, Robert I. Sadly that event was tinged with sadness at the death of Robert's mother who was later interred at the great church.

The Order of Cluny was, like other Benedictine Orders, renowned for their teaching skills and that was no different at Paisley. William Wallace grew up in Elderslie just to the west of Paisley and was thought to have been educated by the Cluniac monks of the abbey. Bearing in mind, only sons of men who had some means to pay, would receive education and, since Wallace's father Malcolm, was said to be a 'minor' noble, he would still have land and the means to finance his son's education.

The influence of the monastery of Cluniacs grew quickly, though mainly due to the Steward's power and wealth, both north and south of the border. In time it became an important trading institution carrying out much business with the northern kingdoms of mainland Europe. Bearing that in mind, it was no surprise when, in 1245, the monks of Paisley founded another abbey, Crossraguel in Ayrshire. Of course, good though things were in the early years, a change, for the worse, was on the way. As we have already seen, when Alexander III died in 1286, followed soon by his heir, Margaret of Norway, Scotland became akin to headless chicken, power hungry men vying for the kingship and a kleptomaniac in London, desperate to get his hands on Scotland or, at least, influence and control

Paisley Abbey - Courtesy of Lairich Rig ©2013

the new king. During the ensuing wars, any building of value and/or influence, was destroyed. Paisley Abbey's 'turn' came in 1307 when soldiers of Edward of England set the wonderful monument alight causing nigh on, total destruction. It was soon built up, partially, before the Stewarts met with the glory of the birth of the future king but the sadness of the death of a princess. Many fires, intentional or otherwise occurred over the centuries but the great Divine was continually being rebuilt, always in a grander fashion. Even as late as 1928, Sir Robert Lorimer was putting the finishing touches to the late Macgregor Chalmers' work. In more recent times, the council and church have been continuously renewing and repairing sections of the building in their ongoing efforts in keeping the beautiful edifice safe, ensuring it will still be a place of worship, wonderment and beauty in the years ahead.

*O*ther notes of interest include, Abbot George Shaw, who, in 1491, stood over the relics of King James III at Cambuskenneth, and, while representing the Pope, granted absolution to James' son, James IV, for his involvement in the death of his father at the Battle of the Sauchie Burn in 1488. The same abbot built a new Pilgrims' Chapel in 1498. George Shaw was succeeded in 1498 by Robert Shaw, who reigned until 1525 when the post was passed to a secular commendator, John Hamilton. Robert Shaw was then created Bishop of Moray, a role he fulfilled for two years. A few of the other abbots included, William in the mid 13th century, James in the 14th century and Richard Bothwell in the 15th century. The last of the commendators was Claude Hamilton, 1st Earl of Paisley who served from 1586 until 1592.

*O*f course, with the coming of the Reformation and the banning of Mass in 1560, Paisley Abbey became part of the new Church of Scotland where it remains to the present day, as the Parish Church of Paisley and is always open to the public who are able to view the magnificent interior, buy at the gift shop or enjoy a coffee in the café. Now we must bid a fond farewell to the gracious building with a tinge of sadness as we say goodbye, for the time being at least but now it is time to head back to the river where a crossing to Clydebank awaits. Before we do though, I must say, Paisley really is, overall, a lovely town with all the necessities required for good comfortable living. Some beautiful churches are joined by excellent leisure and sports facilities, gardens and parks, a truly magnificent town hall, unsurpassed anywhere, many good schools, colleges and a campus of the West of Scotland University. Good shops, hotels, inns, restaurants and cafés are in abundance catering for all tastes and their pride and joy, the local football team, named in honour of Paisley's saint, St. Mirren Football Club founded in 1877 and members of the Scottish Premiership.

*B*ack to the river and the fulsome confluence of the Clyde and Cart, gleefully embracing in the shadow of the nearby Clyde Titan Crane hovering over Clydebank College on the north bank. Docks look over to Renfrew Golf Course as if beckoning us to come and visit and now it is, once again, time to cross the river to the right bank and say hello to Clydebank so, one more time, I must call my river cab and set sail for one of the old industrial capitals of Scotland.

*C*lydebank, as a town, is not so old having been created a burgh in 1886 when Dalmuir, Kilbowie and Yoker were cojoined to create the 'new town'. In the 128 years since, Clydebank has grown in to a great industrial town and now contains, apart from the aforementioned villages, other districts and villages which have been added over the years, Duntocher where once existed a Roman fortlet, Hardgate, Linnvale, Old Kirkpatrick where another Roman fort existed and Whitecrook to name but a few, some of which are much older and have a longer history than the town, or the administration area to which they are now joined.

*I*n the early years of Clydebank and district, industry consisted mainly of

To the Estuary

agricultural activities but, very quickly, extensive ship building yards, the Singer factory, distilleries, breweries and chemical works were added. If you add the arrivals of post offices and banks and the opening of many shops in a newly created town centre, it is easy to see, Clydebank was not long in 'growing up'. By the end of the 19th century and the very early years of the 20th Clydebank as a whole, contained no less than eleven churches and two schools. Growth had arrived quickly, many migrants were beginning to pour in from nearby Glasgow and some from Ireland and eastern European countries which was not such a bad thing, since so many workers were needed, skilled and unskilled, and the population of that time, just under 10,000, could not cope with the volume of work. That meant, in time, more schools, more services, shops and most of all, more houses, Clydebank grew and grew.

The largest of all the shipyards was John Brown's and that company, perhaps as much as any other, gave the expression 'Clyde Built' to the world which, as we

Queen Elizabeth 2, built at John Brown's of Clydebank, off Greenock in 2008
Courtesy of Thomas Nugent ©2008

have seen, was an expression of 'excellence, work of the highest order'. A list of ships constructed at the yard is like a *who's who* of the shipping world. Ships like the Lusitania, Queen Mary, Queen Elizabeth and the Queen Elizabeth 2 ships are only a very small number of the vast amount of ships of all varieties, merchant, passenger and military, built at the yard. John Brown became part of the Upper Clyde shipyards and was known as the place of a 'work-in' during the 1970s when the workers decided, rather than walk out on strike, they stayed within the yard. Jimmy Reid, one of the Trades Union officials at the yard, urged his members to act with the greatest dignity, not to damage any of the yard's fixtures and fittings, and definitely 'no bevvying' or to non Scots, no drinking. That man became one of the great orators in Scottish history as well as being one the most famous sons of Glasgow. He became world renowned for his words and passion. Apart from being a proud man and proud Scot who cared for all, his greatest passion was ensuring the working men were treated how they should be, like worthy and dignified human beings. Jimmy, born in Govan in 1932, later went on to be a broadcaster, journalist and Rector of Glasgow University; the great man died in 2010, his place in Scottish history assured. John Brown's shipyard closed in 2000 and the yard has been totally 'reclaimed' from industry and is being developed for tourism with the gigantic Titan crane the centre piece, hovering over the whole area including Clydebank College. The most beautiful walkway has been created along the entire site attracting many to the area, increasing in popularity year on year.

Singer Corporation, another huge employer, closed in 1980 and the factory totally demolished, I don't think, anyone who ever saw the magnificent clock tower of the works will ever forget it. That area has now been rebuilt as a business centre providing many priceless jobs in the town.

Work, naturally, is not so plentiful as it once was but there are still jobs to be had at the Singer Business Park, Clydebank Industrial estate, a distillery and much, much more including the magnificent Golden Jubilee Hospital situated on one of the old Beardmore sites of airship fame. While unemployment in the area is said to be only 6%, according to the Scottish National Statistics, 20% of the population of the town are 'employment deprived'. Having said that, the town is next door neighbour to Glasgow, meaning opportunities for jobs nearby are still good and travel in to the city is easy with good road, bus services and five rail stations.

From the outset, Clydebank grew, and as industry arrived as we have seen, so did the population to its present, nearly 30,000 souls. More shops opened and now contains all the nationals and so many local shops. Shopping centres and retail parks have opened including one which straddles the Forth and Clyde Canal which flows through the town providing another attraction in a place desperately attempting to reinvent itself after the demise of its glorious industrious past. There are no shortage of fine eateries, inns and hotels, all waiting with the open arms of welcome, whether to local or visitor. The town too, is full of sports and leisure centres and other facilities including parks with sports pitches are plentiful meaning the townsfolk have plenty to keep them busy, the envy of many larger towns in the area. Centres exist too, for BMX biking, kart racing, two golf courses and several bowling clubs.

There are many fine churches in Clydebank, situated in so many lovely buildings, serving most members of the community and contains places of worship for Roman Catholics, Church of Scotland, Free, Episcopal, Wesleyan, Salvation Army, Congregational, Memorial, Methodist, Pentecostal and Christian Fellowship. All those churches have formed Churches Together in Clydebank, a show of togetherness and wonderful ecumenism in practice but you would expect nothing less from the caring community Clydebank is. I believe this Christian act

To the Estuary

of 'holding the hands of friendship and togetherness', added to the efforts of the authorities, will bring the town out of the industrial wilderness and in to the bright modern today and tomorrow, encouraging people to visit, and admire. There are many lovely reminders, like model ships, made of steel, around the town, reminding us of the town's *'proud past and promising a dynamic future'* the motto of a proud community.

Notable buildings in the town, including many fine churches are, the Town Hall, the Municipal Buildings (now a museum) the library and the more modern, including the Clyde Shopping Centre, the college buildings and the Golden Jubilee Hospital. (below)

The town's football team have had a chequered career being formed, fading away, being re-formed then being bought out and removed to Airdrie. Clydebank Football Club presently play in the Western Super League in the Scottish semi-pro,

Golden Jubilee Hospital Courtesy of Danny Kearney ©2012

junior set up. The present club, formed in 2003 have roots in 1899 while the senior version of the club, now playing at Airdrie under that name, briefly united with East Stirlingshire FC under the name of ES Clydebank but that was short lived and the club survived only until 2002. The club did nurture some notable players with the most famous being the legendary, the late Davie Cooper who went on to Rangers and Scotland fame and is widely regarded as one of Scotland's most skilful players of all time. Others included Ken Eadie, Jim Fallon, Gerry McCabe and Bill Munro to name a few

Clydebank is well blessed with so many fine schools with several nursery, pre-school, primary and secondary covering non denominational and Roman Catholic education. The town too, possesses colleges and the Veterinary School of Glasgow University.

Sadly, and shockingly, Clydebank, suffered the biggest and most horrifying attack in Scottish history when, on the 13th and 14th March 1941, the German Luftwaffe launched unprecedented attacks on the town and surrounding areas; their targets of course, were the shipyards, the Singer factory which was deployed for the war effort, armament factories and a large oil depot. They wreaked havoc destroying everything in sight, killing many. A total of 528 innocent civilians were killed in the town with many more seriously injured during an act of gross atrocity

**A sail-thru fish and chip shop on the Forth & Clyde Canal
'A world first for Clydebank' - Courtesy of Thomas Nugent ©2010**

and verging very much on being illegal. It takes a long time to recover from such an act of mass murder. Buildings can, eventually, be rebuilt but the hearts and minds of ordinary people will never fully heal. Thankfully the right side won the war and the forces of evil who governed Germany in those dark days, have been extinguished.

As noted before, Clydebank has no ancient history but some of the areas in the town do, including Old Kilpatrick, an ancient town and Burgh of Barony (1679) in its own right and probably the earliest settlement in the immediate area. Furthermore, the town was the mother of the old parish which included Clydebank and Old Kilpatrick or West Kilpatrick which is said to have been the birthplace of St. Patrick, Patron Saint of Ireland. Some may scorn or at best, question, the birthplace of the saintly Patrick, saying nothing has been so called in his name and yet the word Kilpatrick from the Gaelic, Cille Phàdraig means '*Church of Patrick*'

According to a book ascribed to him, in his own words, the *Book of Confession,* St. Patrick wrote "My Father was Calphurnius a deacon, son of Potitus, a presbyter of the town of Bonaven of Tabernia" According to later writings of the life of Patrick by Jocelin of Furnes in the 12th century, Tabernia was one the Roman names for the province which lay near the end of the Antonine Wall. The occupations of Patrick's forebears, deacon and presbyter, strongly suggest, that some kind of religious establishment had already been founded in *Bonaven*...the future Kilpatrick? Tarbenia was also referred to as Valentia.

Born in 372, Patrick was thought to have been a child captive in Ireland for a time but returned home to contemplate his future life. His family were obviously wealthy and important and, according to their names, suggest they were descendants of Roman stock or, at least, adopted Roman names. Patrick himself referred to his mother by name, Conquessa and, with the best will, we cannot ascribe any of the names of Patrick's forebears to anything other than Latin.

At around the age of 19 or 20, Patrick travelled to Italy and France where he spent more than 35 years, 18 of which were studying under St. Germanus. It is believed, he was in his sixties when he went to preach the Gospel, the length and breadth of the Emerald Isle where he is said to have founded 365 churches, ordained as many bishops and more than 3,000 priests.

Having said all that, there is virtually no mention of the place which became known as Kilpatrick, until the 12th century when the Earl of Lennox confirmed the church. The next mention did not appear until the second decade of the 13th century when Maldoven or Maol Domhnaich a later Earl of Lennox or should I say, Mormaer of Lennox, granted the church and lands to Paisley Abbey. That situation existed, with the church in the Deanery of Lennox and Diocese of Glasgow until the Reformation. An interesting note of those early times came when Dufgal, the rector of the kirk and a brother of the Mormaer, disputed the rights of the church as belonging to Paisley. The confrontation dragged on until the Pope, Gregory IX took an interest in the proceedings then, finally, in 1233, a court of Papal delegates ruled the church, from 1227, and in to perpetuity, belonged to Paisley Abbey.

Another chaplain we know of at Kilpatrick, was Patrick who served in the mid 13th century while later that century, Stephen of Kilpatrick paid homage to Edward at Berwick in 1296. Another mention during that century was of the existence of a chapel at Drumry which was still 'working' in the late 15th century.

In 1812, a new church was built at Kilpatrick on the site of the old church, which, in its day, had a wonderful view of the river. Kilpatrick Church, complete with a majestic clock tower, is still working but has been co-joined with Bowling Church since 1975. The old church, like many other buildings in the area, was damaged during the dastardly German attack in 1941.

Modern day Kilpatrick where once Roman soldiers strutted to and from their nearby fort, though part of the bigger district of Clydebank, is fiercely independent; it is a lovely place with its own shops, post office, nursery and primary school, two churches, one Church of Scotland, the other Roman Catholic, restaurants, inns and cafés while all leisure facilities are nearby. It is a close knit community and many family functions are held throughout the year including two fêtes. Kilpatrick is a lovely place to be at any time of the year and it is good to see the old swing bridge over the Forth and Clyde Canal, now back in full operation after many years of inaction.

Old Kilpatrick was the principal settlement in an extremely busy parish of the day where industry consisted of agriculture, quarrying both red and white sandstone, an extensive weaving industry, coal mining, paper making, bleachfields, printing, dyeing works, with logging and distilling at Auchentoshen.

River Clyde

So it is clear to see, the wee place on the Clyde, which we are about to bid farewell to, was a very important locale, ecclesiastically and industrially in the old Barony of Colquhoun.

The Parish Church of Old Kilpatrick

The people of Clydebank are known as *Bankies,* many of whom have achieved something which sets them apart from us mere mortals. Here is a small selection of a long list of Bankies and others associated with the area. Duncan Bannatyne, entrepreneur, the comedian Kevin Bridges, actor, James Cosmo, two footballers by the name of Johnny Divers, Kevin Gallacher, international footballer, and another, Asa Hartford of Scotland fame, Marti Pellow, singer and member of local band, Wet, Wet, Wet and the barrister, Sir James Beveridge. Now though, it is time to head back to the Erskine Bridge and the town of the same name. It will make a change crossing by road rather than boat but it is such a wonderful bridge and good to be on with so many beautiful views up and down the river. As I write, the bridge is undergoing necessary repairs meaning only one lane of traffic is able to use the north bound route. This crossing will be my second last after dozens of crossings of the great river since her source at Watermeetings. Once we have visited Erskine, Langbank and Port Glasgow, it will be back to the north bank, to visit Bowling, Dumbarton and Cardross.

Back to Inchinnan where we left earlier and where I met the skipper of another river boat who kindly offered me a lift. Sailing down the Clyde at that point, to use my new found, *'parliamo Glasgow'* is *'pure dead brilliant'* and beats walking anytime. Now we are sailing the short distance west to Erskine witnessing a deep basin on our way, an awesome sight as we coast on passing Freeland which skirts on the western reaches of the Inner Clyde Nature Reserve

To the Estuary

The waters there cut their way in during high tide at Newshot Island, passing under footbridges on the way. We have now reached a beautiful stretch of parkland which was created on the site of the old Rashielee Quay in 1993, by using earth which was removed from the construction site of the Erskine swimming pool. That is a sure fire signal that we have reached Erskine and time now to step back on to terra firma at Park Quay.

Old Erskine is of ancient standing and for long in the hands of a family, who, in keeping with the times, adopted the name of the lands on which they lived. Sometimes the lands were spelled Ariskyn or Hyreskin meaning 'green rising lands', and were first mentioned around 1202 when Florence, bishop-elect of Glasgow, confirmed the church as one of the churches of Strathgryffe which Walter Fitzalan granted to Paisley Abbey. When we consider, Walter, the first High Steward, died in 1177, that tells us, the church at Erskine was already established by that time.

In later times, Yrskin (yet another spelling) was gifted by Paisley to Glasgow where it became a prebend of the cathedral.

The old church appeared, with so much reparation and renewal, to stand within its own kirkyard, until the present parish church at Bishopton (pictured right) was erected in 1828 on the same site as its predecessor. We only know one of the mediaeval parsons, William, who witnessed an agreement between the Bishop of Glasgow and the canons of Gyseburn, Lancashire in 1223. Another note of interest arrives in 1300 when James the 5th High Steward granted the lord of the manor, Johane Erskine, liberties and lands at Largs, with the right to erect twenty brew houses if he so wished.

Over the years, the Ireskin (Erskine) family witnessed many charters which appeared to be an everyday occurrence for important families of the day. The Erskines owned great swathes of land and both ferry ports but they, by no means, had it all their own way. Areas like Park was owned by a family of that name during the reign of James IV, while the mighty Maxwell family owned Balgarran, Bishopton and Durvagel where they built a great house, which still stands though until recently belonged to the BAE Systems as part of the now closed Royal Ordnance Factory but there is some mention of the great house coming in to a form of community use: the Maxwells also owned nearby Newark Castle for some time.

*H*ave you noticed how important families of the day, adopted the title of the lands they owned? Well that also applied to the ordinary man who was generally known by his trade since surnames, as such, were still not in common use. Names like farmer, baxter, wright, mason, carpenter, baker...the list goes on, while others adopted their fathers names as in 'son of', fitz or mac.

*T*he family of Erskine held the lands, probably until the early 18th century, before selling them to the Hamiltons of Orbiston, One, Henry de Erskine witnessed many church charters during the early 13th century while his grandson Johane de Irskyn swore fealty to Edward I at Berwick towards the end of the same century. Johane's grand daughter, Mary, married Sir Thomas Bruce, brother of Robert, the king, while another of the family, Sir William, Mary's brother, was a faithful and trusted ally and friend of the same king. William's son, Robert was created the keeper and constable of Stirling Castle and that title passed through the family for many years. The Erskines spread their wings and power throughout the country and were always in the midst, or on the fringes of Scottish history, gaining land and title in the process.

*T*he Hamiltons of Orbiston built a new, more homely, Erskine House and, in the 18th century greatly extended the house before selling the manor to the Stuart, Lords Blantyre. That family built another house in 1828 and was still in their hands in to the 20th century when they passed it over for the care of badly injured soldiers who were sent there from the fields of carnage during the Great War of 1914 – 1918. The final Blantyre owner was Sir David Baird, grandson of the 12th and last Lord, Charles Stuart who died in 1900. That great house contained many ancillary buildings which were retained, and added to, by the hospital, buildings like cottages, a farm steading, kennels, piggery, stables, cowsheds, an ice house all surrounded by magnificent, formal gardens, some of which still stand to the present day in its new guise as Mar Hall Hotel. Near the hotel, in the old policies of Erskine House, there stands a monument in memory of Robert Walter Stuart, 11th Lord Blantyre who was killed in Brussels. The lord, a major-general under the Duke of Wellington, had served in many campaigns including Waterloo where he fought with great courage but in Brussels in 1830, he was hit by a stray bullet during a street riot and died. His friends and comrades erected the monument as a sign of the esteem in which they held him.

*T*hat great hospital, which has now moved to modern, state of the art premises, was a ground breaking institution, particularly in the creation of new limbs for those poor boys who lost arms or/and legs. Today, that great Erskine foundation has spread across Scotland, still caring and providing for the needs of our injured ex servicemen. One man of special note who was instrumental in the provision of so many good things in the early days of the hospital, was the chief surgeon, Sir William McEwan who was helped in his quest, to find and develop better and more functional artificial limbs, by some of the engineers at local shipyards like, for instance, Yarrows, a really touching gesture for our heroes.

To the Estuary

Combined, Erskine and nearby Bishopton are well served by churches including Church of Scotland, Roman Catholic, Baptist, a Gospel Hall and the Cornerstone Church Centre.

Modern design

St. John Bosco Roman Catholic Church in Erskine

Modern beauty

Local Primary Schools care for the children before moving on to the Secondary School, Park Mains High while sport facilities are plentiful including the Community Sports Centre, leisure centre, swimming pool all joined by a spa and leisure centre at the Erskine Bridge Hotel. Sports grounds, parks and gardens are everywhere and there is too, old Erskine Harbour which is a haven for wildfowl and adventurers, an atmospheric playground of a different kind without being troubled too much by boats. The Pandemonium Play Centre is another popular venue for the children of the district. Shopping is adequate within the two communities and no one really needs to travel, though Glasgow is at hand as is Renfrew and Paisley with Dumbarton across the mighty Erskine Bridge. Nearby motorways, railway stations and an excellent bus network mean, that if the locals must travel, they do have many choices.

There is a service reservoir on Craigend Hill on the site of Old Bargarran House once home to the Lairds of Bargarran, the Shaw family. A daughter of that house, Christiana, a clever and very Christian girl who loved nothing more than to attend church. When she was eleven, she began acting very strangely, blaming all and sundry for her uncharacteristic carry on. In those days, Scotland was bedevilled by the King's witch hunt and soon 21 people accused by the girl, were accused of witchcraft including a servant whom Christiana caught drinking the milk. Seven of the accused including the servant were executed. Nothing more is known of that girl who, because of her own misgiven infidelity, cost so many people their lives; the witch hunt ordered by James VI, was one of Scotland's darkest eras when many hundreds, possibly thousands, were tried and executed for witch craft; even owning a cat was classified as evil.

A bit like the ford we talked of earlier at Glasgow Green, here is another important crossing point at Erskine Bridge which has also attracted a growing community, and business. A very large electronic equipment manufacturer is the largest private employer in an area which boasts one of the highest rates of employment in Scotland.

*O*n we go round Longhaugh Point, still on the mudflats and still in the Inner Clyde Wildlife Reserve. At this point, a beacon and a series of pillars can be seen running along on top of what looks like a line of rocks in the river. In actual fact it is the beginning, or east end, of the Lang Dyke, a man made construction devised, designed and developed by John Golborne in the 18th century in an attempt to deepen a channel along the river, to allow larger vessels to reach nearer the city centre. Another interesting feature of this section of the river is the remains of a Roman Causeway which can be seen at low tide, crossing to Dumbarton.

A view of the river and Dumbarton Rock, the Lang Dyke can be seen top middle of the photograph - Courtesy of Thomas Nugent ©2010

To the south at this section is the Cora Campus, a specialist Roman Catholic school with the Ingliston Equestrian Centre and Country Club and the Whitemoss Dam beyond. Now, even more mud and sandbanks await as we make our way, further west below the Ferryhill Plantation on the left bank and directly south of Dumbarton Rock and the confluence with the River Leven. That meeting of waters means the river is a little more affluent than the shallow waters on the

To the Estuary

south bank where walking is a little easier.

Only a few yards on and we have arrived at Langbank. One thing I have noticed here, are the two crannogs on the river with even more up and down the western fringes. A crannog, as you know, was a man made 'island' supported by stilts dug deep in to the mudflats, they were part home, part defensive, with the water their principal defence. Judging by the locations of the ones I have just witnessed, it would appear the river was much wider in times gone, than it is now, meaning the crannogs would be that much further from the dry land. However, if that is the case, the water must have rippled right up and over the main road heading for Port Glasgow, and no further since Langbank is built at the foot of a steep hill.

Langbank is a lovely village hanging as it does, over the banks of the river on the lowest slopes of a wooded hill. There are many fine houses from social, to bungalows, villas and mansion houses, all making up the quiet dormitory community and that appears to have be the case since the village, formerly a series of farms, was founded in the mid 19th century.

At one time, the village contained two churches, the Parish Church and a United Presbyterian Church but the former, which itself was the old parish church, has long since closed and is now in domestic use. A chapel for St. Vincent's College also existed at Langbank but that too has closed. At present, the village boasts a fine inn/restaurant, a popular hotel complete with golf course, a well stocked village shop situated on the main street, and a village hall with function suite. It also has something money cannot buy, wonderful views over the River Clyde to Dumbarton, the Rock and castle with the dramatic scene of the mighty Ben Lomond in the background. Sadly on my last visit, a haze hung over large sections of the river and the view of the north bank was virtually obscured.

A little further along the beach, to the west, we encounter the dramatic sight of countless logs, known as *Timber Ponds,* sticking out of the mud and sand. They were used to store wood, allowing it to 'season', for the shipbuilding industry of old when all ships were built of wood. The wood was imported from North America and stored by tying the logs to large rafts which were held in place by the timber ponds we now see, literally, hundreds of them stretching for miles, forming an incredible scene as we head away from lovely Langbank on our way to Port Glasgow. You may have noticed I mentioned beach, that is what it now is, rather than a river bank, as the waters rush forward at the estuary of the river and the meeting with the tidal waters of the firth.

Barely a mile to the west of Langbank, hovering high above the timber ponds, is gracious, 18th century Finlaystone House with a history said to stretch back to the 14th century when Robert I of Scots, granted the lands to Sir John de Danylstone who, in turn left them to his eldest son, Robert, now known as de Dennistoun. Robert, at that point, was keeper of Dumbarton Castle and was also in possession of Newark Castle to the west. On Robert's death in 1399, his castles at Finlaystone and Newark, passed to his daughters, Margaret and Elizabeth respectively. Margaret later married Sir William Cunningham and he maintained the castle as the Caput of the Clan Cunningham which existed until the 19th century, though, in 1746, a new house was built, still retaining parts of the old fortalice, During that period, William's grandson, was created Earl of Glencairn. Incidentally, the other sister, Elizabeth of Finlaystone, Finlawstane or

Finlaystone House Courtesy of Lairich Rig ©2003

Fynlanstone, married Sir Robert Maxwell of the family of Calderwood and Pollock of whom we shall hear more of at Port Glasgow. Another castle of the Dennistouns, which later came in to the hands of the Maxwells, was Stanely Castle to the south of Paisley, the ruins of which now sit, partly submerged, in Stanely Reservoir.

In the late 18th century, John Cunningham, 15th of Glencairn, died without issue and, though it passed to a cousin, Finlaystone was sold twice before it came in to the own of the Kidston family. They had the house remodelled in 1903, still retaining much fabric of the old buildings, before it passed to Marian Kidston who later married Major, Sir Gordon Macmillan, Chief of the Clan MacMillan, in whose family, the great castle mansion, the magnificent grounds and the chiefdom, remains. From, virtually the beginning of the MacMillan tenure, members of the public have been invited to visit the great house and grounds, not only was this a place of privilege for the gentry but also a playground of the people. Finlaystone Estate is now one of the top destinations in Renfrewshire, offering atmospheric woodland walks, picnic, play and BBQ areas, simply magnificent gardens and much more including holiday flats for rent, all set in 140 acres of paradise overlooking the Clyde and Dumbarton beyond.

Onward we trudge until we reach Finlaystone Point where ample car parking is provided for visitors including local boatmen and many walkers. Continue along the banks and soon Kelburn Park is in sight, a business park, producing many valuable jobs...and space for travelling people, who often turn up unannounced to the annoyance of the business people, though the council are currently considering creating a site for their exclusive use.

To the Estuary

*F*urther to the west, some small craft are at anchor near a long jetty then, just beyond, Port Glasgow's Newark Castle & doocot (pictured below) the remains of which stretch back to the 15th century though it is believed a fortification of sorts from a much earlier period may have existed. George Maxwell, a descendant of the afore mentioned Robert and Elizabeth, began work on the present castle, consisting

of a keep surrounded by a barmkin, in 1478, but later generations would create additions and many alterations, particularly, Sir Patrick in the latter part of the 16th century. Patrick was a powerful ally of James VI but gained notoriety for his murder of two rivals and the beating of his wife, the mother of his 16 children, who eventually left him. Patrick removed much of the barmkin walls retaining the north-east tower and built an early form of Scots Baronial mansion house while retaining the north-east tower which he converted to a doo'cot, one of the most unusual in the country. The last of the Maxwell lairds, Sir George, died in 1698. Newark Castle, at the edge of some fine grass and wood lands offering more good walks, is now in the care of Historic Scotland and is a popular tourist destination.

*T*he Glasgow Corporation leased the lands around the castle in 1688 in order to develop them and build a harbour for the trading ships delivering to the city since the Clyde beyond that point, at that time, was not navigable for larger ships and that spot was considered the most suitable considering its location in Newark Bay. The creation of that harbour or port, was really the beginnings of the larger settlement in the area which would join, and subsequently engulf, the small village of Newark. The shipping authorities named the place, Newport, the New Port of Glasgow, before the present day, Port Glasgow title came in to being.

*T*here has been a settlement at Newark, it's believed, since before the building of the first castle and as we said earlier, another fortification may have been in situ before the building of that castle in the late 15th century. Considering its situation at the Clyde estuary, it would have been invaluable in the defence of Glasgow and the entrance to the river. We have already seen Somerled's attacks of the 12th century, simply following in his Norse predecessors' warlike path of the 8th and 9th centuries when they 'ran riot' over the islands off the west coast before turning their attentions, and ambitions to the mainland.

*I*n the early days, Newark viewed from the Clyde, must have formed an enchanting scene with a row of cottages, grasslands and woodlands to the east, orchards to the west with the steep hills and cliffs forming a dramatic backdrop, it would have looked as though it had been created by divine hands forming a little piece of paradise overlooking the waters of Clyde.

*W*ith the widening of the river's shipping channel in the latter part of the 18th and early 19th centuries, trade was gradually removed from Port Glasgow heading further upstream. What could be done at the Port to make safe jobs and the future of the community? The answer came in converting the three harbours of the port in to ship building yards which further enhanced the size of the wee town, the foundations of which had already been laid.

*P*ort Glasgow's present town centre is much the same as it has been since the late 17th century, a square grid setting with several streets running parallel with each other, with other streets crossing over forming the grid. It is unusual in as much, unlike so many other towns, even ones of a similar age to Port Glasgow, the town centre was very much planned. It is compact making life so much easier for the townsfolk both then and now. This functional, people-friendly town is a good place to shop and, even on a Sunday, on my latest visit, the centre of town was busy with shoppers. Good shops are available including local and national, joining

inns and cafés with a large supermarket and an even larger superstore nearby on one of the old docks. Other shops can be found around and more on the hill behind the town centre. The town is ideal for walking, built on flat lands as it is though more housing has been built on the hills

behind, from relatively recent times, forming another community overlooking the town centre and the scenic vista beyond.

*F*ine buildings are everywhere including the Town Building of 1816, St. Andrews Kirk in Church Street (pictured above) and the many other churches. Other features to be seen, are the lovely War Memorial, a replica of the world

To the Estuary

renowned ship, *Comet,* the nearby water feature and the magnificent, if unusual, *Endeavour* sculpture. Coronation Park too is well worthy of a visit, and where nice walks can be had. In fact several fine parks exist in the town, both near the centre and others 'up the hill' but all provide leisure, play and relaxation adding to some fine walks along the river side towards Greenock to the west. It is difficult to believe so much went on there in terms of ship building compared to how it is today.

The town is served by eight churches, for anyone who may visit on a Sunday, or any other day for that matter, including Roman Catholic, Church of Scotland, Scottish Episcopal, United Reformed, and the Salvation Army. Education is served by non denominational and Roman Catholic primary and secondary schools and there are also exciting works underway to create a 'super campus' with four schools, two high schools and two special needs schools sharing the same campus on the site of the former Port Glasgow High School.

When shipbuilding arrived in Port Glasgow, it really did, and a roll call of some of the finest ships, both wooden and steel, to sail the seven seas, were built at the yards of the town. First to arrive was Thomas McGill in 1780 but the most famous of the early ship builders was local man, John Wood, who built the Comet in 1812, the replica of which we now see. The Comet was built for Henry Bell who ran a regular service around the Clyde and up as far as Oban and Fort William, it was the said to be first commercially viable steamship of its kind in Europe but it all came to a sad end in 1821 when the Comet was wrecked in

Replica of the legendary Comet

strong currents of Craignish near Oban. Bell tried again with another, Comet II, but that ship sank off the Ayrshire coast after a collision. The building of steel hulled ships grew when the great steel works of Lanarkshire opened and this brought the best out of the Port's shipyards, more particularly, Lithgow's yard. As an important incidental, the first dry dock in Scotland was designed by James Watt and opened at Port Glasgow in 1762. We have not seen the last of industry at the town though and there are several business and industrial areas in the town...and at the docks.

William Lithgow began work as an apprentice draughtsman in a yard at Port Glasgow but was soon proprietor of his own ship building yard. He, his sons, Sir James and Henry and his grandson, William, raised the yard to legendary status almost from the beginning. With an inheritance, he bought a share in Russell & Co. but in time, he became sole owner and later changed the name to Lithgows. That company built over a thousand ships in the 20th century until nationalisation arrived in 1977. Nationalisation was more like rationalisation when it was hoped, by yards combining, the industry could be saved but sadly that only delayed the inevitable. Because of cheaper alternatives, not better products, especially in the Far East, the Clyde shipping industry collapsed, including Port Glasgow. Thankfully, one yard survives to carry on a great industry with all its traditions. Ferguson's are now the sole proprietors and bearers of a long and proud shipbuilding industry in Port Glasgow and it is they who are left today, to add to the glories of yesterday with some more of their own, today and tomorrow.

Many other industries were busy in the town, serving the shipping industries, including the Gourock Rope Works and sail making, but they have, like their more illustrious neighbours, sailed beyond the most distant horizons.

With the demise of the great industry, the population of the town dwindled but it is making a come back and many new housing developments have been completed in recent years, forming the fine town we see today as it gradually realigns itself in the business world as a tourist town...and it is beginning to make inroads in to that sector. A fine waterfront with good walks, the parks as we have already mentioned and, of course, the atmospheric old castle and doo'cot. Sports facilities are in abundance particularly at Parklea including football, in the shape of Port Glasgow Juniors who were founded in 1948, a fine sports and gym centre at Birkmyre Park and a swimming pool while another community centre exists at Boglestone. There is an excellent golf course, two bowling clubs, a rugby club, tennis courts and putting course. The great Kilmacolm and Port Glasgow Agricultural Show is held every year as is the Bulb Show and the Art and Needlework exhibition not forgetting the eternal sailing and boating enthusiasts who are always looking for fresh faces and, could we forget?..fishing.

Boglestone is a very interesting name, it is the name of a stone, once situated on the beach and now near the Bogle Stone roundabout. It is known, with some affection, as the mainstay, or even the founding stone of both Newark and the New Port. Some say it is a place of witchcraft where locals believe it was, in ancient times, a haunt of witches and warlocks but, it would seem, they were of the benevolent variety.

Depending on which chronicle you read, both Newark and Newport were

burghs but whatever is the case, Burgh of Barony was bestowed
whole in 1775 and the status of Parliamentary Burgh in 1832, mak
quite independent of all others and now had the ability to appoint a P
major milestone in the town's history since, apart from its new status, it
officially, known as Port Glasgow.

Above : Port Glasgow – The Town building and the Endeavour sculpture
Below: Newly launched from Ferguson's yard at Port Glasgow. The diesel electric
hybrid ferry, Hallaig, a world first of its type and now in service in the Western Isles.
Courtesy of Thomas Nugent ©2013

Overall, Port Glasgow is a nice clean town with a lot going for it, including
good communications by road and rail and close to the airport, but with hopes of
much more in the future. The people are considerate, friendly and helpful and they

on the town as a
ing the town
ovost, a
as now

, which I am sure will arrive in time.
eas call the town, dirty wee Port but
ngs and goings, full of industry. With
s that very dirt which brought thousands
tive, Port Glasgow has a bright,
can never be quite so bright as the
s she slips in to the bracing waters of the
nsfolk are moving with those times. Put
ess, the people of the port have got the
as, it's back across the Erskine Bridge.
alk along the riverside past the great
docks and basins, the mouth of the Dunocher Burn and the Forth and Clyde Canal
entering in to the River Clyde almost hand in hand with the Gavin Burn as she too

**Leaf covered
basin at the end
of the Forth and
Clyde Canal
at Bowling**

makes her way to her very own 'estuary', On the walk, there are lovely carvings
of swans, the 'owl bench' and the Millenium Link Memorial, linking the Forth and
Clyde Canal with the Falkirk Wheel, we are now at the village of Bowling, or
originally Bowling Bay in West Dunbartonshire. In the Kilpatrick Hills to the
north of Bowling, exist many small reservoirs and their waters produce several
exciting waterfalls as they crash down towards Clyde and the Firth beyond. The
old harbour is pretty much disused now but in recent times, the Bowling Basin has
been re-developed to provide a safe haven and sanctuary for boats travelling the
canal and river and what a beautiful haven it is, especially when it is full of small
craft. The boating fraternity do bring a lot of benefits to the village and does the
local economy no harm at all.

    *B*owling is at the extreme north-western boundary of the great Roman
Empire or so we are told and a play *The Romans stopped at Bowling* emphasised
that, this was near the end of the line for the Latin invaders, the western end of the

To the Estuary

Antonine Wall but was it? We shall see. It is one of those places where access is made easy, whether by sea, canal, walking, cycling, road or rail, fine facilities cater for all forms of transport. The village once boasted a thriving boat building industry but that all closed forever in 1997 when the last boat, the Laggan, built for Forth Tugs at Grangemouth was launched. The village also contained, at one time, a distillery, post office, a church and free church. Fragments of the old wharf can be seen along the riverside as a reminder of a proud past.

There are a few community activities which mainly take place in Bowling Hall or at the Railway Inn, the only inn in the tiny village. The hall, once the Buchanan Institute, also served as a Free Church of Scotland in days gone by. The distillery has long since departed the scene but new housing is being built on the site but nothing yet has been decided regarding the now closed church situated on the Dumbarton Road. The only shop provides most of the villagers' every day needs but they do have to travel further afield for much of their requirements. There is a playpark for the kiddies while a lovely garden is laid out around the village's War memorial. More development for business and residential is planned for the near future which would further sustain the facilities of the community.

Housing at Bowling consists of two blocks of red sandstone flats and some, more modern flats have been recently built, with lovely cottages in between. Just west of the peaceful wee place and down towards the river is old Dunglass Castle, where once a Roman fortlet stood, and the imperious obelisk monument dedicated to Henry Bell. He was the man who, more than anyone else, pioneered the shipping industry on the Clyde when he first designed the steamship, Comet, as we noted at Port Glasgow. Even though many of his business ventures failed, he was one of the leading lights in the roller coaster that was Clyde shipping. The great monument, another part of Clyde Waterway Heritage, was opened in 1838.

Dunglass Castle sits near the beach at the west end of the village but is hidden from view behind an oil depot, as is the Henry Bell monument. The castle was built in the late 14th early 15th century by the Colquhoun family but began to fall into disrepair after the family moved in to a more modern house of the Scots Baronial style, adjacent to the castle, and which contains some Charles Rennie MacIntosh touches. In the latter part of the 18th century, sections of the castle walls were removed to repair a nearby quay leaving the ruin in such a sorry state of disrepair with only fragments remaining though some sections stand to a height of more than eight feet. An old beehive style doo'cot, also ruined, is thought to have began life as a tower to the south-east corner of the castle. The newer house has been much restored in recent times though the interior still contains large sections of the original fabric of the building. High upon the Kilpatrick Hills to the north-west of the castle, the remains of the private family chapel of Colquhoun can be seen.

To the west, we now head in search of Dumbarton, the road rising well above the shoreline now as we head along the foothills of the Kilpatricks. On our way, we pass through Milton on the east side of Dumbarton and home to several hotels, garage services, car sales and some very fine homes. Tucked as it is, below hills to

River Clyde

the east, west and north, it is also home to several burns which pass through, and under the main road in their eagerness to join Clyde for the final fling of the 'river dance' as her own flow reaches out for the open seas.

On the road in to the Dumbarton Town Centre, there is row after row of what looks like an old army training base but is, in fact, bonded whisky warehouses which were once protected by, would you believe? a flock of geese known as the *Scotch Watch.* Down on the river side, cobbled remains of the Roman causeway we mentioned earlier, can be clearly seen as can the pillars on the Lang Dyke as we approach mighty Dumbarton Rock and the powerful bastion of Dumbarton Castle. To the right, towering high above the eastern edges of the town is Dumbuck Hill, spliced virtually in to two separate hills by a huge quarry where yet another Roman Fort once stood and which was the destination for the Roman causeway and road. In much more recent times, excavation finds in the region show us, the Romans also had a base at what became known as Dumbarton including a naval station and look out point at the Rock.

The coastline cuts in to the north, forming a bay where the strangely named Gruggies Burn flows in to the Clyde which, at this stage, is a trifle sluggish during the low tides of the firth. We are almost at the Rock now and time to step on to the grasslands below the daunting castle which sits high on a promontory squeezed between the Gruggies, the Clyde and the River Leven. The great rock and the fortifications thereon, was the most important place in what became known as Strathclyde and was seat of the chiefs, later kings, of the local British tribe of the Damnonii. At that time, the rock was known as Alt Clut. *height above the Clyde* which would survive as their capital until 870AD when it was taken by a huge Viking force before being occupied by a combined army of Scots and Picts ensuring the old British tribe would never return to their old castle of Dùn Breatainn, *fort of the Britons,* a castle with a longer known history than any other in Britain. We have looked at the Kingdom of Strathclyde throughout our journey and some of the confusion which it has caused with regards to names of kings at certain times and so on. While some say, Alt Clut was the capital of Ystrad Clut, other students of the subject believe, Alt Clut, rather than be the capital of Ystrad Clut, was a kingdom all of its own and they, like Strathclyde, had their own kings.

The history of that area may stretch as far back as the time when man first walked on the land which would become known as Scotland, and that would be no later than the Neolithic period some 6,500 years ago. From then until the coming of the Romans virtually nothing is known; more is known, from the times of the Romans but is somewhat fragmented and full of contradiction. It is possible to read up to a dozen accounts on various parts of the history, of the Romans, the church, Alt Clut or Dumbarton, and of Strathclyde itself, all with different tales to tell, all with contradicting dates.

What we do know, or think we know, is, the Romans arrived in 71AD, were involved in many scuffles and one serious battle, Mons Graupius in 83AD, then built the Antonine Wall from 142AD, and a fort on the great rock, the last of a line of forts they built which stretched across central Scotland after they decided they would, or could not overpower the Picts. We have been told, they subsequently left in 220AD after attempting to rebuild the Antonine Wall during the reign of Emperor Severus, but did they? I have mentioned the Roman Province of Valentia earlier in this journey but the emperor from whom that title came, was Valentininian I, who ruled from the mid 4th century AD. If that is the case, then the Romans did indeed have some influence over the lands which stretched from the northern shores of the Clyde and down through, what is now Cumbria, long beyond 220AD.

The Kingdom of Ystrad Clywd or Clud (Strathclyde) would not come to pass until the latter part of 5th century when Ceretic Guletic was crowned king at his capital of Alt Clut. He, according to *St. Patrick's Chronicles*, received a letter from Patrick who pleaded with him to stop his vendetta against people who were baptised Christians and whom the king either sold as slaves or executed them. In that letter, Patrick referred to Ceretic as Coroticus. Patrick's letter to Ceretic was as follows :

"Soldiers whom I no longer call my fellow citizens, or citizens of the Roman saints, but fellow citizens of the devils, in consequence of their evil deeds; who live in death, after the hostile rite of the barbarians; associates of the Scots and Apostate Picts; desirous of glutting themselves with the blood of innocent Christians, multitudes of whom I have begotten in God and confirmed in Christ"

More contradiction arrives later, more in the terms of dating, through the medium of the early church and the *Annals of Ulster* which tell us of the death of Cathal MacFergus, Bishop of Alcluyd (Dumbarton) in 554AD. Others mention bishops of Alt Clud attending conferences in France in the very early 4th century but I find that quite baffling since, at that time, no known arrival of Christianity in the area came until St. Ninian spread the word in the latter part of the 4th century and even that story is based, mainly on legend. Ninian or Ringan, as he was also known, is not verified by anything at all other than a legend being passed from generation to generation and from the writings of St. Bede the Venerable, in the 7th and 8th centuries. As we have seen, the king, Ceretic was not a Christian and, if the king was not Christian, neither was his kingdom, and any Christians of that time, would be too frightened to 'out' themselves for obvious reasons. It is interesting however, to note Patrick's letter to Ceretic where he mentions Roman saints. What is for certain, there were no definite Christian establishments as such until Columba's arrival at Iona in 563AD, before spreading across southern Scotland as far as Coldingham on the Berwickshire coast and Lindisfarne, off the coast of Northumberland. Furthermore, Monks as such, were not ordained priests and did not lead worship, their monastic life was more to do with solitude, meditation and prayer. The earliest mention in Strathclyde of Jesus, may have come from some of the converts within the Roman army and later, from wandering Culdees like Baldred and Kentigern who lived hermit-like lives in between their spells of spreading the good word. The Roman way of universal worship arrived in the Vale of Clyde in the very late 9th century or early 10th but the first solid evidence of a church in the town Dumbarton is 1296 when it was mentioned in the *Rotuli Scotiæ* and the fact it was granted to the monks of Kilwinning where it remained until the Reformation. In time, as we shall learn, there may have been a church on the site of the present parish church at an even earlier time.

The Britons of Alt Clut would war with both the Scots of Dal Riata and the Picts of Pictland and later, when the Scots and Picts had 'merged', were again at war with their neighbours now collectively known as the Kingdom of Alba. The Britons, through all their trials and tribulations, still managed to hold on to their capital, Alt Clut but in 756AD, they did lose it for some months after a joint force of Northumbrians from the south-east of Scotland and Picts captured the Rock. By 870AD, as we have learned, the Kingdom of Strathclyde was all but dead when a sea faring force of Danes arrived and laid siege to the castle for four months before starving the garrison out of food and water, causing the defenders to surrender. A year later, the Viking leader, Olaf, returned to his kingdom of Dublin with more than 200 slaves aboard his boats.

Dumbarton Rock and the Castle-Courtesy of Danny Kearney ©2013
More buildings, are dotted all over over the Rock, front and back,
top and bottom. Historic Scotland's work is continuous in keeping the castle safe for
generations to come.

In the meantime, the king of Strathclyde retreated to Govan to set up new headquarters there, meaning the powers of the kingdom of Strathclyde had left Dumbarton forever and, though the kings appeared to carry on for another century, their power and influence was virtually worthless. The last king, Dunwallen, left Scotland in 974AD and spent the rest of his life in Rome.

Now that the Scots and Picts had united, and the Kingdom of Alba founded, it was still a long and troubled road which led to the founding of the Kingdom of Scotland. That conversion to a unification of the whole country, I am convinced, never wholly arrived nor was ever truly completed until, perhaps, after the Union

To the Estuary

of the Crowns in 1603 and, even then, there were divisions still to come. Different cultures existed north and south of the country and even the later introduction of the Episcopacy in 1584 by King James, further divided the people. Many Highlanders still, covertly, worshipped in the old ways and were more willing to embrace the Episcopal form of worship much more so than the Lowlands or Borders. In 1638, the General Assembly took the decision to ban the new Common Book of Prayer and evicted the bishops installed by Charles II. The king decided to use force to subdue his Scottish subjects, a decision which led to two brutal wars, the Bishops' Wars of 1638 and 1639, very often Scot against Scot. A few years later, the civil war in England was underway ending in 1649 when the king was executed. We then had the 'privilege' of Cromwell's occupation for ten years until, in 1660 and the Restoration of the king, Charles II who then further thrust his Episcopal ways on the people of Scotland which led to a period known as the *Killing Times*. Many ministers refused to adhere to the king's wishes and were hounded out of their churches and in to the fields. This happened at Dumbarton too with ministers taking to the fields or even the seas, to preach in what became known as *Blanket Sermons*.

*F*ollowing the Union of 1707, we had the two Jacobite rebellions which, as we learned in Glasgow, further emphasised there were still divisions in the country, with the Highlanders supporting the Stuarts but not the people in the south of the country. That was a strong indication that the peoples of Scotland never truly united even though the major differences were now as much about religion as they were political. What the Union did do though, was galvanise most of the people, to fight, and save the Scottish identity and culture for all time and, I believe, those aims have been fruitful. Men and women of Scotland gave so much to the world during the years of the Enlightenment and beyond, helping make Scotland one of very few nations, within a federation, still known and regarded as an individual people with a unique identity and a long and noble history, a large part of which belongs to old Alt Clut and Ystrd Clwyd.

*F*rom the reign of Malcolm III in 1058, Dumbarton once more, became an important 'city' with successive kings using the castle on the rock as a royal residence. It was a place where Malcolm, some times known as *big head*, or Canmore, and his wife, Margaret, the saintly princess of Wessex, could play, both at land and sea, a place where they could feel safe and probably more importantly, they could worship within the castle walls in a chapel which was dedicated, probably in the early 7th century to St. Patrick and founded by Ryderrich Hael the first Christian King of Alt Clut. Later kings used the castle including all of Malcolm's sons, Edgar, Alexander I and David I. David actually designated Dumbarton as his own *Royal Castle* before, in 1222, his great grandson, Alexander II, raised the town to the status of Royal Burgh.

*I*n 1138, when the king granted the lands of Lennox to the earl of that domain, he specifically kept the castle within the domain of the royal family, even the fishing rights around the confluence of Leven and Clyde were denied the nobleman.

River Clyde

*C*omings and goings over years meant different lords being granted Dumbarton but never the castle nor harbour until eventually in the 16th century, when the town was finally returned to the patronage of the king, rejoining the castle, fishings and rivers, solely in royal hands. During the Wars of Succession, the castle came in to the hands of Edward of England who, in turn, awarded it to his puppet, King John Baliol in 1298. By this time, the Wars of Independence were underway and the castle again changed hands several times until it was back in the hands of Edward by 1305. Edward, in turn, granted Dumbarton to Monteith, the traitor who betrayed William Wallace, but that arrangement would never last thanks to the intervention of Robert Bruce.

*I*n 1481, the English were back, placing the fortress under siege and, for weeks, the great bastion withstood all that was thrown at them until, eventually, the siege was lifted. Sir Andrew Wood, the Constable of the Castle, was later granted title and lands in Fife by King James III for his courage and steadfastness in his stubborn refusal to surrender. Later comings and going saw more changes of stewardship including an ill fated tenure of the Earl of Lennox.

*M*any Scottish lords fled to safety after the debacle of Pinkie in 1547, where did they go for safety? the great strength of Dumbarton, but they were only following in the footsteps of many of their predecessors, common and royal, including David II and his queen, Joan, who fled to Dumbarton in fear of their lives after the fateful Battle of Halidon Hill in 1333. It was obvious even from those early days that Dumbarton was truly royal, not just in name but in actual fact. In August, 1548, six years old Mary Stewart left the castle to sail to France where she would one day be queen; she would return one day to seek safe refuge just as so many other royal persons had done for centuries.

*T*he castle continued being a royal fortress, right to the end of the Stuart dynasty and was strengthened during the reign of James VI before being visited and financed by both Charles I & II. It was attacked several times during that period, before being occupied during the republican days of the Cromwell era when his troops were in command during his unwanted occupation of Scotland in the mid 17th century. Even after the Treaty of Union, the castle was improved and garrisoned as a requirement of the Articles of Union for the purpose of national defence and was further strengthened during the Napoleonic Wars, when a prison was built...and used. More strengthening followed during the American Wars of Independence, and though it was garrisoned during World War Two, it could not prevent the battering of the town and shipyards at the hands of the German Luftwaffe. Still the great and mighty fort stands but is now garrisoned by the staff of Historic Scotland and is proud host to the many thousands of visitors every year. A fort has stood on the Rock, almost certainly for up to 2,500 years and more; it was the place of the kings of two long gone kingdoms, Strathclyde and Scotland and still the old lady stands supreme, guarding, as she does, the entrance to the River Clyde. The great castle on the rock was the caput of a new Royal Town which survives in her shadow to the present day and where every man, woman and child are proud, to call themselves, *Sons or Daughters of the Rock.*

To the Estuary

*O*ne other note of interest regarding the Rock is, the higher of the two peaks is known as Wallace's Seat and the tower which was built thereon was known as Wallace's Tower. A great double handed sword, which was found on the Rock was, according to legend, the sword wielded by the great man himself. The ancient settlement is full of intrigue and mystery and it would be inappropriate to go forward to modern times without looking again at the past and relate some more of the legends, or myths of Dumbarton.

Legends of the rock include, St. Patrick consecrating an Irish nun, St. Monenna before she went on to found seven churches in Scotland. Ossian is said to have identified his Balclutha with the Roman naval base at Dumbarton known as *Theodosia* and *Urbs Legionis, (City of the Legions)* as the place where the 9th Arthurian battle, the Battle of the City of Legion, which was fought against the Saxons early in the 6th century. So much has been said about Arthur, defender of Britain against the marauding Saxons, and his many famous battles, some of which were in the northlands which became Scotland. He is even said to be living under the Eildon Hills in Roxburghshire, awaiting the call to return when Britain is at her most needy. He, his *Knights of the Round Table* and Thomas

de Ercildune (*Thomas the Rhymer)* await the fateful day when they must return to our aid.

*T*he chapel at the castle was the first religious establishment at Dumbarton though only for the use of the castle residents, and, as we know, the first solid mention of a church in the town did not arrive until 1296, but there has, most certainly, been a church there since no later than the 11th century. Today's parish church, Riverside (pictured above) is the direct descendant of a mediaeval kirk and, remarkably still stands on the same spot after more than 900 years of holy worship from the Catholic era through the Reformation to the present day. If any proof was ever needed to substantiate the church's antiquity, it was found in 1848 in the shape of a stone bearing a sword and cross, when new piping was being installed below the floor of the church. Later, a local historian, Donald Macleod confirmed it was from the time of the crusades of the late 11th or early 12th century seemingly confirming a place of worship was already in place at that time. Now after, at least two re-builds, we have a church with the most inspiring spire and clock dominating the crescent shaped High Street as it has always done. Riverside Church is a new name for the old Parish Church since the unification with the North Church and High Church in 1972. Another early establishment stands in today's Levengrove Park, St Serf's Church, in the old parish of Cardross, the ruins of which, though very scant, can still be viewed.

We are blessed with the knowledge of some early names from that church and chapel at the castle including Adam, chaplain at the castle, Alan de Dunfries, the parson of the church who swore fealty to Edward I in 1296 in the company of John the clerk. Others are Robert, a baillie and William Fleming who was a local land owner.

Other religious establishments of early times in Dumbarton included, a chapel dedicated to the Virgin near the town at an area which was then known as Chapelton and a holy hospital founded for the care of the infirm, the old and

College Bow from Isabella's Collegiate Church
Courtesy of Lairich Rig ©2010

Christian travellers in need of a rest. A collegiate church dedicated to St. Mary, was founded in 1450 by Isabella, Duchess of Albany and Countess of Lennox and continued up to the Reformation though many believe, the College building was added to the above mentioned chapel. The only part left of that church, a gracious arch, can be seen at the town's municipal buildings and really is an eye catcher, of sublime beauty and craftsmanship of the highest order. The one special and unusual note I can add to Isabella's church, it is one of the very few, if not the only one, collegiate church which was not taken away from the parish congregation. In so many other cases, lords of the manor applied to the bishop and pope for permission to convert parish churches for the purpose of erecting a college of priests for the sole use of the lord and his family with little or no regard to the congregation; happily that was not the case at Isabella's chapel.

Many holy houses of today, waiting with open arms of welcome, regardless of denomination, include Roman Catholic, Church of Scotland, United Reformed, Episcopal, Evangelical and a Church of Latter Day Saints

In the early years of the 'modern' town, the major industries were agriculture,

To the Estuary

weaving and fishing including localised fishing-boat builders but most of all, glass manufacture. So large was that industry, in the mid 19th century, the factory owners were paying up to nearly £120,000 a year to the Government in taxes and duties. Add that to small, home based craftworks, rope works, quarries, brick and tile works, foundries, tanneries, distilleries, three ship building yards, boiler works, brass foundry and an import/export trade was carried out with quays on the Clyde and Leven which were both navigable to larger vessels during high tide. It is easy to see, a thriving community existed below the great castle during those heady years of industry. Dumbarton, with its regal rights, hosted a market every Tuesday and no less then six fairs every year encouraging visitors from near and far to come to town and perhaps dig out a bargain or two, look for work on the hiring days, sell their cattle or simply enjoy the fun of the fair. Many of the fairs were opened every year during their tenure, by George snr. and George jnr, 1st and 2nd Earl of Dumbarton who 'reigned' from 1675

The River Leven with Dumbarton Rock beyond

until 1749 when the latter died without issue. The 1st earl, an army officer, defected the country with the court of James VII of Scots and II of England when the king was dethroned. The king and his entourage went to the court of Paris St. Germains where the 1st earl died but in terms of power or importance however, the Dumbartons were not in the same league as the mighty Lennox Mormaers or Earls as they later became. They were the most important and powerful of all families in the region of Lennox which contained Dumbarton. They, more than anyone else, were the real power of that region though sometimes allowing others to battle it out before they arrived and picked up the pieces, a form of scavenging I know but probably the right way to go in those unpredictable days of the Middle Ages.

While most of the old industries have gone, some remnants linger on, like a small shipyard on the River Leven, the bonding sheds are the last of the once huge whisky industry and a little small time fishing. Nearby Faslane submarine base is a large employer as is a large generator suppliers which has recently increased its volume in the town. Small remnants of the Polaroid company remain but the great

River Clyde

Burroughs electrical calculator company has gone. All the other jobs are provided in the service sector, warehousing, offices, private and local government (Dumbarton is headquarters of West Dunbartonshire Council) There is too, a BBC television studio containing the set for the popular River City where the programme is recorded and shown on BBC Scotland throughout the year but, more importantly, providing a few more jobs and, in summer, tours of the studios are available for visitors and locals alike. Other sources of work are to be found at shops, hotels, cafés, restaurants, leisure centres and schools.

On the subject of schools, Dumbarton is well equipped to provide a high standard of education for the children of the town and district. Most of the town's districts have primary schools serving as Roman Catholic and non denominational while two secondary schools, Dumbarton Academy and Our Lady and St. Patrick's High, serve children's higher education. Joining the schools, is the recently installed Dumbarton Campus of the Clydebank College which is situated on the town's High Street.

Dumbarton Academy in particular, is a long established school, opening its doors for the first time near the end of the 16th century or early 17th and has been regarded so highly as a place of excellence ever since. People educated at the school include, A.J.Cronin, physician and novelist of the early 20th century, John MacAusland Denny, Member of Parliament and ship builder of the late 19th and early 20th century. Others were David Steel, politician and once Presiding Officer of the Scottish Parliament, William Strang, the engraver and painter and Jackie Stewart, world champion formula one racing driver. Many others of course were educated at the school including more of the Denny family who did so much for the town through their shipbuilding acumen including the financing, laying out and the building of the Knoxland area of the town,

**Left :
TS Queen
Mary built by
the William
Denny
Shipyard at
Dumbarton
Seen here on
the River
Thames
©Ryan Kirk
– Wikimedia
Commons**

To the Estuary

Others with strong connections to the town were the Smollets, grandfather and grandson. Sir James Smollett was a great politician of his day, being a burgess then provost of the town before representing Dumbarton at the commission which decided on the Treaty of Union in 1707. His grandson, Tobias, was a writer and generally accepted as one of the founders of the written novel during the 18th century. The Dixon family who also did so much for the people of Dumbarton, now occupy a mausoleum in the old church of St. Serf in Levengrove Park.

Dumbarton is a good place to visit on occasion whether it be for shopping, sailing or sightseeing and there is much to see including so many fine, historic buildings and of course, some lovely walks on the waterfront and parks not forgetting the mighty castle on the rock.

All the national shops exist in the town and on the periphery retail parks joining so many locally independents, everything is here. The High Street provides a wide pavement offering safe walking while shopping, allowing everyone to stop and admire some lovely buildings and atmospheric pends.

Buildings worth seeing include those I have already mentioned, the 19th century parish church, the castle and the wonderful arch from St. Patrick's Collegiate. Others are the façade and tower of the old Burgh Hall and Academy which was badly burnt in the 1970s and presently held in place by steel frames. The Old Suters building on High Street, the magnificent West Kirk, Municipal Buildings, St. Serf's Kirk in Levengrove Park, the remains of the old prison which closed in 1863 and, not forgetting, Glencairn's Greit Hoose, former home of the Earl of Glencairn, another old classic on the High Street. Those are only a few of the many in the old town.

The Cutty Sark, The greatest of all clippers, now a museum at Greenwich, London. Built at Dumbarton in 1869 by Scott and Linton Courtesy of Stephen Craven ©2012

There are many fine parks and sporting facilities in the town with Levengrove the biggest and most popular of them all and where the organs of Robert Bruce were buried in 1329. Sporting facilities cater for all field and court sports while the area is well served by swimming pools, excellent golf courses and bowling clubs including one, immediately at the foot of Dumbarton Rock. There is too, the Scottish Maritime Museum containing the world famous *Denny Tank,* the world's first commercial ship model experiment tank. The best known sports club in

River Clyde

Dumbarton however, is the senior, professional football club, Dumbarton F.C. who play at the Bet Butler Stadium situated at the end of Castle Street, in the shadow of the Rock. Dumbarton were founded in 1872 and are the fourth oldest club in Scotland arriving just a little later than Queens Park, Kilmarnock and Stranraer. The club won the Scottish League Championship in each of the first two seasons of existence but now have the dubious 'honour' of being the only former champions not currently playing in the top flight. The club's colours are essentially gold, black and white and their badge incorporates an elephant representing the Rock with the castle on its back. The club have the distinction of being the first Scottish club to form a supporters trust and currently play in the Championship, the second tier of Scottish football.

Dumbartion Football Club has produced some fine players over the years including, Willie Wallace who went on to play for Hearts, Celtic and Scotland, Tom McAdam who then played for Celtic, Colin McAdam who later played with Rangers joining so many others. They have also had some great managers including, Billy Lamont, Bertie Auld, Alex Totten, Willie Toner and Gerry McCabe.

The town is well equipped with services, a fine library, one of the oldest in the country, community centres, health clinics and a hospital, Dumbarton Joint

Old Dumbarton Bridge ©2006 Eddie Mackinnon
Built in the mid 19th century by John Brown to allow the Duke of Argyll to move his goods more quickly to Glasgow.

Hospital which we pass on our way to Cardross. Communications are excellent considering the proximity to Glasgow Airport and nearby motorways. Bus services are better than most and three rail stations mean local communication to Glasgow and surrounds is not difficult. Dumbarton is especially lucky in the sense, it has more than 'one egg in its basket'. It is near to the metropolis that is Glasgow, yet more rural countryside is at hand. It is blessed with being part of the River Clyde communities yet is not much more that a good walk to the seaside of

To the Estuary

the Firth of Clyde. Loch Lomond with all its splendours, is half an hour away while beautiful Helensburgh is 'just round the corner', It is as idyllic a situation any one could wish for but now it is time to push on to our final destination, Cardross, and the estuary of the River Clyde.

Cardross awaits. A good walk on a hard path with railing protections above the embankments, takes us west with sand and mud banks below as the river gently sweeps between Levengrove and Port Glasgow. Over the years, sections of the path have been subject to erosion and breakage as powerful winds blow fiercely along the estuary but nothing can take away from the simple beauty of the place. On below Brucehill and Castlehill, we reach the district of Havock. or Havoc where rock features appear on the beach including what appears to be an ancient jetty of sorts. Now we are officially in the district of Argyll and Bute and the river has decidedly opened up as the tide comes sweeping in from the west and south. We are now, without doubt, walking along the shores of open water and the river is now becoming overwhelmed by the tidal waters.

The man made pathway has gone and a makeshift path trampled down by the many travellers is now our way forward below the tiny hamlet of Ardoch. The coastline is a little more interesting at this point with more varieties of rock and stone, lichen and algae giving some enthusiasts a little more interest on their way. Beyond Ardoch there are remains of an old 'yair', a fish trap, and, when in its 'working days' would be a relatively profitable location for the 'foot fishers' of the region. Walking on the sand and mudflats is a little safer now, the tide is out and we have reached another ruined jetty at the east end of the beach at Cardross. Just offshore are the remains of boundary posts which existed to help navigation in and out of the great river. Again we are amidst another section of the Inner Clyde Nature Reserve, another home to a wide array of wild fowl but don't be surprised to see some inquisitive seals in their never ending search for food. Out on the estuary, the Pillar and Cockle Banks can be seen at lower tides and just beyond, even more yairs, On land there are many ruins of concrete artillery buildings including six gun emplacements and a camp, built for defence during the Second World War, and even more boat landings. This particular section of the coast, known as Murrays, was obviously a scene of great importance in the defence of the approaches to Glasgow in wartime. The site of an old cottage known as Seabank, now replaced by a much more modern house comes in to view, near the forlorn ruins of Murrays farm but before going to the point of our destination, let us have a look at old Cardross.

Cardross was once home of a great parish in Dunbartonshire but now is part of Argyll and Bute. In the old Parish of Cardross, lived a man who changed the course of Scottish history forever. He founded a new royal house and set a thousand legends in motion, legends which live long in the heart of every Scot. King Robert Bruce built a manor house, the Queen's Quarters, and a chapel at Pillanflatt on the west bank of the River Leven, on the fields of the Mains of Cardross, where in recent times, some evidence was found to mark the spot. Others believe it was in a slightly different area but researchers of the Bruce story

185

appear adamant this is the place where the king lived from 1326 until his death in 1329. This is where the great knight who sent the English homeward in disarray, spent his last years enjoying fishing, hawking and, would you believe? building boats. When he died, his body lay in state in St. Serf's Church before being interred in a secret vault in Dunfermline Abbey, his heart was taken on crusade to the Holy Land but was finally buried at Melrose Abbey and his other organs were buried at St. Serf's which, as we have seen, is situated in Levengrove Park. Such was the lengths the Scottish Hierarchy had to go to, in order to ensure our sovereigns' bodies were not stolen and desecrated by the English.

The village is very much an upmarket location and exists in the most wonderful spot overlooking another 'water meetings' as the river and firth come together to the south with hills stretching ever higher to the north. The old parish contained the district of Dumbarton to the west of the Leven, Dalreoch, Renton, Ardoch and Ardmore. The name 'Cardross' known as Cardinros in the 11th century, is thought to mean *'wooded promontory'* from the Brythonic language and that

The St. Just on the river with Cardross beyond
Courtesy of Thomas Nugent ©2008

beautiful promontory attracted many wealthy families during the great days of industry at Dumbarton, who built many lovely homes. When the railway arrived, many more fine houses were built as was some social housing.

Cardross was never a place of great industry though there was some works, but the only 'ship builder' we know of was the King, Robert Bruce. There existed some agricultural activity, yair fishing, logging, quarrying, a distillery, a brewery and three mills joining the workings of the bleaching and print fields which caused so many from the village to move a little to the north to be nearer their work. The place to which they transferred was on the lands of the Smollett family who financed the building of a farm village in 1782 and named it *Rentoun* now known as Renton.

At least four ferries operated, for centuries, across the Clyde at this point, but that has gone long beyond living memory. Those must have been wonderful times,

To the Estuary

when tons of local produce was shipped across the firth with tons of horse manure coming back on the return journey. At the end of each trip, the jolly tars were able to enjoy a glass of ale at one of the inns at the ferry stations. Each ferry meant, there was always busy times at the side of the water, on both sides and every one had its very own inn. Apart from the business of the ferries, it was, and is, a peaceful place and it seemed, always to avoid the unwanted visitors but perhaps its location, just beyond Dumbarton was the reason behind that. Once invaders had their fill of attacking the Rock, they had had enough and went home or stayed to defend the fortress whichever way the battle went, without bothering too much of the wee place along the coast.

The church arrived early in the form of St. Serf's which, as we have seen, was located on the eastern fringes of the parish in, what is now, Levengrove Park. That church was built in the early 13th century and granted to Walter, Bishop of Glasgow, along with fishing rights, in January, 1229, by Maldoven, Mormaer of Lennox. Of the early parsons only one is known; that chaplain, Adam Seton, was one of the witnesses to the charter granting Cardross to Glasgow.

The tower of the old church

The old parish church was abandoned in 1643 when a much larger building was built within the confines of the village. That church underwent major repairs in 1775 before, in 1791, large scale repairs were carried out on the church offices and the manse. The first minister after the Reformation was Simon Shaw in 1560 with the next ordained minister arriving in 1570 in the shape of Thomas Archibald who presided over the parishes of Cardross and Kilmahew which were united soon after the Reformation. The church of 1643 was replaced in 1827, on the same site, by a truly majestic church with the most wonderful square tower. A Free Church was opened in 1872 but was destined to become the new parish church during the Second World War when the existing parish church was destroyed at the same time as many houses, by German bombing. Miraculously the tower survived and still stands supreme to the present day. The old Free Kirk still serves the parish where a wonderful suite of church halls serves the community for so many meetings, clubs and of course, social occasions

The church of Kilmahew at Kirkton survived until just beyond the Reformation before it was abandoned and fell in to ruin. It is not entirely clear when the chapel, which was dedicated to St. Mahew, the last disciple of St. Patrick, was built but there is mention of it having been rebuilt in 1467. The chapel stood on the lands of the Cochranes who later changed their name to Napir or Napier. It was reconsecrated on the 10th May 1467 by George, Bishop of Argyle with the full blessing of the Napier family, and a chaplain appointed with the handsome grant of 40 shillings and ten pence annually.

*I*n 1948, with the old chapel and burial ground in what appeared to be terminal decay, the Archdiocese of Glasgow purchased the lands with a view of resurrecting the old Divine. After much work and a lot of dedicated effort, the old church was opened again in 1955 and was once more in a fit state to reintroduce itself to the world and carry out its noble function, spreading the word of the Lord to the local Roman Catholic population and, of course, anyone at all, who wished solace and well being at such a holy spot.

St. Mahew's Chapel – Courtesy of Lairich Rig ©2010

Today, the church is, once again, a fixture, just a few hundreds yards north of the village of Cardross in the most idyllic setting with wonderful views over the Clyde. The church joined the newly opened St. Peter's Seminary located in Kilmahew House and Darleith House. An incredible building was erected, wrapped around Kilmahew House and was widely hailed as the most magnificent architecture of 20th century Scotland. Sadly things began to go wrong both with the buildings and declining numbers of students at the Seminary which finally closed in 1980. The building was later used as a drug rehabilitation centre but a devastating fire in 1995 put paid to that initiative. Today the sad remnants of a great building, listed as Grade A by the Royal Commission, lies empty, lost and totally forlorn. The Catholic Church invested heavily in the centre and it is such a sad tale for everyone concerned that it has not worked out as hoped but at least, thankfully, the beautifully renovated mediaeval church of St. Mahew, remains.

*T*he Napier family were the proprietors of nearby Kilmahew Castle, a 16th century, heavily fortified tower house, which, as a ruin, can still be seen. The lands went through many families including the Maxwells of Newark until finally, it

To the Estuary

came in to the own of the Burns family of Cumbernauld who, in the shape of James, built the wonderful Kilmahew House in 1858. The Burns' are now interred in a wonderful burial ground at Vale of Leven. Other great houses in the area included Cardross Park, Ardoch, Ardmore, Geilston, Moorpark, Drumhead, Lyleston and Ardenvhor, many of which contained walled gardens and some can still be seen and admired to this day. Geilston in particular, part of the National Trust for Scotland, is a very popular destination for many admiring visitors. Ardadan Farm is another popular spot where local produce can be purchased, enjoy a coffee in the tearooms, marvel at the walled garden or simply go for a refreshing walk along the river

Cardross today contains most facilities required for modern day living including a busy, recently refurbished library, shops, inn and hotels while local children attend pre-school and primary school before heading to Helensburgh for secondary education. The village boasts excellent communications with regular bus and train services and is close to top tourist spots like Helensburgh and Loch Lomond. While most of the old industries have gone, though a sawmill remains, some farms still fight the uphill battle against the ever increasing foreign imports. Sports facilities too are excellent for a village of its size and the people of Cardross are rightly proud of their tennis, bowls, football and golfing venues. The golf club was founded in 1895 and the course, which was laid out by Willie Fernie, was later upgraded by James Braid. Cardross Golf Club played host to the Scottish Professional Golf Championship in 1992 when the winner was Paul Lawrie who would go on to win the Open Championship.

Cardross, village and parish, is beautiful and it is not difficult to guess why so many large houses and estates were founded in the locale. From the days of the Earls of Lennox and King Robert, Cardross has attracted so many of means to set up home, overlooking the coming together of the river and firth but now it is time to see more of the coastline on our walk to Ardmore Point. A walk round the Point is a refreshing diversion from the towns and city and where so much wildlife is to be seen. Over the years Whitethroats and Red-breasted Merganisers have been seen along with a wide array of other ducks, swans and gulls of all varieties. Look out too for shoals of porpoises cruising along providing a supreme show of stealth and agility. The path can be narrow in places and sometimes a little overgrown but the walk is well worthwhile. When the tide is out, a walk on the beach can sometimes be a little easier but take care, it can also be very rocky in places. Rock cliffs, the old ferry jetty, old fish yairs and rocks of all varieties are all around. A cave located on the cliffs on the west side of the Point has as been used for shelter over the centuries and a central hearth of seas shells and carbonised wood has been tentatively attributed to the Iron Age. A ruined tower of later times sits against the cliff edge to the south-west. On the heavily afforested Hill of Ardmore is the most wonderful country house which stands in strictly private lands.

The walk round the peninsula of Ardmore Point which, at one time was an island, is the most fitting end to my journey of discovery. The views across the

River Clyde

Clyde and up the Gare Loch are quite breathtaking with Greenock, Port Glasgow, Helensburgh and the Rosneath Peninsula all coming in to view and looking so close, you feel as though you could reach out and touch them. The breeze cools the summer sun, seagulls are swooping denying the porpoises their next meal as a great blast from a ship's horn rings out as she sails round Greenock making her way south-west, away from Glasgow and on in to the Firth of Clyde.

**Syncline rock formation at Ardmore Point
with Rosneath Peninsula in the background
Courtesy of Lairich Rig ©2009**

I have reached the end of my trip and as mentioned earlier, Greenock would be the starting point for my next journey around the rivers and coasts of Scotland; it would be a little foolish of me however, not to give some mention to one of Scotland's great sea faring towns.

*S*ome confusion reigns over early mentions of Greenock particularly in 1296 and the call to Berwick to swear fealty to King Edward. Two men, Hugh de Grenock and William de Schawe attended to pay their homage and both are thought to have represented Greenock but I find that, in both cases, to be questionable since Greenock as such, did not exist at that point.

*A*round 1404, in the reign of Robert III, Malcolm de Galbraith died with no male heirs and his lands were left to his two daughters, the Wester lands to one the Easter to the other. The two girls married, one to Malcolm de Crawfurd of Loudoun who received the easter barony and the other daughter to Sir John Schawe of Sauchie. More than two centuries later, the Schawes purchased parts of the Crawfurd lands, including a recently built castle, from a female heiress, and it was they, the Schawes, who now reigned supreme and would begin to create the earliest areas of what we now call Greenock. But before that, the Shaws were already making their mark, not only with the influential people of the day but also the common people. Before the Reformation, what is now Greenock, contained three Catholic Chapels, St. Lawrence's and St. Blane's and another in an area which became known as Chapelton and they were all in the parish of Inverkip. In those days, before the coming of the 'new' town, the people celebrated two fairs every year, one dedicated to St. Helen and the other to St. Lawrence; both fairs were held near St. Lawrence's Church. When the Shaws purchased much more of the lands, other sections were sold off to another branch of the Crawfurd family, the Crawfurds of Cransburn.

The West Kirk, Greenock-Courtesy of Thomas Nugent ©2007

Within a year of the Reformation however, the chapels had closed meaning local people would need to make the trek to Inverkip for holy worship. That prompted Sir John to petition the commissioners to have a church of the reformed faith built at Greenock. That petition had to go before the king, James VI, for his approval which came in 1590 with the words "Only people who worship in the new way shall use this church" - the church opened on 5th October 1591 and was disjoined from Inverkip thus creating a new parish of Greenock on 8th June, 1594 by Act of Parliament. The first minister at the new church was Andrew Murdoch who was translated from St. Andrews but only two years later, Patrick Shaw was installed as minister by the church's patron, the king. The West Kirk, or as it is now known, Lyle Kirk is the original parish church but, in 1925, was moved, stone by stone to its present site when the shipbuilding company of Harland and Wolff extended their ship yards. The church's website tells us, the church of 1925 was built on a different shore but still retained its view of the northern mountains and the seas but most importantly of all, the *Sailors Kirk* was still in full view of the passing ships.

River Clyde

*S*t. Mary's Roman Catholic Church lays claim to the being the *Mother Church* of the Roman Catholic community in the area and why not? It was the first Catholic Church built in Greenock since the Reformation and priests from that mission served a wide area including parts of Ayrshire. It would not be wrong to say, that church is a continuation of the Catholic Chapels which closed soon after the coming of the Reformed Church

.   *T*hat is a very small section of the history of the formation of the great industrial town and the early churches. Of course, education arrived early and now so many schools and colleges are in place to cover most educational needs for all. Great industries have come and gone but the town retains strong association with the sea and still many jobs are connected with the seafaring traditions. Great strides were made to house people and extraordinary constructions were put in place to provide the populace with fresh water. Work was ongoing as the population exploded over the years. People do of course need something more than work and, in time, leisure facilities and parks were opened to meet needs. Since the beginning of that programme, sporting and leisure facilities have been provided and have grown in the ensuing years until now, they abound in one of Scotland's most famous industrial towns.

The beautiful entrance to St. Mary's Church
Courtesy of Thomas Nugent ©2012

*O*n my return to the Clyde coast in the near future, we can take a longer look at the town as part of a new journey down the *Coast of Clyde* but now it is back to Ardmore Point for another look down the estuary.

*T*o my amazement, the ship I mentioned earlier is now between Greenock and Rosneath Peninsula, once again, the great horn sounds, as if in celebration of a new adventure but it is not just any ship, it is the PS Waverley, the great paddle steamer, heading out on another voyage of discovery. The PS Waverley personifies exactly what the Clyde means to all men. Great ships, sailing to all corners of the world though, in the case of Waverley, it is trips to and from all parts of the British Islands and of course what she became famous for, taking Glaswegians and anyone else who wished, the time and the pleasure to sail with her, *Doon the Watter.*

Sailing
doon
the watter

PS Waverley passing Port Glasgow
with Rosneath Peninsula in the background
Courtesy of Thomas Nugent ©2012

The Song of the Clyde

I sing of a river I'm happy beside
The song that I sing is a song of the Clyde
Of all Scottish rivers it's dearest to me
It flows from Leadhills all the way to the sea
It borders the orchards of Lanark so fair
Meanders through meadows with sheep grazing there
But from Glasgow to Greenock, in towns on each side
The hammers ding-dong is the song of the Clyde

Oh the river Clyde, the wonderful Clyde
The name of it thrills me and fills me with pride
And I'm satisfied whate'er may betide
The sweetest of songs is the song of the Clyde

Imagine we've left Craigendoran behind
And wind-happy yachts by Kilcreggan we find
At Kirn and Dunoon and Innellan we stay
Then Scotland's Madeira that's Rothesay, they say
Or maybe by Fairlie and Largs we will go
Or over to Millport that thrills people so
Maybe joumey to Arran it can't be denied
Those scenes all belong to the song of the Clyde

When sun sets on dockland, there's beauty to see
The cry of a seabird is music to me
The blast of a horn loudly echoes, and then
A stillness descends on the water again
Tis here that the sea-going liners are born
But, unlike the salmon, they seldom return
Can you wonder the Scots o'er the ocean so wide
Should constantly long for the song of the Clyde

Oh the river Clyde, the wonderful Clyde
The name of it thrills me and fills me with pride
And I'm satisfied whate'er may betide
The sweetest of songs is the song of the Clyde

Bibliography

Douglas Archives – douglashistory.co.uk

Catholic Online – catholic.org/saints

Education Scotland – educationscotland.gov.uk/

William Wallace – thesocietyofwilliamwallace.com

Documents illustrative of Sir William Wallace : his life and times – Joseph Stevenson – 1841 – Printed for the Maitland Club

Topographical Dictionary of Scotland – Samuel Lewis – 1841 – S. Lewis & Co. London

Libberton & Quothquan Parish Church website

Discovering the River Clyde – Innes Macleod amd Margaret Gilroy - 1991 – ISBN 0 85976 333 1 – John Donald Publishers, Edinburgh.

Origines Pariochales Scotiae – *The Antiquities Ecclesiastical and Territorial of the Parishes of Scotland* – Bannatyne Club, Edinburgh – 1851 – W.H. Lizars, Edinburgh.

Picts, Gaels and Scots: Early Historic Scotland – Sally M. Foster – 2004 – ISBN 0 7134 8874 3 – Batsford, London.

St. Patrick – *Saints and Angels* – *Catholic Online* – catholic.org/saints

Roman Scotland – romanscotland.org.uk

Various Wikipedia articles where reliable sources have been identified.

Cairngryffe Parish Church website – cairngryffeparishchurch.org.uk

Clydesdale's Heritage – Clydesdalesheritage.org.uk/

The Lanimers website – lanarklanimers.co.uk

Fasti Ecclessiæ Scoticannæ, Volume III – Hew Scott D.D. 1920 – Oliver & Boyd, Edinburgh : Tweeddale Court.

Lanark – lanark.co.uk

New Lanark World Heritage site – newlanark.org/

Scan Weights and Measures Guide – scan.org/weights/measures.asp

Valley International Park – visitlanarkshire.com.attractions

Milton-Lockhart House and Carluke – carlukecommunity/history.com

Royal Commission on Ancient & Historical Monuments of Scotland - various

Blantyre's Ain Website – blantyre.biz

A Blast from the Past – Andrew Paterson – 2005 – ISBN 0-9550000-0-9 – Airdrie Print Services – Andrew MacAnulty Paterson

West Dunbartoshire website - west-dunbarton,gov.uk/media

Wishaw Curling Club – wishawcurlingclub.com/

Hamilton Academical F.C. - acciesfc.co.uk/

Abandoned Communities website – Bothwellhaugh

Motherwell Athletics Club – motherwellac.com/

Colville Park Golf Club – Colvillegc.co.uk

Motherwell Hockey Club – motherwellhc.co.uk

Dalziel Rugby Club – dalzielrugby.com/

Motherwell Football Club – motherwellfc.co.uk/

Dalziel St. Andrews Parish Church – dalzielstandrews.org.uk

St. Mary's Parish Church – stmarysmotherwell.org.uk

Bibliography (cont)

*North Lanarkshire Leisure – many sites in various locations
*South Lanarkshire Leisure & Culture – many sites in various locations
*Bellshill Golf Club – bellshillgolfclub.com
*River Clyde | Fishingnet
fishingnet.com/angling/category/rivers-scotland/river-clyde/
*Lanarkshire Muslim Welfare Society – lanarkshiremosque.com
*Visit Lanarkshire – various sites – visitlanarkshire.com/
*Castles of Glasgow and the Clyde – Gordon W. Mason – 2013 - ISBN
19781899874590 – Goblinshead, Musselburgh – printed by Bell & Bain, Glasgow
*Cambuslang Rangers F.C. – clubwebsite.co.uk.cambuslangfootballclub/#
*Clyde Football Club – clydefc.co.uk/
*The Scottish Mining Website – scottishmining.co.uk
*Rutherglen Glencairn F. C. - freewebs.com/rutherglenglencairn/
*Third Lanark Football Club – thirdlanark.co.uk
*History of the Christian Church, Volume IV – Medieval Christianity, AD590-
1073 – ccel.org/ccel/schaff/hcc4.html/
*The Devil's Plantation – Trip Twenty Four –
devilsplantaton.co.uk/blog/the-devils-plantation-trip-twenty-four/
*Paisley Abbey – paisleyabbey.org.uk/
*Renfrew – The Royal Burgh – freewebs.com/renfrew
*Inverclyde Leisure – inverclydeleisure.gov.uk/
*The Port, Past and Present, 1775-1975 – Janetta Bowie,
imverclydeleisure.org.uk
*History of Port Glasgow, Geograph – Thomas Nugent
*History of Riverside Parish Church – www.dumbartonriverside.org.uk/about-
riverside/parish-church-history
*Scottish Maritime Museum – scottishmaritimemuseum.org
*Cardross Parish Church – cardrossparishchurch.org
*Fasti Ecclesiæ Scoticanæ, The Succession of ministers in the Church of Scotland
from the Reformation – New Edition, Volume III – Hew Scott D.D. - Oliver &
Boyd, Edinburgh. Tweeddale Court. - 1920
*A Gazetteer of Scotland – Francis Groome - 1896
*The Statistical Accounts of Scotland – 1791-1845 Parish – Parish Ministers –
Patron : Sir John Archibald Sinclair, 3rd Viscount Thurso
*Clyde Waterfront Heritage – clydewaterfront heritage.com
*Dumbarton Football Club – dumbartonfootballclub.com
*Cardross Golf Club – cardross.com
*Visit Scotland – visitscotland.com (several sites)
*People of Medieval Scotland 1093 – 1314 – poms.ac.uk (accesses several times
between September 24th 2013 and December 9th 2013.
*Scottish Association for Country Sports – sacs.org.uk
*Old West Kirk, Greenock (Lyle Kirk) – www.lylyekirk.org
*Village Kirks of the Borders of Scotland – James Denham, 2011 – ISBN 978-1-
4477-4293-4 Galashiels